Proceedings of the
10th Italian Conference on

THEORETICAL

COMPUTER

SCIENCE

ICTCS'07

EDITORS

GIUSEPPE F ITALIANO

University of Rome "Tor Vergata", Italy

EUGENIO MOGGI

University of Genova, Italy

LUIGI LAURA

"Sapienza" University of Rome, Italy

Rome, Italy   3 – 5 October 2007

Proceedings of the
10th Italian Conference on

THEORETICAL

COMPUTER

SCIENCE

ICTCS'07

World Scientific

NEW JERSEY • LONDON • SINGAPORE • BEIJING • SHANGHAI • HONG KONG • TAIPEI • CHENNAI

Published by

World Scientific Publishing Co. Pte. Ltd.

5 Toh Tuck Link, Singapore 596224

USA office: 27 Warren Street, Suite 401-402, Hackensack, NJ 07601

UK office: 57 Shelton Street, Covent Garden, London WC2H 9HE

British Library Cataloguing-in-Publication Data
A catalogue record for this book is available from the British Library.

THEORETICAL COMPUTER SCIENCE
Proceedings of the 10th Italian Conference on ICTCS '07

ISBN-13 978-981-277-098-1
ISBN-10 981-277-098-4

Printed in Singapore

PREFACE

The 10th Italian Conference on Theoretical Computer Science (ICTCS 2007) was held on 3-5 October 2007 in Rome, Italy. Previous conferences took place in Pisa(1972), Mantova (1974 and 1989), L'Aquila (1992), Ravello (1995), Prato (1999), Torino (2001), Bertinoro (2003), Siena (2005).

The conference covers all fields of Theoretical Computer Science. The Program Committee, consisting of 16 members, received 34 submissions, and selected 15 papers for inclusion in the scientific program. All the work of the PC was done electronically. The selection was based on originality, quality and relevance to theoretical computer science. Each submission was reviewed by at least 3 reviewers.

The first day of ICTCS 2007 (October 3) hosted a colloquium, entitled "Types and Computations", to celebrate the 60th birthday of Mario Coppo, Mariangiola Dezani-Ciancaglini and Simona Ronchi Della Rocca. Stefano Berardi, Ferruccio Damiani, Ugo de'Liguoro and ourselves felt appropriate to honor them in conjuction with ICTCS 2007, since they are distinguished researchers within the Theoretical Computer Science community, and because of the important services they have offered to EATCS and the Italian Chapter over the years.

These proceedings contain the revised versions of the 15 papers selected by the PC; the invited talks by Giorgio Ausiello (Clairvoyance and laziness for on line travelling agents) and Rocco De Nicola (Session Centered Calculi for Service Oriented Computing); and the invited presentations for the "Types and Computations" colloquium by Chantal Berline (Can a proper lambda-model have an r.e. equational theory?), Giuseppe Longo (Symmetries in Foundations), and Henk Barendregt (Proving the range property for lambda theories and models).

We wish to thank all authors who submitted papers, the PC, and the external reviewers. A special thanks to the Organizing Committee for a very dedicated work.

June 2007

Giuseppe F. Italiano
Eugenio Moggi
Luigi Laura

A SHORT RESEARCH BIOGRAPHY OF MARIO COPPO, MARIANGIOLA DEZANI-CIANCAGLINI, AND SIMONA RONCHI DELLA ROCCA

The 60th birthdays of Mario Coppo, Mariangiola Dezani-Ciancaglini, and Simona Ronchi Della Rocca all take place between 2006 and 2007. These three researchers are widely known in the world community of theoretical computer scientists, and especially among the researchers in λ-calculus, type theory and semantics of programming languages.

All of them have been students of Corrado Böhm in the early 70's, and got a professorship of Computer Science by the University of Torino, where they have been the first members of the "λ-group", still the largest group in the field.

Since then they worked on interleaving fields over thirty years and more. For the common part of the large bibliography that will appear in a forthcoming volume dedicated to them, it seems worthy to mention the introduction of intersection types, a fruitful extension of Curry's assignment system allowing for a deep understanding of the relation between syntax and semantics of the λ-calculus. Among the results we mention separability and approximation theorems, the studies on typability and principal type schemes for polymorphic systems, the completeness theorem for Curry assignment systems and the construction of filter λ-models.

Beside the common kernel of interests and research work, each of them has pursued her/his own investigation into several aspects of the semantics of calculi and type systems. Coppo contributed on recursive types proposing a new denotational interpretation; he used assignment systems for the static analysis of programs, with applications to strictness, totality and dead-code analysis; he also investigated the connection between type assignment and abstract interpretation. Dezani investigated union types, both for the λ-calculus and for its nondeterministic and parallel extensions. She exploited type systems to study the behaviour of concurrent and mobile processes, enforcing safe and structured interaction. She studied type systems for object oriented languages allowing for strong forms of polymorphism and modularity; these eventually meet the foundational work on typing process calculi when concurrent objects and session types are involved. Ronchi has studied typability in the case of polymorphic and dependent types, both with respect to the characterization of the set of typable terms, and to (semi)algorithms for type reconstruction. She introduced and studied a hierarchy of assignment systems that parallels Barendregt's λ-cube. Concerning λ-calculi denotational semantics she established the incompleteness of topological models, and extended the notion of filter models to qualitative domains and to coherent spaces, in view of understanding in particular the lazy and call-by-value λ-calculi. This led both to works on linear logic, and to a systematic presentation of "parametric λ-calculi".

June 2007

Stefano Berardi
Ferruccio Damiani
Ugo de'Liguoro

ICTCS 2007
October 3-5 2007, Rome, Italy

Program Co-chairs

Giuseppe F. Italiano, Rome "Tor Vergata" University, Italy
Eugenio Moggi, Genova University, Italy

Program Committee

Nadia Busi, Bologna University, Italy
Ferruccio Damiani, Torino University, Italy
Paola Inverardi, L'Aquila University, Italy
Giuseppe F. Italiano (Co-Chair), Rome "Tor Vergata" University, Italy
Irit Katriel, Brown University, USA
Giovanni Manzini, Piemonte Orientale University, Italy
Alberto Marchetti-Spaccamela, "Sapienza" Rome University, Italy
Dimitrios Michail, MPI Saarbrücken, Germany
Eugenio Moggi (Co-Chair), Genova University, Italy
Alberto Momigliano, Edinburgh University, UK
Piotr Sankowski, Warsaw University, Poland
Roberto Segala, Verona University, Italy
Francesca Toni, Imperial College, UK

Organizing Committee

Fabio Dellutri, Rome "Tor Vergata" University, Italy
Luigi Laura, "Sapienza" Rome University, Italy
Michela Loja, Rome "Tor Vergata" University, Italy
Maurizio Saltali, Rome "Tor Vergata" University, Italy

Sponsoring Institutions

European Association for Theoretical Computer Science (EATCS)
Dipartimento di Informatica e Sistemistica - "Sapienza" Università di Roma

External Reviewers

Robert Atkey	Jesper Jansson
Davide Bacciu	Kanela Kaligosi
Stefano Berardi	William Knottenbelt
Lennart Beringer	Lukasz Kowalik
Anna Bernasconi	Ivan Lanese
Annalisa De Bonis	Lap Chi Lau
Andrea Bracciali	Josef Lauri
Franco A. Cardillo	Kenneth MacKenzie
Nicolò Cesa-Bianchi	Maria Madonia
Marco Cesati	Paul-Amaury Matt
Alessandra Cherubini	Giovanna Melideo
Stelvio Cimato	Carlo Mereghetti
Marco Comini	Monica Nesi
Massimo De Gregorio	Luca Padovani
Gianluca De Marco	Beatrice Palano
Michael Domaratzki	Giovanni Pighizzini
Susanna Donatelli	G. Michele Pinna
Lavinia Egidi	Giovanni Resta
Mohammad Farshi	Andrea Ribichini
Camillo Fiorentini	Roberto Solis-Oba
Maurizio Gabbrielli	Fausto Spoto
Travis Gagie	Jeremy Sproston
Serge Gaspers	Thomas Stuetzle
Silvio Ghilardi	Wing-Kin Sung
Massimiliano Goldwurm	Stefan Szeider
Roberto Gorrieri	Laurent Théry
Szymon Grabowski	Mauro Torelli
Fabrizio Grandoni	Marco Trubian
Giuliano Grossi	Eli Upfal
Andrea Grosso	Rosalba Zizza
Giovanna Guaiana	Enrico Zoli
John Hershberger	Daniele Zucchelli

CONTENTS

PART A

Invited Talks

CLAIRVOYANCE AND LAZINESS
FOR ON LINE TRAVELLING AGENTS

G. AUSIELLO

(JOINT WORK WITH L. ALLULLI, V. BONIFACI, AND L. LAURA)

Dipartimento di Informatica e Sistemistica,
"Sapienza" Università di Roma,
Via Ariosto 25 — I-00185 Roma, Italy
E-mail: ausiello@dis.uniroma1.it

In several circumstances we have to solve a problem whose instance is not completely known in advance. Situations of this kind occur in computer systems and networks management, in financial decision making, in robotics etc. Problems of this kind are called on-line problems. In most applications (e.g. paging) an agent is required to serve requests in an on line fashion and a request has to be served by the agent before a new request is revealed. In such cases the notion of time is simply used to refer to a totally ordered sequence of discrete instants $(t_0, t_1, \ldots, t_n)$. Both requests and agent's service actions occur instantaneously in one of these moments. The actual time elapsed between two instants is not specified and inessential under any respect. A different situation occurs instead in other problems where the time dimension is continuous and plays a specific role. We call this kind of problems real time on-line problems. We address a specific class of real time on-line problems: vehicle routing problems. By examining the properties of this paradigmatic type of problems, we put in evidence the role of real time in the design of competitive algorithms, in the construction of adversarial arguments and in the definition of clairvoyance and laziness.

PROVING THE RANGE PROPERTY FOR LAMBDA THEORIES AND MODELS

H. BARENDREGT

Institute for Computing and Information Sciences,
Radboud University Nijmegen,
6500 GL Nijmegen, The Netherlands
E-mail: henkATcs.ru.nl

The range property states that the range of a definable map has cardinality either one or infinite. In several situations this has been proved by different means: topology, computability, analysis of reduction. Is there a common pattern?

CAN A PROPER LAMBDA-MODEL HAVE AN R.E. EQUATIONAL THEORY?

C. BERLINE

UFR de Mathmatiques de l'Universit Paris 7,
175 rue du Chevaleret,
75013 PARIS (mtro Chevaleret)
E-mail: berline@pps.jussieu.fr

By a proper lambda-model we understand here a model M of untyped lambda-calculus whose construction makes no reference to the syntax of lambda-calculus. I will present here several results obtained jointly with Antonino Salibra and Giulio Manzonetto, and which all argue in favour of the following conjecture, where "r.e." stands for "recursively enumerable": *Conjecture*: No proper lambda-model can have an r.e. equational theory. Variant: No lambda-model living in Scott's semantics or in one of its refi nement (e.g. the stable or strongly stable semantics) can have an r.e. equational theory. Note that this conjecture encompasses the longstanding open question of the existence of a proper model having lambda-beta as its equational theory. We will see in particular that we can prove that no "effective" lambda-models can have an r.e theory, at least if it lives in the stable or in the stable semantics; concerning Scott's continuous semantics, we have only partial results, even for effective graph models. Nevertheless, these partial results cover all the lambda-models which have been introduced "individually" in the literature.

Bibliography

Chantal Berline, Giulio Manzonetto and Antonino Salibra. Lambda theories of effective lambda models. Accepted at CSL'07, (2007), preprints available at http://www.pps.jussieu.fr/~berline/.

SESSION CENTERED CALCULI
FOR SERVICE ORIENTED COMPUTING

R. DE NICOLA

Dipartimento di Sistemi e Informatica, Università di Firenze,
Firenze, I-50136, Italy
* E-mail: denicola@dsi.unifi.it

Within the European project SENSORIA, we are developing formalisms for service description that lay the mathematical basis for analysing and experimenting with components interactions, for combining services and formalising crucial aspects of service level agreement. One of the outcome of this study is ρSCC, a process calculus with explicit primitives for service definition and invocation. Central to ρSCC are the notions of session and pipelining. Sessions are two sided and can be equipped with protocols executed by each side during an interaction and permit interaction patterns that are more structured than the simple one-way and request-response ones. Pipeline permits exchange of values between among sessions. The calculus is also equipped with operators for handling (unexpected) session closures that permit programming smooth propagation of session closures to partners and subsessions, so as to avoid states with dangling or orphan sessions. In the talk we will present SCC and discuss other alternatives that are (or have been) considered within the project.

Keywords: Process Algebras, Service Oriented Computing, Process Calculi

1. Introduction

The EU funded SENSORIA project [1] aims at developing a novel, comprehensive approach to the engineering of software systems for service-oriented overlay computers. Specifically, SENSORIA focuses on methods and tools for the development of global services that are context adaptive, personalisable, possibly with different constraints on resources and performance, and deployable on significatively different platforms over a global computer. SENSORIA seeks for full integration of foundational theories, techniques and methods in a pragmatic software engineering approach.

Within SENSORIA, a workpackage is devoted to the development of calculi for service specifications and analysis that comply with a service-oriented approach to business modeling, allow for modular description of services, support dynamic, ad-hoc, "just-in-time" composition.

During the first eighteen months of the project a few proposals have emerged [2–6]. Most of the considered calculi are based on process algebras but enhanced with primitives for manipulating semi-structured data, mechanisms for describing safe client-service interactions, operators for composing (possibly unreliable) services, techniques for query and discovery of services. The comparison, assessment, refinement and integration of the proposed calculi will constitute a prominent research activity for the prosecution of the project. Here, we will concentrate on one of the proposed calculi [2] named SCC.

SCC has been influenced by Cook and Misra's Orc [7], a basic programming model for structured orchestration of services, and by π-calculus, [8] the by now classical representative of name passing calculi. Indeed one could say that SCC combines the service oriented flavour of Orc with the name passing communication mechanism of π-calculus. SCC supports explicit modeling of sessions that are rendered as private bi-directional channels created upon services invocation and used to bind caller and callee. The interaction is programmed by two communication protocols installed at each side of the bi-directional channel. This session mechanism permits describing and reasoning about interaction patterns that are more structured than the classical *one-way* and *request-response* pattern..

Apart for the intra-session communication, a calculus for services has to have the possibility of handling inter-session communications. Different opinions on how to model this kind of communications have led to the definition of three variants [9–11] of SCC that essentially differ only for the chosen inter-session communication mechanism:

pSCC is *dataflow* oriented and makes use of a pipelining operator (a la ORC) to model the passage of information between sessions [11].

SSCC is *stream* oriented and has primitives for inserting/retrieving data in/from streams [9].

CSCC has explicit and distinct message passing primitives to model inter and intra session communication [10].

In the rest of this presentation, we shall concentrate just on the pSCC [11] variant. Within this calculus, services are seen as passive objects that can be invoked by clients and service definitions can be seen as specific instances of input prefixed processes. Indeed, service definitions are rendered as

$$s.A$$

where s is the service name and A is the *abstraction* defining the service behaviour. A can be seen as a process that waits for a value from the client side and then activates the corresponding computational activities. For instance,

$$\texttt{succ.}(?x)\langle x + 1 \rangle$$

models a service that, after receiving an integer, returns its successor.

Service invocations can be seen as specific instances of output prefixed processes and are rendered as

$$\overline{s}.C$$

Here, service s is invoked with the value carried by the *concretion* C. This is a process that emits a value and then implements the client-side protocol for interacting with the new instance of s. As an example, a client for the simple service described above will be written in pSCC as

$$\overline{\texttt{succ}}.\langle 5 \rangle (?y)\langle y \rangle^{\uparrow}$$

After succ is invoked, argument 5 is passed on to the service side and the client waits for a value from the server: the received value will be substituted for y and returned as the result of the service invocation.

A service invocation causes activation of a new session. A fresh, private, name r is used to bind the two sides of the session. For instance, the interaction of the client and of the service described above triggers the session

$$(\nu r)\big(r \rhd \langle 5 + 1 \rangle \,|\, r \rhd (?y)\langle y \rangle^{\uparrow}\big)$$

The value 6 is computed on the service-side and then received at the client side, that reduces first to $r \rhd \langle 6 \rangle^{\uparrow}$ and then to $6 \,|\, r \rhd nil$ to return the result outside of the session.

More generally, within sessions, communication is bi-directional, in the sense that the interacting peers can exchange data in both directions. Values returned outside of the session (to the enclosing environment) with the return operator $\langle . \rangle^{\uparrow}$ can be used for invoking other services. Indeed, processes can be composed by using the *pipeline* operator

$$P > A$$

A new instance of abstraction A is activated in correspondence of each of the values produced by P. For instance, what follows is a client that invokes the service succ and then prints the obtained result:

$$5 > (?x)\overline{\texttt{succ}}.\langle x \rangle (?y)\langle y \rangle^{\uparrow} > (?z)\overline{\texttt{print}}.\langle z \rangle$$

To improve usability, structured values are permitted; services are invoked using structured values that, via pattern matching, drive usage of the exchanged information. Using this approach, each service can provide different *methods* corresponding to the exposed activities. For instance:

$$calculator. \; (\text{``}sum\text{''}, ?x, ?y)\langle\text{``}result\text{''}, x + y\rangle$$
$$+ \; (\text{``}sub\text{''}, ?x, ?y)\langle\text{``}result\text{''}, x - y\rangle$$
$$+ \; (\text{``}mul\text{''}, ?x, ?y)\langle\text{``}result\text{''}, x * y\rangle$$
$$+ \; (\text{``}div\text{''}, ?x, ?y)\langle\text{``}result\text{''}, x/y\rangle$$

models a service *calculator* that expose the methods for computing the basic arithmetic operations. This service can be invoked as follows:

$$\overline{calculator}.\langle\text{``}sum\text{''}, 2, 4\rangle(\text{``}result\text{''}, ?y)\langle y\rangle^{\uparrow}$$

A similar approach is used for session interaction. Indeed, thanks to tags and pattern matching, more sophisticated protocols can be programmed for both the server and client side of a session. For instance, a service can reply to a request with different values denoting the status of the execution:

$$\ldots |r \rhd (\text{``}fail\text{''}, ?x)P_1 + (\text{``}result\text{''}, ?y)P_2| \ldots$$

After presenting syntax and semantics of pSCC, we shall consider possible behavioral semantics and linguistic extensions to deal with programmed or unexpected session closures. We shall then analyze policies that guarantee controllable behaviors and permit the necessary actions or compensations in such situations.

Acknowledgments

I would like to thank all members of the SENSORIA projects that have been involved in Workpackage 2 and have contributed to the discussion on Service Oriented Calculi. Michele Boreale, Roberto Bruni and Michele Loreti deserve special thanks for having gone through many discussions on pSCC.

Bibliography

1. Sensoria Project, Public web site http://sensoria.fast.de/.
2. M. Boreale, R. Bruni, L. Caires, R. De Nicola, I. Lanese, M. Loreti, F. Martins, U. Montanari, A. Ravara, D. Sangiorgi, V. Vasconcelos and G. Zavattaro, Scc: a service centered calculus, in *Web Services and Formal Methods, Third International Workshop, WS-FM 2006*, Lecture Notes in Computer Science Vol. 4184 (Springer, 2006).
3. N. Busi, R. Gorrieri, C. Guidi, R. Lucchi and G. Zavattaro, Sock: a calculus for service oriented computing, in *Proc. of 4th Int. Conf. on Service-Oriented Computing*, Lect. Notes in Comput. Sci. Vol. 4294 (Springer, 2006).
4. G. Ferrari, R. Guanciale and D. Strollo, Jscl: a middleware for service coordination, in *Proc. of FORTE'06*, Lect. Notes in Comput. Sci. Vol. 4229 (Springer, 2006).

5. A. Lapadula, R. Pugliese and F. Tiezzi, A calculus for orchestration of web services, in *16th European Symposium on Programming*, Lect. Notes in Comput. Sci. Vol. 4421 (Springer, 2007).

6. M. Bartoletti, P. Degano and G. Ferrari, Types and effects for secure service orchestration, in *Proc. of 19th IEEE Computer Security Foundations Workshop (CSFW'06)*, 2006.

7. J. Misra and W. R. Cook, *Journal of Software and Systems Modeling* **6**, 83 (2007).

8. R. Milner, J. Parrow and J. Walker, *Information and Computation* **100**, 1 (1992).

9. I. Lanese, V. T. Vasconcelos, F. Martins and A. Ravara, *Disciplining Orchestration and Conversation in Service-Oriented Computing*, Tech. Rep. (2007).

10. L. Caires and H. Viera, *A note on a Model for Service Oriented Computation*, Tech. Rep. (2007).

11. M. Boreale, R. Bruni, R. De Nicola and M. Loreti, *A Service Oriented Process Calculus with Sessioning and Pipelining*, Draft - Tech. Rep. (2007).

SYMMETRIES IN FOUNDATIONS

G. LONGO

CNRS & Dpartement d'Informatique
Ecole Normale Suprieure
45, rue d'Ulm (Etage 3, Escalier A)
75230 Paris Cedex 05 - France
E-mail: longo@di.ens.fr

Our mathematical relation to space originated by the symmetries at the core of Greek geometry as well as Riemann's manifolds. Symmetries continued to provide the conceptual tools for further constructions of mathematical structures, from Poincare's Geometry of Dynamical Systems to Category Theory, but were disregarded in logical foundations as Arithmetic has been considered, since Frege, the (only or paradigmatic) locus for foundational analyses. They are back now also in Logic, but a direct link to their role in Physics is still missing. As a matter of fact, geodetic principles, in Physics, originate in symmetries and provide an effective foundational frame for the main theoretical approaches, since the work by E. Noether and H. Weyl. The common 'construction principles", largely grounded on symmetries, may renew the foundational links between these two disciplines. Can computability fi t into this renewed frame? What can it tell us about physical dynamics?

Bibliography

Bailly F., Longo G. Mathmatiques et sciences de la nature. La singularit physique du vivant. Hermann, Paris, 2006 (Introduction in English downloadable from http://www.di.ens.fr/~longo/).

PART B

Regular Contributions

ON THE APPROXIMABILITY OF
DENSE STEINER TREE PROBLEMS

M. HAUPTMANN

Institute of Computer Science, University of Bonn,
53117 Bonn, Germany E-mail: hauptman@cs.uni-bonn.de

The ϵ-Dense Steiner Tree Problem was defined by Karpinski and Zelikovsky [9] who proved that for each $\epsilon > 0$, this problem admits a PTAS. Based on their method we consider dense versions of various Steiner Tree problems. In particular, we give polynomial time approximation schemes for the *ϵ-Dense k-Steiner Tree Problem*, the *ϵ-Dense Price Collecting Steiner Tree Problem*, the *ϵ-Dense k-Steiner Tree Problem* and the *ϵ-Dense Group Steiner Tree Problem*. For the dense version of the *Steiner Forest Problem* we obtain an approximation algorithm that performs well if the number of terminal sets is small compared to the total number of terminals.

1. Introduction

Given a graph $G = (V, E)$, a cost function $c \colon E \to \mathbb{R}_+$ and a subset $S \subseteq V$ of the vertices of G, a Steiner Tree T for S in G is a subtree of G that all vertices from S. The elements of S are called terminals. The Steiner Tree Problem (STP) is: Given G, c and S as above, find a Steiner Tree T for S in G of minimum cost $c(T) = \sum_{e \in E(T)} c(e)$.

The Steiner Tree Problem is one of the fundamental network design problems with applications ranging from transportation networks, energy supply and broadcast problems to VLSI design and Internet Routing. The currently best known Steiner Tree approximation algorithm is due to Robins and Zelikovsky [11] and achieves a ratio of ≈ 1.55. On the other hand, Chlebik and Chlebikova [3] proved that the Steiner Tree Problem is NP-hard to approximate within ratio 1.01063.

Numerous results for special cases of the Steiner Tree Problem are known. Robins and Zelikovsky [11] obtain a better approximation ratio for the quasi-bipartite case. Arora [2] gives a polynomial time approximation scheme (PTAS) for geometric instances in constant dimension. Karpinski and Zelikovsky [9] construct a PTAS for the ϵ-Dense Steiner Tree Problem.

In this paper we consider dense versions of the Steiner Tree Problem and of some of its most important generalizations, namely the Steiner Forest Problem, the k-Steiner Problem, the Price Collecting Steiner Tree Problem and the Group Steiner Tree Problem. Let us give the definitions of these problems and of their dense versions and state results that are known for these problems.

The ϵ-Dense Steiner Tree Problem. The ϵ-Dense Steiner Tree Problem was introduced by Karpinski and Zelikovsky [9]. An instance of the Steiner Tree Problem in Graphs consisting of graph $G = (V, E)$ and terminal set $S \subseteq V$ is called ϵ-dense if each $s \in S$ has at least $\epsilon \cdot |V \setminus S|$ neighbours in $V \setminus S$. Karpinski and Zelikovsky show that for every $\epsilon > 0$ there is a polynomial time approximation scheme for the ϵ-Dense Steiner Tree Problem. The idea of their algorithm is to perform first a number of greedy steps contracting stars, where a star always consists of a non-terminal and all the terminals that are connected to it. The greedy phase reduces the number of terminals to a constant while adding extra cost $\delta \cdot |S|$. In a second phase, the remaining problem is solved by the Tree Enumeration Algorithm.

However, the following problem occurs. The greedy contractions used in [9] are not necessarily disjoint such that the density condition is not preserved under these greedy picks. We will fix this problem, using a slightly modified approach where the greedy contractions are disjoint, hence the density condition is preserved. This ends in a remaining instance of $O(\log(|S|))$ terminals, and hence using the Dreyfus-Wagner algorithm we can solve the remaining problem to optimality. This yields a PTAS which is not efficient.

However, we will show that after such a greedy phase in a sense the density is not completely destroyed, and after $O(\log^*(|S|))$ such greedy phases we obtain a remaining instance with a constant number of terminals. This approach gives an efficient PTAS for the ϵ-Dense Steiner Tree Problem.

We also consider a relaxation of the density condition which we call log-density. An instance is called log-dense if all subsets of the terminal set of size at least $\log(|S|)$ satisfy the average-density condition. The precise definition is given in the next section. For this density condition we will also obtain a PTAS.

Steiner Forest Problem: Given a graph $G = (V, E)$ with edge costs $c \colon E \to \mathbb{R}_+$ and pairwise disjoint nonempty terminal sets $S_1, \ldots, S_n \subseteq V$, find a forest F in G of minimum cost such that for all $1 \leq i \leq n$, S_i is contained in a connected component of F. The best known approximation algorithms for the Steiner Forest Problem achieve ratio $2 \cdot (1 - |S|^{-1})$, based on the primal-dual method (see for instance [10], [6]). An instance of the Steiner Forest Problem is called ϵ-dense if the edge costs are all equal to 1 and for $1 \leq i \leq m$, every $s \in S_i$ has at least $\epsilon \cdot |V \setminus S_i|$ neighbors in $V \setminus S_i$. We give a polynomial time approximation scheme for ϵ-dense instances where the number of terminal sets is small compared to the total number of terminals. The precise statement is given below.

Price Collecting Steiner Tree Problem (PSTP): Given a graph $G = (V, E)$ with edge costs $c \colon E \to \mathbb{R}_+$ and a terminal set $S \subseteq V$ with price function $p \colon S \to \mathbb{R}_+$, find a tree $T \subseteq G$ connecting a subset S' of S such as to minimize $c(T) + p(S \setminus S')$. Again, the best known approximation ratio for the general case is 2, based on the primal-dual method [6] Here we take the same density condition as for the Steiner Tree Problem: An instance is called ϵ-denes if every terminal has at least $\epsilon \cdot |V \setminus S|$ neighbours in $V \setminus S$. We will give a polynomial time approximation scheme for the ϵ-Dense PSTP.

k-Steiner Tree Problem (k-STP): Given a graph $G = (V, E)$ with edge costs $c \colon E \to \mathbb{R}_+$, a terminal set $S \subseteq V$ and a number $k \in [1, |S|]$, find a tree T in G of minimum cost $c(T)$ which connects at least k terminals from S. We will consider the same density condition as for the Steiner Tree Problem and for the Price Collecting Steiner Tree Problem. We will give a PTAS for the ϵ-Dense k-Steiner Tree Problem.

Group Steiner Tree Problem: Given a graph $G = (V, E)$ with edge costs $c \colon E \to \mathbb{R}_+$ and a system of pairwise disjoint subsets $S_1, \ldots, S_n \subseteq V$ called *groups*, find a minimum cost tree T in G such that for each $1 \leq i \leq n$ T contains at least one vertex from S_i. Halperin and Krauthgamer give a polylogarithmic lower bound for approximability [8]. The best approximation algorithm is due to Garg and Konjevod [5], obtaining a polylogarithmic approximation ratio. For the ϵ-dense case we obtain a PTAS. Here an instance is called ϵ-dense if it consists of a graph $G = (V, E)$ (i.e. all edge weights are 1) and groups $S_1, \ldots, S_n$ such that each $s \in S := \bigcup_{i=1}^{n} S_i$ has at least $\epsilon \cdot |V \setminus S|$ neighbors in $V \setminus S$.

Let us list known results and compare them to our new results.

Steiner Problems: General Case vs. Dense Case

Problem Definition	General Case		ϵ-Dense
	Upper	Lower	Upper
Steiner Tree Problem	≈ 1.55 [11]	≈ 1.01 [3]	PTAS [9]
Group Steiner Tree	polylog. [5]	polylog. [8]	**PTAS**
k-Steiner Problem	$2 + \delta$ [1]	≈ 1.01 [3]	**PTAS**
Price Collecting STP	$2 \cdot \left(1 + \frac{1}{|S|}\right)$ [6]	≈ 1.01 [3]	**PTAS**
Steiner Forest Problem	$2 \cdot \left(1 + \frac{1}{|S|}\right)$ [6]	≈ 1.01 [3]	**improved**

Steiner Tree Problem:
Density, Everywhere-Density, Average Density

Problem	Density Condition	Result
in ϵ-Everywhere Dense Graphs	$\forall\, v \in V\ d_G(v) \geq \epsilon \cdot n$	**PTAS**
in ϵ-Average Dense Graphs	$\|E\| \geq \epsilon \cdot n^2$	**APX-hard**
(ϵ, c)-log Density	$\forall S' \subseteq S,\ \|S'\| \geq c \cdot \log(\|S\|)$ implies $\|E(S', V \setminus S)\| \geq \epsilon \cdot \|S'\| \cdot \|V \setminus S\|$	**PTAS**

The paper is organized as follows. In section 2 we mention two exact algorithms for the Steiner Tree Problem, the Spanning Tree Heuristic and the Dreyfus-Wagner algorithm. In section 3 we consider the ϵ-Dense Steiner Tree Problem and the relaxation to the log-density mentioned above. Section 4 deals with the Dense Steiner Forest Problem, two open problems are stated in the Conclusion (section 5). The hardness results as well as the polynomial time approximation schemes for dense versions of the Price Collecting STP, k-Steiner Tree and Group Steiner Tree Problem will be given in the full version of the paper.

2. Exact Algorithms for the Steiner Tree Problem

We mention here only two exact algorithms for the Steiner Tree Problem, the Tree Enumeration Heuristic and the Dreyfus-Wagner Algorithm.

The Tree Enumeration Heuristic [7] enumerates all subsets of $V \setminus S$ of size at most $\|S\| - 2$ and for each of them tries to compute a minimum spanning tree (MST). The running time is $O(\|S\|^2 \cdot 2^{n - \|S\|} + n^3)$, hence exponential in the number of non-terminals but polynomial in the number of terminals.

The Dreyfus-Wagner Algorithm [4] is based on a dynamic programming approach and achieves a running time of $O(3^{\|S\|}n + 2^{\|S\|}n^2 + n^3)$, hence exponential in the number of terminals but polynomial in the number of vertices in the graph.

For the rest of the paper, by *THD* we denote the Tree Enumeration Heuristic and by *DWA* the Dreyfus-Wagner Algorithm.

3. The ϵ-Dense Steiner Tree Problem

In this section we will construct an efficient polynomail time approximation scheme for the ϵ-Dense Steiner Tree Problem. Furthermore we consider a relaxation of the density condition "towards average-density" which we call log-density.

We start with the ϵ-Dense Steiner Tree Problem. If an instance $G = (V, E)$, $S \subseteq V$ satisfies the ϵ-density condition, then there exists some $v \in V \setminus S$ such that $\|N_S(v)\| \geq \epsilon \cdot \|S\|$ [9]. Here $N_S(v)$ denotes the set of all neighbors of v in S. If we pick such a node v and remove all its terminal neighbors from S, the resulting instance $G, S \setminus N_S(v)$ is still ϵ-dense. Hence we can iterate these greedy picks and collect the stars consisting of such a node v and the set $N_S(v)$. After i picks, the size of the terminal set is reduced to at most $(1 - \epsilon)^i \cdot |S|$. Afterwards we contract all the stars picked so far and add these supernodes to the terminal set. This gives an instance of the Steiner Tree Problem with a terminal set of size at most $(1 - \epsilon)^i \cdot |S| + i$. Hence after $O(\log |S|)$ greedy steps we are left with an instance of the Steiner Tree Problem with only $O(\log(|S|))$ terminals, which can be solved to optimality using the Dreyfus Wagner Algorithm DW [4]. This gives the following modified version of the Karpinski-Zelikovsky algorithm.

Algorithm DST
Input: $G = (V, E)$, $S \subseteq V$, $\delta > 0$
Output: $(1 + \delta)$-approx. Steiner Tree for S in G
Phase 1: Greedy Picks
    while $|S| > k_\delta$
        $v := \mathrm{argmax}\{|N_S(u)|, u \in V \setminus S\}$
        $ST_v :=$ the star consisting ov v and $N_S(v)$
        $S := S \setminus N_S(v)$
Phase 2:
    for each star ST_v collected in Phase 1
        Contract ST_v into s_v
        $S := S \cup \{s_v\}$
    Solve the remaining instance using
    the Dreyfus-Wagner Algorithm, obtain tree T_2.
Return $T_{DST} := T_2 \cup \bigcup_{\text{Phase 1}} ST_v$

Analysis. Let S_i denote the terminal set after i greedy picks in phase 1. Due to the density condition, $|S_i| \le (1 - \epsilon)^i \cdot |S|$. Hence after $i \ge \frac{\log(|S|/k_\delta)}{\log(1/(1-\epsilon))}$ greedy steps, $|S_i| \le k_\delta$. The remaining instance consists of at most $i + k_\delta$ terminals. For each star ST_v picked in phase 1, we add edges that form an MST for the terminals of ST_v. This does not increase the cost of an optimum Steiner tree. We may assume that the optimum Steiner tree for this modified instance consists of the MSTs for the stars and a tree T_0 connecting these. Note that the cost of T_2 is bounded by the cost of T_0. Let T^* denote an optimum Steiner tree for S in G. Let $ST_1, \ldots, ST_i$ be the stars collected in phase 1, let S_j denote the terminal set of ST_j ($1 \le j \le i$). Hence we obtain $\frac{(T_{DST})}{c(T^*)} \le \frac{\sum_{j=1}^{i} |S_j| + i + k_\delta}{\sum_{j=1}^{i} |S_j| + k_\delta}$ We want to choose k_δ such as to bound the right hand side of this inequality by $1 + \delta$. It suffices to choose $k_\delta \ge \frac{|S|}{2^{\log(1/(1-\epsilon)) \cdot |S| \cdot \delta - 1}}$, which can be bounded by a constant only depending on ϵ and δ. The running time of phase 1 is polynomial in the size of G and S. Since $i = O(\log(|S|))$ for fixed δ, the running time of phase 2 is also polynomial in the input size. Hence we obtain

Theorem 3.1. *Algorithm DST is a polynomial time approximation scheme for the ϵ-Dense Steiner Tree Problem.*

Since each terminal is involved in at most one contraction, afterwards each of the new terminals has at least $\epsilon|V \setminus S| - 1$ non-terminal neighbors and the number of non-terminals is $|V \setminus S| - i$. Hence the resulting instance is ϵ'-dense for $\epsilon' = \frac{\epsilon \cdot |V \setminus S| - i}{|V \setminus S| - i}$. We can now iterate the greedy process $O(\log^*(|S|))$ times, where the j-th run of the greedy phase takes as its terminal set the remaining terminals and the contracted stars from the previous phase. This reduces the number of terminals to a constant, and therefore we can afterwards use the Tree Enumeration Algorithm [7] instead of the Dreyfus-Wagner algorithm to solve the remaining instance. This yields the following result, the complete proof of which will be given in the full version of the paper.

Theorem 3.2. *For each $\epsilon > 0$, there is an efficient polynomial time approximation scheme for the ϵ-dense Steiner Tree Problem.*

3.1. *Towards Average-Density: Relaxing the Density Condition*

We may now ask for a polynomial approximation scheme for average-dense versions of the Steiner Tree Problem. A natural definition of average density is as follows: We call an instance $G = (V, E), S \subseteq V$ of the Graph Steiner Tree Problem *average ϵ-dense* if

$$|E(S, V \setminus S)| \geq \epsilon \cdot |S| \cdot |V \setminus S|. \tag{1}$$

Note that ϵ-Density as defined in [9] implies Average-ϵ-Density. Furthermore average ϵ-density implies existence of a vertex $v \in V \setminus S$ with at least $\epsilon \cdot |S|$ neighbours in S, i.e. a *good pick*. Unfortunately, average ϵ-density is not preserved under good picks. Here is an easy example: If there exists a subset S' of S of size $\epsilon \cdot |S|$ such that every vertex $v \in V \setminus S$ is connected to all terminals from S' and to none of the terminals from $S \setminus S'$, this instance is average ϵ-dense. However after one good pick the density condition is not valid anymore.

Nevertheless we will at least relax the density condition "towards average-density" and give a PTAS for this relaxed version. Let us first give some motivation. We observe that ϵ-density not only implies (1) but the following more general property:

$$|E(S', V \setminus S)| \geq \epsilon \cdot |S'| \cdot |V \setminus S| \quad \text{for all } S' \subseteq S \tag{2}$$

Indeed (2) is equivalent to ϵ-density. We may now ask how far we can relax (2). Relaxing here means to consider instances where (2) does not necessarily hold for all subsets S' of S but for all subsets with cardinality at least some prespecified lower bound. In (2) the lower bound is 1 (or 0) while in the average-density condition (1) it is $|S|$. The question now is: How much can we increase the lower bound (starting from 1) and still get a PTAS ? Actually we do not know the answer but at least we can relax up to logarithmic size:

Definition 3.1. (log-**Density**) An instance $G = (V, E), S$ of the Graph Steiner Tree Prolem is called $(\epsilon, c) - \log$-**dense** iff for all subsets $S' \subseteq S$ of the terminal set with $|S'| \geq c \cdot \log(|S|)$

$$|E(S', V \setminus S)| \geq \epsilon \cdot |S'| \cdot |V \setminus S|. \tag{3}$$

Theorem 3.3. *For each $\epsilon > 0, c > 0$ there is a PTAS for the $(\epsilon, c) - \log$-Dense Steiner Tree Problem.*

Let us first give some ideas and then give the precise proof of Theorem 3.3. Our approach is quite similar to that of Karpinski and Zelikovsky [9]. The most important difference is that when performing greedy steps and picking Steiner points, after contracting a star consisting of a vertex from $V \setminus S$ and all its neighbours in S, the resulting supernode will be removed from S and hence not be considered in further greedy steps anymore. This alternative method has basically two effects: First the density condition for the actual terminal set is preserved and second afterwards we are left with a "residual" terminal set of logarithmic instead of constant size. Hence in order to solve the remaining problem we will take the Dreyfus Wagner algorithm instead of the Tree Enumeration algorithm since its running time is polynomial in the number of non-terminals (and exponential in the number of terminals, hence polynomial in the initial input size). We are now ready to describe our algorithm.

Algorithm LDSTP

Input: an instance of the (c, ϵ)-log-dense Steiner Tree Problem
             consisting of graph $G = (V, E)$, terminal set $S \subseteq V$

Output: Steiner tree T for S in G

(0) $\mathcal{C} := \{\{s\} : s \in S\}$ set of terminal components
    $\mathcal{C}_a := \mathcal{C}$ set of active terminal components

(1) **while** $E(\mathcal{C}_a) \neq \emptyset$ **do**
    Pick $e \in E(\mathcal{C}_a)$ connecting two terminal components $C_1, C_2 \in \mathcal{C}_a$.
    Let $\mathcal{C}_a := (\mathcal{C}_a \setminus \{C_1, C_2\}) \cup \{C_1 \cup C_2\}$, update $\mathcal{C}$ accordingly.

(2) **while** $|\mathcal{C}_a| \geq c \cdot \log(|S|) \cdot K$ **do**
    Find $v \in V \setminus S$ with the maximum number of neighbours in $\mathcal{C}_a$.
    Contract the star $T(v)$ consisting of v and its neighbours $N(v, \mathcal{C}_a)$
    in $\mathcal{C}_a$. Update $\mathcal{C}$ and $\mathcal{C}_a$ accordingly:
    $\mathcal{C}_a := \mathcal{C}_a \setminus N(v, \mathcal{C}_a), \ \mathcal{C} := (\mathcal{C} \setminus N(v, \mathcal{C}_a)) \cup \{\bigcup_{C \in N(v, \mathcal{C}_a)} C\}.$

(3) Find an optimum Steiner tree T^* for $\mathcal{C}$.

(4) **Return** $T_{LD} := T^* \cup \bigcup_{v \text{ picked in (1)}} T(v) \cup \{e|\ e \text{ picked in (1)}\}$.

Analysis. The log-density condition directly implies that initially

$$|E(\mathcal{C}', V \setminus \mathcal{C}_a)| \geq \epsilon \cdot |\mathcal{C}'| \cdot |V \setminus \mathcal{C}_a| \tag{4}$$

for all subsets $\mathcal{C}'$ of $\mathcal{C}_a$ of size at least $c \cdot \log(|S|)$. We will now prove that (4) is preserved by the picks of edges in phase (1) and stars in phase (2) of algorithm LDSTP. Indeed, if an edge connecting two active components is picked, then subsets $\mathcal{C}'$ of $\mathcal{C}_a$ of size at least $c \cdot \log(|S|)$ after the pick correspond to subsets of $\mathcal{C}_a$ of size $\in [\ |\mathcal{C}'|, |\mathcal{C}'| + 1]$ before the pick with the same neighbourhood in $V \setminus \mathcal{C}$, and since $|V \setminus \mathcal{C}|$ does not change, (4) still holds. On the other hand, if a vertex $v \in V \setminus \mathcal{C}$ is picked and the star consisting of v and $N(v, \mathcal{C}_a)$ is contracted, then the resulting supernode is removed from $\mathcal{C}_a$ and the cardinality of $V \setminus \mathcal{C}_a$ remains the same, hence also in this case (4) is preserved.

Let k be the number of picks of stars $T(v, N(v, \mathcal{C}_a))$ in phase (2), let $T_1 = T(v_1, N_1), \ldots, T_k = T(v_k, N_k)$ denote these stars and let $e_1, \ldots, e_l$ denote the single edges connecting active components picked in phase (1) of algorithm LD-STP.

Now construct graph G' from G by adding edges connecting the set $N(v, \mathcal{C}_a)$ by a spanning tree for each pick v in phase (1) of algorithm LDSTP. Note that $OPT(G', S) \leq OPT(G, S)$. There exists an optimum tree T^{**} in G' consisting of spanning trees T_i' for the sets $N_i = N(v_i, \mathcal{C}_a)$ of picks in phase (2), the set E_1 of all edges connecting two active components in phase (1) and a tree T' connecting the set of components $\mathcal{C}$ at the end of phase (2). Hence we can bound the approximation ratio of algorithm LDSTP as follows:

$$\frac{\text{cost}(T_{LD})}{\text{cost}(T^{**})} \leq \frac{\text{cost}(T^*) + \sum_{i=1}^{k} \text{cost}(T_i) + |E_1|}{\text{cost}(T') + \sum_{i=1}^{k} \text{cost}(T_i') + |E_1|} \leq \frac{\sum_{i=1}^{k} |N_i|}{\sum_{i=1}^{k}(|N_i|-1)} \leq 1 + \frac{k}{(\sum_{i=1}^{k} |N_i|)-k}.$$

Hence let us assume we start with a (c, ϵ)-dense instance with no edges between terminals. Each pick of a star reduces the cardinality of $\mathcal{C}_a$ by a factor ϵ. Let $\mathcal{C}_a(i)$ denote the set $\mathcal{C}_a$ after i picks of a star, then $|\mathcal{C}_a(i)| \leq (1-\epsilon)^i |S|$. We obtain $|\mathcal{C}_a(k)| < c \cdot \log(|S|) \cdot K$ for $k \geq \frac{|S|}{c \cdot \log(|S|) \cdot K} \cdot \frac{1}{\log(1/(1-\epsilon))}$, hence we assume $k \leq \frac{|S|}{c \cdot \log(|S|) \cdot K} \cdot \frac{1}{\log(1/(1-\epsilon))} + 1$. Since

$$\sum_{i=1}^{k} |N_i| \geq \sum_{i=1}^{k}(1-\epsilon)^i \cdot \epsilon \cdot |S| = \epsilon \cdot |S| \cdot \sum_{i=1}^{k}(1-\epsilon)^i = \epsilon \cdot |S| \cdot \frac{1-(1-\epsilon)^k}{\epsilon}$$

we obtain the following bound for the approximation ratio of algorithm LDSTP:

$$\frac{\text{cost}(T_{LD})}{\text{cost}(T^{\star\star})} \leq 1 + \frac{2k}{\sum_{i=1}^{k} |N_i|} \leq 1 + \frac{2k}{|S| \cdot (1 - (1 - \epsilon)^k)}$$

$$\leq 1 + \frac{2 \cdot (\frac{|S|}{c \cdot \log(|S|) \cdot K} \cdot \frac{1}{\log(1/(1-\epsilon))} + 1)}{|S| \cdot (1 - (1 - \epsilon)^k)}$$

$$\leq 1 + \frac{2 \cdot (\frac{|S|}{c \cdot \log(|S|) \cdot K} \cdot \frac{1}{\log(1/(1-\epsilon))} + 1)}{|S| \cdot \epsilon} \qquad (5)$$

since we may assume $k \geq 1$ (in case $k = 0$ algorithm LDSTP computes an optimum solution, namely a spanning tree for S). Using $\frac{1}{|S|} \leq \frac{1}{\log(|S|)}$ we obtain $\frac{\text{cost}(T_{LD})}{\text{cost}(T^{\star\star})} \leq 1 + \frac{1}{\epsilon} \cdot \left(\frac{1}{c \cdot K \cdot \log(\frac{1}{1-\epsilon})} + 1 \right) \cdot \frac{1}{\log(|S|)}$. For given $\delta > 0$ we will now choose K such that the approximation ratio is bounded by $1 + \delta$, i.e. $K \geq \left(c \cdot \log\left(\frac{1}{1-\epsilon}\right) \cdot (\epsilon \cdot \delta \cdot \log(|S|) - 1) \right)^{-1}$. Hence choosing $K = \left(c \cdot \log\left(\frac{1}{1-\epsilon}\right) \right)^{-1}$, solving the Steiner Tree instance exactly by brute force for $|S| \leq 2^{2/(\epsilon \cdot \delta)}$ and applying LDSTP for all other instances yields a PTAS for the (c, ϵ)-log-dense Steiner Tree Problem. $\qquad \square$

4. The Dense Steiner Forest Problem

Concerning the ϵ-Dense Steiner Forest Problem, we are currently not able to provide a PTAS for this problem, for the following reason: All the variants of the methods of [9] we have discussed so far (and will discuss in subsequent sections) are based on the approach of performing greedy steps until the problem size is sufficiently small and then applying some exact algorithm for the remaining instance. In the Steiner Forest Case the kind of greedy steps we may think of reduce each single terminal set to constant size, but the number of terminal sets might not be reduced at all. On the other hand we do not know how to justify contraction steps that reduce the number of terminal sets, since melting j of them into a single terminal set might produce an additional cost of j. However we will give an approximation algorithm for the Dense Steiner Forest Problem with approximation ratio $1 + O((\sum_{i=1}^{n} \log(|S_i|))/(\sum_{i=1}^{n} |S_i|))$, where $S_1, \ldots S_n$ are the given terminal sets. Intuitively this provides good approximation in case sufficiently many terminal sets are large, and we will make this precise in this section.

Definition 4.1. An instance $G = (V, E), S_1, \ldots, S_n$ of the SFP is called ϵ-**dense'** iff for all $1 \leq i \leq n$ and $S' \subseteq S_i$ there exists a vertex $v \in V \setminus S_i$ such that $|N(v) \cap S'| \geq \epsilon \cdot |S'|$.

Lemma 4.1. *For every $\epsilon > 0$, every ϵ-dense instance of the SFP is ϵ-dense'.*

Proof. Let $G = (V, E), S_1, \ldots, S_n$ be ϵ-dense, let $i \in \{1, \ldots, n\}$ and $S' \subseteq S_i$. Then for all $s \in S'$ it holds $|N(s) \cap (V \setminus S_i)| \geq \epsilon \cdot |V \setminus S_i|$.
From $\sum_{v \in V \setminus S_i} |N(v) \cap S'| = \sum_{s \in S'} |N(s) \cap (V \setminus S_i)| \geq |S'| \cdot \epsilon \cdot |V \setminus S_i|$ we conclude that there exists at least on $v \in V \setminus S_i$ such that $|N(v) \cap S'| \geq \epsilon \cdot |S'|$ $\square$

Algorithm A_k:
Input: $G = (V, E), \mathcal{S} := \{S_1, \ldots, S_n\} \subseteq P(V)$ instance of the ϵ-Dense SFP
Output: Set of edges $F \subseteq E$ defining a Steiner Forest for $S_1, \ldots, S_n$

(0) Let $F := \emptyset$ and $S_{i,act} := S_i, 1 \leq i \leq n$.
(1) **while** $\max_{1 \leq i \leq n} |S_{i,act}| \geq k$ **do**
    Pick $i \in \{1, \ldots, n\}$ and $v \in V \setminus S_{i,act}$
    such as to maximize $|N(v) \cap S_{i,act}|$.
    Let $\tilde{S} := N(v) \cap S_{i,act}$ and $F := F \cup \{\{v, s\} : s \in S\}$.
    $S_{i,act} := S_{i,act} \setminus \tilde{S}$. Contract $\tilde{S} \cup \{v\}$.
(2) Solve the remaining instance using the Primal-Dual algorithm.

Lemma 4.2. *At the beginning of every call of the while-loop the sets $S_{i,act}$ are ϵ-dense'.*

Proof. The initial sets $S_{i,act} = S_i$ are ϵ-dense and therefore ϵ-dense'. Since in every iteration the removed set $\tilde{S}$ does not contain elements from $\bigcup_{s \in S_{i,act} \setminus \tilde{S}} N(s) \setminus S_{i,act}$, for every subset S' of $S_{i,act} \setminus \tilde{S}$ existence of a vertex v in $V \setminus S_{i,act}$ and hence in $V \setminus S'$ with many neighbours in S' is not disturbed. $\square$

Analysis of Algorithm A_k. First note that $\sum_{i=1}^{n}(|S_i| - 1) =: L$ is a lower bound for the cost of an optimum solution. We will now estimate the cost of the solution produced by algorithm A_k. For $1 \leq i \leq n$ let $j(i)$ denote the number of contractions of subsets of $S_{i,act}$ in phase (1) of the algorithm, and let $S_i^1, \ldots, S_i^{j(i)}$ be the subsets being contracted. Let $S_{i,rem} := S_i \setminus (S_i^1 \cup \ldots \cup S_i^{j(i)})$ the remaining set of S_i. Then the number of edges added to F in phase (1) is given by $\mathrm{cost}_1 = \sum_{i=1}^{n} \sum_{l=1}^{j(i)} |S_i^l| = \sum_{i=1}^{n}(|S_i| - |S_{i,rem}|)$. At the end of phase (1), for $1 \leq i \leq n$ the size of S_i is given by $s(i) := j(i) + |S_i| - \sum_{l=1}^{j(i)} |S_i^l| = j(i) + |S_{i,rem}|$. Furthermore the size of $S_{i,act}$ after l contractions is bounded by $|S_i|(1 - \epsilon)^l$, hence we have $s(i) \leq j(i) + |S_i|(1 - \epsilon)^{j(i)}$. Hence the number cost_2 of edges picked by the 2-Approximation Algorithm in phase (2) of A_k is bounded as follows:
$\mathrm{cost}_2 \leq 2 \cdot \sum_{i=1}^{n} \left(j(i) + |S_i|(1 - \epsilon)^{j(i)} \right)$. Let $x_{i,l} := |S_i^l|, 1 \leq i \leq n, 1 \leq l \leq$

$j(i)$. An upper bound for the cost of solution generated by algorithm A_k is then given by the following optimization problem:

$$\max \sum_{i=1}^{n} \sum_{l=1}^{j(i)} x_{i,j} + 2 \cdot \left(|S_i| - \sum_{l=1}^{j(i)} x_{i,l} + j(i) \right)$$
$$\text{s.t.} \quad \sum_{l=1}^{j(i)} x_{i,l} \geq |S_i| \cdot \left(1 - (1 - \epsilon)^{j(i)} \right), \; 1 \leq i \leq n$$
$$= \quad \max \sum_{i=1}^{n} \left(2|S_i| - \sum_{l=1}^{j(i)} x_{i,l} + 2j(i) \right)$$
$$\text{s.t.} \quad \sum_{l=1}^{j(i)} x_{i,l} \geq |S_i| \cdot \left(1 - (1 - \epsilon)^{j(i)} \right), \; 1 \leq i \leq n$$

Let $\text{save}_i := \sum_{l=1}^{j(i)} x_{i,l} - 2j(i) \; (1 \leq i \leq n)$. We give a lower bound for save_i as a function of $|S_i|$: Let $X = \sum_{l=1}^{j(i)} x_{i,l}$ the total number of terminals removed from S_i in phase (1) of algorithm A_k, then $X > (\epsilon|S_i| - k)/\epsilon = |S_i| - k/\epsilon$. Furthermore $k > \epsilon \cdot |S_i| \cdot (1 - \epsilon)^{j(i)}$ from which we conclude $j(i) < \frac{\log(k/(\epsilon|S_i|))}{\log(1-\epsilon)}$. Hence the total cost of the solution generated by algorithm A_k is bounded by

$$\sum_{i=1}^{n} \left(|S_i| + \frac{k}{\epsilon} + 2 \cdot \frac{\log\left(\frac{k}{\epsilon|S_i|}\right)}{\log(1-\epsilon)} \right) = \sum_{i=1}^{n} \left(|S_i| + \frac{k}{\epsilon} + 2 \cdot \frac{\log\left(\frac{\epsilon|S_i|}{k}\right)}{\log\left(\frac{1}{1-\epsilon}\right)} \right) =:$$

$tc(\epsilon, k)$. Since $\frac{d}{dk} tc(\epsilon, k) = n \cdot \left(\frac{1}{\epsilon} - \frac{2}{\log\left(\frac{1}{1-\epsilon}\right)} \cdot \frac{1}{k} \right) = 0$ for $k^* = \frac{2\epsilon}{\log\left(\frac{1}{1-\epsilon}\right)}$ and $\frac{d^2}{dk^2} tc(\epsilon, k^*) > 0$, we choose $k = k^*$ and finally obtain

Theorem 4.1. *For each $\epsilon > 0$ there is a polynomial time approximation algorithm for the ϵ-Dense Steiner Forest Problem with approximation ratio $1 + O\left(\frac{\sum_{i=1}^{n} \log(|S_i|)}{\sum_{i=1}^{n} |S_i|} \right)$.*

5. Conclusion

We have presented polynomial time approximation schemes for dense versions of the Steiner Tree Problem and some of its generalizations. One of the most challenging open questions that remain in this field is to prove the NP-hardness of the ϵ-Dense Steiner Tree Problem.

Acknowledgement. We would like to thank Marek Karpinski for valuable discussions.

References

1. S. Arora and G.G. Karakostas. A 2+epsilon approximation for the k-mst problem. In *Proc. SIAM Symp. Discrete Algorithms (SODA)*, 2000.
2. S. Arora. Polynomial time approximation schemes for Euclidean traveling salesman and other geometric problems. *Journal of the ACM*, 45(5):753–782, 1998.
3. M. Chlebikov and J. Chlebikova. Approximation hardness of the steiner tree problem on graphs. In *Proceedings of 8th Scandinavian Workshop on Algorithm Theory (SWAT)*, pages 170–179. LNCS 2368, 2002.

4. S.E. Dreyfus and R.A. Wagner. The steiner problem in graphs. *Networks*, 1:195–207, 1971.

5. N. Garg, G. Konjevod, and R. Ravi. A polylogarithmic approximation algorithm for the group steiner tree problem. In *SODA: ACM-SIAM Symposium on Discrete Algorithms*, 1998.

6. M. Goemans and D. Williamson. A general approximation technique for constrained forest problems. In *SODA: ACM-SIAM Symposium on Discrete Algorithms*, 1992.

7. S.L. Hakimi. Steiner's problem in graphs and its implications. *Networks*, 1:113–133, 1971.

8. E. Halperin and R. Krauthgamer. Polylogarithmic inapproximability. In *In Proc. of STOC*, 2003.

9. M. Karpinski and A. Zelikovsky. Approximating dense cases of covering problems. In *Proc. of the DIMACS Workshop on Network Design: Connectivity and Facilites Location, Princeton University, NJ, April, 1997. DIMACS series in Disc. Math. and Theor. Comp. Sci. 40*, pages 169–178, 1998.

10. R. Ravi. A primal-dual approximation algorithm for the steiner forest problem. *Information Processing Letters*, 50(4):185–190, 1994.

11. G. Robins and A. Zelikovsky. Improved steiner tree approximation in graphs. In *Proc. 11th Ann. ACM-SIAM Symp. on Discrete Algorithms*, pages 770–779. ACM-SIAM, 2000.

WEAK PATTERN MATCHING IN COLORED GRAPHS: MINIMIZING THE NUMBER OF CONNECTED COMPONENTS

RICCARDO DONDI

Dipartimento di Scienze dei Linguaggi, della Comunicazione e degli Studi Culturali
Università degli Studi di Bergamo, Piazza Vecchia 8, 24129 Bergamo - Italy
EMAIL: riccardo.dondi@unibg.it

GUILLAUME FERTIN

Laboratoire d'Informatique de Nantes-Atlantique (LINA), FRE CNRS 2729
Université de Nantes, 2 rue de la Houssinière, 44322 Nantes Cedex 3 - France
EMAIL: guillaume.fertin@lina.univ-nantes.fr

STÉPHANE VIALETTE

Laboratoire de Recherche en Informatique (LRI), UMR CNRS 8623
Université Paris-Sud 11, 91405 Orsay - France
EMAIL: stephane.vialette@lri.fr

In the context of metabolic network analysis, Lacroix *et al.* [11] introduced the problem of finding occurrences of motifs in vertex-colored graphs, where a motif is a multiset of colors and an occurrence of a motif is a subset of connected vertices which are colored by all colors of the motif. We consider in this paper the above-mentioned problem in one of its natural optimization forms, referred hereafter as the MIN-CC problem: Find an occurrence of a motif in a vertex-colored graph, called the *target graph*, that induces a minimum number of connected components.

Our results can be summarized as follows. We prove the MIN-CC problem to be **APX**–hard even in the extremal case where the motif is a set and the target graph is a path. We complement this result by giving a polynomial-time algorithm in case the motif is built upon a fixed number of colors and the target graph is a path. Also, extending recent research [8], we prove the MIN-CC problem to be fixed-parameter tractable when parameterized by the size of the motif, and we give a faster algorithm in case the target graph is a tree. Furthermore, we prove the MIN-CC problem for trees not to be approximable within ratio $c \log n$ for some constant $c > 0$, where n is the order of the target graph, and to be **W[2]**–hard when parameterized by the number of connected components in the occurrence of the motif. Finally, we give an exact efficient exponential-time algorithm for the MIN-CC problem in case the target graph is a tree.

1. Introduction

In the context of metabolic network analysis, Lacroix *et al.* [11] introduced the following vertex colored graph problem (referred hereafter as the GRAPH-MOTIF problem): Given a vertex-colored graph G and a multiset of colors $\mathcal{M}$, decide whether G has a connected subset of vertices which are exactly colored by $\mathcal{M}$. There, vertices correspond to chemical compounds or reactions, and each edge (v_i, v_j) corresponds to an interaction between the two compounds or reactions v_i and v_j. The vertex coloring is used to specify different chemical types or functionalities. In this scenario, connected motifs correspond to interaction-related submodules of the network which consist of a specific set of chemical compounds and reactions. A method for a rational decomposition of a metabolic network into relatively independent functional subsets is essential for a better understanding of the modularity and organization principles in the network [5,11]. Notice that Ideker considered a related relevant work [10].

Unfortunately, it turns out that the GRAPH-MOTIF problem is **NP**–complete even if the graph is a tree and the motif is actually a set [8,11]. Moreover, the GRAPH-MOTIF problem is fixed-parameter tractable when parameterized by the size of the motif, but **W[1]**–hard when parameterized by the number of distinct colors in $\mathcal{M}$ [8]. Finally, Lacroix *et al.* [11] gave an exact algorithm dedicated to solve small instances.

For metabolic network analysis, the GRAPH-MOTIF problem appears, however, to be too stringent. Indeed, due to measurement errors, it is often not possible to find a connected component of the graph G which corresponds exactly to the motif $\mathcal{M}$. Hence one needs to relax the definition of an occurrence of a motif in a metabolic network. Therefore, aiming at dealing with inherent imprecise data, we consider in this paper the above-mentioned problem in one of its natural optimization form, referred hereafter as the MIN-CC problem: Find an occurrence of a motif in a vertex-colored graph, that induces a minimum number of connected components.

The paper is organized as follows. Section 2 provides basic notations and definitions that we will use in the paper. In Section 3, we prove the MIN-CC problem to be **APX**–hard even if the motif is a set and the target graph is a path. Extending recent research [8], we prove in Section 4 that the MIN-CC problem is fixed-parameter tractable when parameterized by the size of the motif, and we give a faster algorithm in case the target graph is a tree. In Section 5 we present a polynomial-time algorithm in case the motif is built upon a fixed number of colors and the target graph is a path. Section 6 is devoted to hardness of approximation in case the target graph is a tree and we present in Section 7 an exact efficient exponential-time algorithm for trees. Section 8 concludes our work and suggests future directions of research.

2. Preliminaries

We assume readers have basic knowledge about graph theory [6] and we shall only recall basic notations here. Let G be a graph. We write $\mathbf{V}(G)$ for the set of vertices and $\mathbf{E}(G)$ for the set of edges. For any $V' \subseteq \mathbf{V}(G)$, we denote by $G[V']$ the subgraph of G induced by the vertices V', that is $G[V'] = (V', E')$ and $(u, v) \in E'$ iff $u, v \in V'$ and $(u, v) \in \mathbf{E}(G)$. Let $\mathcal{M}$ be a multiset of colors, whose colors are taken from the set $\mathcal{C} = \{c_1, c_2, \ldots, c_q\}$. Let G be a connected graph, where every vertex $u \in \mathbf{V}(G)$ is assigned a color $\lambda(u) \in \mathcal{C}$. For any subset V' of V, let $C(V')$ be the multiset of colors assigned to the vertices in V'. A subset of vertices $V' \subseteq \mathbf{V}(G)$ is said to *match* a multiset of colors $\mathcal{M}$ if $C(V')$ is equal to $\mathcal{M}$. A *color-preserving injective mapping* θ of $\mathcal{M}$ to G is an injective mapping $\theta : \mathcal{M} \to \mathbf{V}(G)$, such that $\lambda(\theta(c)) = c$ for every $c \in \mathcal{M}$. The subgraph induced by a color-preserving injective mapping $\theta : \mathcal{M} \to \mathbf{V}(G)$ is the subgraph of G induced by the images of θ in G.

We are now in position to formally define the MIN-CC problem we are interested in. Given a set of colors $\mathcal{C}$, a multiset (motif) $\mathcal{M}$ of size k of colors from $\mathcal{C}$ and a target graph G of order n together with a vertex-coloring mapping $\lambda : \mathbf{V}(G) \to \mathcal{C}$, find a color preserving injective mapping $\theta : \mathcal{M} \to \mathbf{V}(G)$, *i.e.*, $\lambda(\theta(c)) = c$ for every $c \in \mathcal{M}$ that minimizes the number of connected components in the subgraph induced by θ. In other words, the MIN-CC problem asks to find a subset $V' \subseteq \mathbf{V}(G)$ that matches $\mathcal{M}$, and that minimizes the number of connected components of $G[V']$. The MIN-CC problem was proved to be **NP**–complete even if the target graph is a tree and the occurrence is required to be connected (the occurrence of $\mathcal{M}$ in G results in one connected component) but fixed-parameter tractable in this case when parameterized by the size of the given motif [11].

3. Hardness result for paths

In this section we show that the MIN-CC problem is **APX**–hard (not approximable within a constant) even in the simple case where the motif $\mathcal{M}$ is a set and the target graph is a path in which each color in $\mathcal{C}$ occurs exactly twice. Our proof consists in a reduction from a restricted version of the PAINTSHOP-FOR-WORDS problem [2,3,15].

First, we need some additional definitions. Define an *isogram* to be a word in which no letter is used more than once. A *pair isogram* is a word in which each letter occurs exactly twice. A *cover* of size k of a word u is an ordered collection of words $C = (v_1, v_2, \ldots, v_k)$ such that $u = w_1 v_1 w_2 v_2 \ldots w_k v_k w_{k+1}$ and $v = v_1 v_2 \ldots v_k$ is an isogram The cover is called *prefix* (resp. *suffix*) if w_1 (resp. w_{k+1}) is the empty word.

A *proper 2-coloring* of a pair isogram u is an assignment f of colors c_1 and c_2 to the letters of u such that every letter of u is colored with color c_1 once and colored with color c_2 once. If two adjacent letters x and y are colored with different colors we say that there is a *color change* between x and y. For the sake of brevity, we denote a pair isogram u together with a proper 2-coloring f of it as the pair (u, f).

The 1-REGULAR-2-COLORS-PAINT-SHOP problem is defined as follows: Given a pair isogram u, find a 2-coloring f of u that minimizes the number of color changes in (u, f). Bonsma [2] proved that the 1-REGULAR-2-COLORS-PAINT-SHOP problem is **APX**–hard. We show here how to reduce the 1-REGULAR-2-COLORS-PAINT-SHOP problem to the MIN-CC problem for paths. We need the following easy lemmas.

Lemma 3.1. *Let u be a pair isogram and C be a minimum cardinality cover of u. Then C cannot be both prefix and suffix.*

Lemma 3.2. *A pair isogram has a proper 2-coloring with at most k color changes iff it has a cover of size at most $\left\lceil \frac{k}{2} \right\rceil$.*

Combining Lemma 3.2 with the fact that the 1-REGULAR-2-COLORS-PAINT-SHOP problem is **APX**–hard, we state the following result.

Proposition 3.1. *The following problem is **APX**–hard : Given a pair isogram u, find a minimum cardinality cover of u.*

Corollary 3.1. *The MIN-CC problem is **APX**–hard even if $\mathcal{M}$ is a set and P is a path in which each color appears at most twice.*

4. Fixed-parameter algorithms

Corollary 3.1 gives us a sharp hardness result for the MIN-CC problem. To complement this negative result, we first prove here that the MIN-CC problem is fixed-parameter tractable [7,9] when parameterized by the size of the pattern $\mathcal{M}$. The algorithm is a straightforward extension of a recent result [8] and is based on the *color-coding* technique [1]. Next, we give a faster fixed-parameter algorithm in case the target graph is a tree.

4.1. *The* MIN-CC *problem is fixed-parameter tractable*

We only sketch the fixed-parameter tractability result. Let G be a graph and k be a positive integer. Recall that a family $\mathcal{F}$ of functions from $\mathbf{V}(G)$ to $\{1, 2, \ldots, k\}$ is *perfect* if for any subset $V \subseteq \mathbf{V}(G)$ of k vertices there is a function $f \in \mathcal{F}$ which is injective on V [1]. Let $(G, \mathcal{M})$ be an instance of the MIN-CC problem, where $\mathcal{M}$ is a motif of size k. Then there is an occurrence of $\mathcal{M}$ in G, say $V \subseteq \mathbf{V}(G)$, that results in a minimum number of connected components. Furthermore, suppose we are provided with a perfect family $\mathcal{F}$ of functions from $\mathbf{V}(G)$ to $\{1, 2, \ldots, k\}$. Since $\mathcal{F}$ is perfect, we are guaranteed that at least one function in $\mathcal{F}$ assigns V with k distinct labels. Let $f \in \mathcal{F}$ be such a function. We now turn to defining a dynamic programming table T indexed by vertices of G and subsets of $\{1, 2, \ldots, k\}$. For any $v \in \mathbf{V}(G)$ and any $L \subseteq \{1, 2, \ldots, k\}$, we define $T_L[v]$ to be the family of all motifs $\mathcal{M}' \subseteq \mathcal{M}$, $|\mathcal{M}'| = |L|$, for which there exists an exact occurrence of $\mathcal{M}'$ in G, say V, such that $v \in V$ and the set of (unique) labels that f assigns to V is exactly L. We need the following lemma [8].

Lemma 4.1. *For any labeling function* $f : \mathbf{V}(G) \to \{1, 2, \ldots, k\}$, *there exists a dynamic programming algorithm that computes the table T in* $\mathcal{O}(2^{5k}kn^2)$ *time.*

Now, denote by $\mathcal{P}$ the set of all pairs $(\mathcal{M}', L') \in \mathcal{M} \times 2^{\{1,2,\ldots,k\}}$ with $|\mathcal{M}'| = |L'|$ such that there exists an exact occurrence of $\mathcal{M}'$ in G, say V', such that $v \in V'$ and the set of (unique) labels that f assigns to V' is exactly L'. Clearly, $|\mathcal{P}| \leq 2^{2k}$. Furthermore, by resorting to any data structure for searching and inserting that guarantees logarithmic time [4] (and observing that any two pairs $(\mathcal{M}', L')$ and $(\mathcal{M}'', L'')$ can be compared in $\mathcal{O}(k)$ time), one can construct the set $\mathcal{P}$ in $\mathcal{O}(nk^2 2^{2k})$ time by running through the table T. Our algorithm now exhaustively considers all subsets of $\mathcal{P}$ of size at most k to find an occurrence of $\mathcal{M}$ in G that results in a minimum number of connected components. The rationale of this approach is that two pairs $(\mathcal{M}', L')$ and $(\mathcal{M}'', L'')$ with $L' \cap L'' = \emptyset$ correspond to non-overlapping occurrences in G. The total time of this latter procedure is certainly upper-bounded by $\sum_{i=1}^{k} k \binom{2^{2k}}{i} \leq k^2 2^{2k^2}$. Summing up and taking into account the time for computing the table T, the running time for a given $f \in \mathcal{F}$ is $\mathcal{O}(2^{5k}kn^2 + nk^2 2^{2k} + k^2 2^{2k^2})$.

According to Alon *et al.* [1], we need to use $\mathcal{O}(2^{\mathcal{O}(k)} \log n)$ functions $f : \mathbf{V}(G) \to \{1, 2, \ldots, k\}$, and such a family $\mathcal{F}$ can be computed in $\mathcal{O}(2^{\mathcal{O}(k)} n \log n)$ time. For each $f \in \mathcal{F}$ we use the above procedure to determine an occurrence of $\mathcal{M}$ in G that results in a minimum number of connected components. We have thus proved the following.

Proposition 4.1. *The* MIN-CC *problem is fixed-parameter tractable when parameterized by the size of the motif.*

4.2. A faster fixed-parameter algorithm for trees

We proved in Section 3 that the MIN-CC problem is **APX**–hard even if the target graph is a path. To complement Proposition 4.1, we give here a dynamic programming algorithm for trees that does not rely on the color-coding technique (approaches based on the color-coding technique usually suffer from bad running time performances).

Let $(G, \mathcal{M})$ be an instance of the MIN-CC problem for trees where both G and $\mathcal{M}$ are built upon a set of colors $\mathcal{C}$. Let $k = |\mathcal{M}|$ and $q = |\mathcal{C}|$. Furthermore, for ease of exposition, write $\mathbf{V}(G) = \{1, 2, \ldots, n\}$ and assume G is rooted at some arbitrary vertex $r(G)$.

Our dynamic programming algorithm is basically an exhaustive search procedure. The basic idea is to store - in a bottom-up fashion - for each vertex i of G and each submotif $\mathcal{M}' \subseteq \mathcal{M}$ that occurs in $T(i)$, i.e., the subtree rooted at i, the minimum number of connected components that results in an occurrence of $\mathcal{M}'$ in $T(i)$. More precisely, for each vertex i of G, we compute two dynamic programming tables $X[i]$ and $Y[i]$. The dynamic programming table $X[i]$ stores all pairs $(\mathcal{M}', c)$, where $\mathcal{M}' \subseteq \mathcal{M}$ is a submotif and c is a positive integer, such that (1) there exists an occurrence of $\mathcal{M}'$ in $T(i)$ that matches vertex i, (2) the minimum number of connected components of an occurrence of $\mathcal{M}'$ in $T(i)$ that matches vertex i is c. The dynamic programming table $Y[i]$ stores all pairs $(\mathcal{M}', c)$, where $\mathcal{M}' \subseteq \mathcal{M}$ is a submotif and c is a positive integer, such that (1') there exists an occurrence of $\mathcal{M}'$ in $T(i)$ that *does not match* vertex i, (2') the minimum number of connected components of an occurrence of $\mathcal{M}'$ in $T(i)$ that does not match vertex i is c.

We first claim that both $X[i]$ and $Y[i]$ contain at most k^{q+1} pairs. Indeed, the number of submotifs $\mathcal{M}' \subseteq \mathcal{M}$ is upper-bounded by k^q and any occurrence of any submotif in any subtree of G results in at most k connected components. We now describe how to compute - in a bottom-up fashion - those two dynamic programming tables X and Y.

Let i be an internal vertex of G and suppose that vertex i has s_i sons in the subtree $T(i)$ rooted at i, say $\{i_1, i_2, \ldots, i_{s_i}\}$. Notice that $s_i \geq 1$ since i is an internal vertex of G. The entries $X[i]$ and $Y[i]$ are computed with the aid of two auxiliary tables W_i and V_i. Table W_i contains s_i entries, one for each son of vertex

i in the subtree rooted at i, that are defined as follows:

$$\forall\, 1 \leq j \leq s_i,$$
$$W_i[i_j] = \{(\mathcal{M}', c, 1) : (\mathcal{M}', c) \in X[i_j]\} \cup \{(\mathcal{M}', c, 0) : (\mathcal{M}', c) \in Y[i_j]\}.$$

In other words, we merge $X[i_j]$ and $Y[i_j]$ in $W_i[i_j]$, differentiating the origin of a pair by means of a third element (an integer that is equal to 1 for $X[i_j]$ and 0 for $Y[i_j]$). Clearly, each entry $W_i[i_j]$ contains at most $2k^{q+1}$ triples, and hence table W_i on the whole contains at most $2\, s_i\, k^{q+1} \leq 2\, n\, k^{q+1}$ triples. Table V_i also contains s_i entries, one for each son of vertex i in the subtree rooted at i, that are computed as follows: $V_i[i_1] = W_i[i_1]$ and

$$\forall\, 2 \leq j \leq s_i,$$
$$V_i[i_j] = W_i[i_j] \,\cup\, \{(\mathcal{M}' \cup \mathcal{M}'', c' + c'', r' + r'') \subseteq \mathcal{M} \times k \times k :$$
$$(\mathcal{M}', c', r') \in W_i[i_j] \text{ and } (\mathcal{M}'', c'', r'') \in V_i[i_{j-1}]\}.$$

Each entry $V_i[i_j]$ contains at most k^{q+2} triples, and hence table V_i on the whole contains at most $s_i\, k^{q+2} \leq n\, k^{q+2}$ triples. All the needed information is stored in $V_i[i_{s_i}]$, and $X[i]$ and $Y[i]$ can be now computed as follows:

$$X[i] = \{(\mathcal{M}', c - r + 1) : (\mathcal{M}', c, r) \in V_i[i_{s_i}] \text{ and } r > 0\}$$
$$Y[i] = \{(\mathcal{M}', c) : (\mathcal{M}', c, 0) \in V_i[i_{s_i}]\}.$$

The two entries $X[i]$ and $Y[i]$ are next filtered according to the following procedure: for each submotif $\mathcal{M}' \subseteq \mathcal{M}$ that occurs in at least one pair of $X[i]$ (resp. $Y[i]$), we keep in $X[i]$ (resp. $Y[i]$) the pair $(\mathcal{M}', c)$ with the minimum c.

The base cases, *i.e.*, vertex i is a leaf, are defined as follows: $X[i] = \{(\lambda(i), 1)\}$ and $Y[i] = \emptyset$. In other words, $X[i]$ contains exactly one pair $(\mathcal{M}', c)$, where $\mathcal{M}'$ consists in one occurrence of the color associated to vertex i, and $Y[i]$ does not contain any pair. The solution for the MIN-CC problem consists in finding a pair $(\mathcal{M}, c)$ in X or Y with minimum c. If such a pair cannot be found in any entry of both X and Y, then the motif $\mathcal{M}$ does not occur in the tree G.

Proposition 4.2. *The* MIN-CC *problem for trees is solvable in* $\mathcal{O}(n^2 k^{(q+1)^2+1})$ *time, where n is the order of the target graph, k is the size of the motif and q is the number of distinct colors.*

The above result is particularly interesting in view of the fact that the MIN-CC problem for trees parameterized by q is **W[1]**–hard [8].

5. A polynomial-time algorithm for paths with a bounded number of colors

We complement here the results of the two preceding sections by showing that the MIN-CC problem for paths is polynomial-time solvable in case the motif is built upon a fixed number of colors. Observe, however, that each color may still have an unbounded number of occurrences in the motif.

In what follows we describe a dynamic programming algorithm for this case. The basic idea of our approach is as follows. Suppose we are left by the algorithm with the problem of finding an occurrence of a submotif $\mathcal{M}' \subseteq \mathcal{M}$ in the subpath G' of G induced by $\{i, i + 1, \ldots, j\}$, $1 \leq i < j \leq n$. Furthermore, suppose that any occurrence of $\mathcal{M}'$ in G' results in at least k' connected components. This minimum number of occurrences k' can be computed as follows. Assume that we have found one leftmost connected component C_{left} of the occurrence of $\mathcal{M}'$ in G' and let i_2, $i \leq i_2 < j$, be the rightmost (according to the natural order of the vertices) vertex of C_{left}. Let $\mathcal{M}''$ be the motif obtained from $\mathcal{M}'$ by subtracting to each color $c_\ell \in \mathcal{C}$ the number of occurrences of color c_ℓ in the leftmost connected component C_{left}. Then the occurrence of $\mathcal{M}'$ in G' is given by C_{left} plus the occurrence of the motif $\mathcal{M}''$ in the subpath G'' of G' induced by $\{i_2 + 1, i_2 + 2, \ldots, j\}$, which results in $k' - 1$ connected components. From an optimization point of view, the problem thus reduces to finding a subpath $\{i_1, i_1 + 1, \ldots, i_2\}$, $i \leq i_1 \leq i_2 < j$, such that the occurrence of the motif $\mathcal{M}''$ modified according to the colors in $\{i_1, i_1 + 1, \ldots, i_2\}$ in the subpath induced by $\{i_2 + 1, i_2 + 2, \ldots, j\}$ results in a minimum number of connected components.

Let $(G, \mathcal{M})$ be an instance of the MIN-CC problem where G is a (vertex-colored) path built upon the set of colors $\mathcal{C}$. For ease of exposition, write $\mathbf{V}(G) = \{1, 2, \ldots, n\}$ and $q = |\mathcal{C}|$. We denote by m_i the number of occurrences of color $c_i \in \mathcal{C}$ in $\mathcal{M}$. Clearly, $\sum_{c_i \in \mathcal{C}} m_i = |\mathcal{M}|$. We now introduce our dynamic programming table T. Define $T[i, j; p_1, p_2, \ldots, p_q]$, $1 \leq i \leq j \leq n$ and $0 \leq p_\ell \leq m_\ell$ for $1 \leq \ell \leq q$, to be the minimum number of connected components in the subpath of G that starts at node i, ends at node j and that covers p_ℓ occurrences of color c_ℓ, $1 \leq \ell \leq q$. The base conditions are as follows:

- for all $1 \leq i \leq j \leq n$, $T[i, j; 0, 0, \ldots, 0] = 0$ and $T[i, i; p_1, p_2, \ldots, p_q] = \infty$ if $\sum_{1 \leq \ell \leq q} p_\ell > 1$,
- for all $1 \leq i \leq n$, $T[i, i; p_1, p_2, \ldots, p_q] = \infty$ if $\sum_{1 \leq \ell \leq q} p_\ell = 1$ and $\lambda(i) \neq c_\ell$ and $p_\ell = 1$, and $T[i, i; p_1, p_2, \ldots, p_q] = 1$ if $\sum_{1 \leq \ell \leq q} p_\ell = 1$ and $\lambda(i) = c_\ell$ and $p_\ell = 1$.

The entry $T[i, j; p_1, p_2, \ldots, p_q]$ of the dynamic programming table T can be computed by the following recurrence

$$T[i, j; p_1, p_2, \ldots, p_q] = \min_{i \leq i_1 \leq i_2 < j} T[i_2 + 1, j; p'_1, p'_2, \ldots, p'_q] + 1 \qquad (1)$$

where each $p'_\ell \geq 0$ is equal to p_ℓ minus the number of occurrences of color c_ℓ in the subpath of G induced by the vertices $\{i_1, i_1 + 1, \ldots, i_2\}$. The optimal solution is clearly stored in $T[1, n; p_1, p_2, \ldots, p_q]$.

We claim that our dynamic programming table T contains $\mathcal{O}(n^{q+2})$ entries. Indeed, there are q colors in $\mathcal{M}$, each color $c_i \in \mathcal{C}$ has at most n occurrences in G and we have $\mathcal{O}(n^2)$ subpaths in G to consider. We now turn to evaluating the time complexity for computing $T[i, j; p_1, p_2, \ldots, p_q]$. Assuming each entry $T[i', j'; p'_1, p'_2, \ldots, p'_q]$ with $i \leq i' \leq j' \leq j$ and $|j' - i'| < |j - i|$ has already been computed, $T[i, j; p_1, p_2, \ldots, p_q]$ is obtained by taking a minimum number among $\mathcal{O}(|j - i + 1|^2) = \mathcal{O}(n^2)$ numbers, and hence is $\mathcal{O}(n^2)$ time. We have thus proved the following.

Proposition 5.1. *The* MIN-CC *problem for paths is solvable in* $\mathcal{O}(n^{q+4})$ *time, where* n *is the number of vertices and* q *is the number of colors in* $\mathcal{C}$.

As an immediate consequence of the above proposition, the MIN-CC problem is polynomial-time solvable in case the motif $\mathcal{M}$ is built upon a fixed number of colors and the target graph G is a path.

6. Hardness of approximation for trees

We investigate in this section approximation issues for restricted instances of the MIN-CC problem. Unfortunately, as we shall now prove, it turns out that, even if $\mathcal{M}$ is a set and G is a tree, the MIN-CC problem cannot be approximated within ratio $c \log n$ for some constant $c > 0$, where n is the size of the target graph G. As a side result, we prove that the MIN-CC problem is **W[2]**–hard when parameterized by the number of connected components of the occurrence of $\mathcal{M}$ in the target graph G.

At the core of our proof is an L-reduction [12] from the SET-COVER problem. Let I be an arbitrary instance of the SET-COVER problem consisting of a universe set $X(I) = \{x_1, x_2, \ldots, x_n\}$ and a collection of sets $\mathcal{S}(I) = S_1, S_2, \ldots, S_m$, each over $X(I)$. For each $1 \leq i \leq m$, write $t_i = |S_i|$ and denote by $e_j(S_i)$, $1 \leq j \leq t_i$, the j-th element of S_i. For ease of exposition, we present the corresponding instance of the MIN-CC problem as a rooted tree G. We construct the tree G as follows (see Fig. 1). Define a root r and vertices $S'_1, S'_2, \ldots, S'_m$ such that each vertex S'_i is connected to the root r. For each S'_i define the subtree $G(S'_i)$ rooted at S'_i as follows: each vertex S'_i has a unique child S_i and each vertex S_i

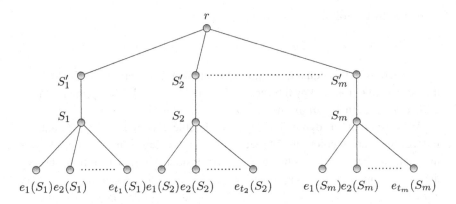

Figure 1.   Construction of the corresponding instance of the MIN-CC problem.

has children $e_1(S_i), e_2(S_i), \ldots, e_{t_i}(S_i)$. The set of colors $\mathcal{C}$ is defined as follows: $\mathcal{C} = \{c(S_i) : 1 \leq i \leq m\} \cup \{c(x_j) : 1 \leq j \leq n\} \cup \{c(r)\}$. The coloring mapping $\lambda : \mathbf{V}(G) \to \mathcal{C}$ is defined by: $\lambda(S_i) = \lambda(S_i') = c(S_i)$ for $1 \leq i \leq m$, $\lambda(x_j) = c(x_j)$ for $1 \leq j \leq n$ and $\lambda(r) = c(r)$. The motif $\mathcal{M}$ is the set defined as follows: $\mathcal{M} = \{c(S_i) : 1 \leq i \leq m\} \cup \{c(x_i) : 1 \leq i \leq n\} \cup \{c(r)\}$.

Proposition 6.1. *For any instance I of the* SET-COVER *problem, there exists a solution of size h for I, i.e., a subset $\mathcal{S} \subseteq \mathcal{S}(I)$, $|\mathcal{S}| = h$, such that $\bigcup_{S_i \in \mathcal{S}} S_i = X$, if and only if then there exists an occurrence of $\mathcal{M}$ in G that results in $h + 1$ connected components.*

It is easily seen that the above reduction is an L-reduction [12]. It is known that SET-COVER cannot be approximated within ratio $c \log n$ for some constant $c > 0$ [14]. Then it follows that there exists a constant $c' > 0$ such that the MIN-CC for trees cannot be approximated within performance ratio $c' \log n$, where n is the number of vertices in the target graph.

As a side result, we also observe that the above reduction is a parameterized reduction. Since the SET-COVER is **W[2]**–hard when parameterized by the size of the solution [13], the following result holds.

Corollary 6.1. *The* MIN-CC *problem for trees is* **W[2]**–*hard when parameterized by the number of connected components of the occurrence of the motif in the graph.*

7. An exact algorithm for trees

We proved in Section 4 that the MIN-CC for trees is solvable in $\mathcal{O}(n^2 k^{(q+1)^2+1})$ time, where n is the order of the target tree, k is the size of the motif and q is the number of distinct colors. We propose here a new algorithm for this special case, which turns out not to be a fixed-parameter algorithm but has a better running time in case the motif k is not that small compared to the order n of the target graph. More precisely, we give an algorithm for solving the MIN-CC problem for trees that runs in $\mathcal{O}(n^2 2^{\frac{2n}{3}})$, where n is the order of the target tree. Due to space constraints, we skip the proof details.

Let T be the target tree. For any vertex x of T, denote by $T(x)$ the subtree of T rooted at x. The first step of our algorithm splits the target tree in a *balanced way*, so that T is rooted at a vertex r having children, $r_1, r_2, \ldots, r_h$ such that none of the trees $T(r_i)$, $1 \leq i \leq h$, has order greater than $\lceil \frac{n}{2} \rceil$. Such a vertex r can be found in $\mathcal{O}(n^2)$ time. We then construct two disjoint subsets R_1 and R_2 of $r_1, \ldots, r_h$ with the property that

$$\frac{1}{3}|T| \leq \sum_{r_i \in R_1} |T(r_i)| \leq \lceil \frac{1}{2}|T| \rceil \text{ and } \lceil \frac{1}{2}|T| \rceil \leq \sum_{r_i \in R_2} |T(r_i)| = \frac{2}{3}|T|$$

Given V' a subset of nodes of V, we say that V' does not violate $\mathcal{M}$ if the multiset of colors $C(V')$ is a subset of $\mathcal{M}$. Given a subtree T' of T, we define a *partial solution* F of MIN-CC over instance $(T', \mathcal{M})$ as a set of connected components of T' that does not violate the multiset $\mathcal{M}$.

The algorithm computes an optimal solution for MIN-CC by first computing all the partial solutions S_1 over instance $(R_1, \mathcal{M})$ and all the partial solutions S_2 over instance $(R_2, \mathcal{M})$ and then merging a partial solution F_1 of S_1 and a partial solution F_2 of S_2 into a feasible solution for the MIN-CC over instance $(T, \mathcal{M})$. Since there are $2^{\frac{n}{2}}$ and $2^{\frac{2n}{3}}$ possible subsets of vertices of R_1 and R_2 respectively, it follows that the set of partial solutions over instance $(R_1, \mathcal{M})$, $(R_2, \mathcal{M})$ can be computed in time $\mathcal{O}(2^{\frac{n}{2}})$ and $\mathcal{O}(2^{\frac{2n}{3}})$ respectively. Then set S_1 is ordered and by binary search we can find in time $\mathcal{O}(n \log 2^{\frac{n}{2}}) = \mathcal{O}(n^2)$ a solution F_1 of S_1 that, merged to a solution F_2 of S_2, produces a feasible solution of MIN-CC over instance $(T, \mathcal{M})$. Since $|S_2| = \mathcal{O}(2^{\frac{2n}{3}})$, it follows that the overall time complexity of the algorithm is $\mathcal{O}(n^2 2^{\frac{2n}{3}})$.

8. Conclusion

We mention here some possible directions for future works. First, approximation issues of the MIN-CC problem are widely unexplored. In particular, is the MIN-CC problem for paths approximable within a constant ? Also, most parameterized complexity issues are to be discovered. Of particular importance: is the

MIN-CC problem for paths **W[1]**–hard when parameterized by the number of connected components in the occurrence of the motif in the target graph ?

Bibliography

1. N. Alon, R. Yuster, and U. Zwick. Color coding. *Journal of the ACM*, 42(4):844–856, 1995.
2. P. Bonsma. Complexity results for restricted instances of a paint shop problem. Technical Report 1681, Dept of Applied Maths, Univ. of Twente, 2003.
3. P. Bonsma, T. Epping, and W. Hochstättler. Complexity results on restricted instances of a paint shop problem for words. *Discrete Applied Mathematics*, 154(9):1335–1343, 2006.
4. T.H. Cormen, C.E. Leiserson, R.L. Rivest, and C. Stein. *Introduction to algorithms.* McGraw Hill, New York, 2001.
5. Y. Deville, D. Gilbert, J. Van Helden, and S.J. Wodak. An overview of data models for the analysis of biochemical pathways. *Briefings in Bioinformatics*, 4(3):246–259, 2003.
6. R. Diestel. *Graph Theory.* Number 173 in Graduate texts in Mathematics. Springer-Verlag, second edition, 2000.
7. R. Downey and M. Fellows. *Parameterized Complexity.* Springer-Verlag, 1999.
8. M. Fellows, G. Fertin, D. Hermelin, and S. Vialette. Sharp tractability borderlines for finding connected motifs in vertex-colored graphs. In *Proc. 34th Int. Colloquium on Automata, Languages and Programming (ICALP)*, 2007. To appear.
9. J. Flum and M. Grohe. *Parameterized Complexity Theory.* Springer-Verlag, 2006.
10. T. Ideker, R.M. Karp, J. Scott, and R. Sharan. Efficient algorithms for detecting signaling pathways in protein interaction networks. *Journal of Computational Biology*, 13(2):133–144, 2006.
11. V. Lacroix, C.G. Fernandes, and M.-F. Sagot. Motif search in graphs: application to metabolic networks. *IEEE/ACM Transactions on Computational Biology and Bioinformatics (TCBB)*, 3(4):360–368, 2006.
12. C.H. Papadimitriou and M. Yannakakis. Optimization, approximation and complexity classes. *J. of Computer and System Sciences*, 43:425–440, 1991.
13. A. Paz and S. Moran. Non deterministic polynomial optimization problems and their approximations. *Theoretical Computer Science*, 15:251–277, 1981.
14. R. Raz and S. Safra. A sub-constant error-probability low-degree test, and sub-constant error-probability PCP characterization of NP. In *Proc. 29th Ann. ACM Symp. on Theory of Comp. (STOC)*, pages 475–484, 1997.
15. W. Hochstättler T. Epping and P. Oertel. Complexity results on a paint shop problem. *Discrete Applied Mathematics*, 136(2-3):217–226, 2004.

WEAK MARKOVIAN BISIMILARITY:
ABSTRACTING FROM PRIORITIZED/WEIGHTED
INTERNAL IMMEDIATE ACTIONS

M. BERNARDO and A. ALDINI

Università di Urbino "Carlo Bo" – Italy

Markovian process calculi constitute a useful framework for reasoning about the functional and performance aspects of concurrent systems. This is achieved by means of behavioral equivalences that take into account both the action names and their exponentially distributed durations. A notable extension to the expressiveness of Markovian process calculi derives from the adoption of GSPN-like immediate actions, i.e. actions with a zero duration and equipped with a priority level and a weight. Since internal immediate actions are unobservable both from the functional viewpoint and from the performance viewpoint, in this paper we tackle the problem of defining a weak variant of Markovian bisimilarity that abstracts from such actions. We show that the proposed equivalence is a congruence and admits a sound and complete axiomatization for the class of well-prioritized process terms.

1. Introduction

Markovian process calculi have been developed as performance-oriented extensions of traditional calculi (see, e.g., Refs. 4,6,7). In essence, they introduce exponentially distributed delays governed by the race policy, can be equipped with behavioral equivalences that take into account such stochastic delays besides the action names, and provide continuous-time Markov chain (CTMC) models for performance evaluation purposes.

When using pure Markovian process calculi to model concurrent systems in practice, the availability of only exponentially distributed delays may be too restrictive. Although proper combinations of exponential distributions (called phase-type distributions) can approximate most of the general distributions arbitrarily closely, some useful distributions are left out, specially the one representing a zero duration. The capability of expressing zero durations would also constitute a good performance abstraction mechanism, similar to the internal action name τ on the functional side.

In the modeling process it often happens to deal with choices among logical events (like the reception of a message vs. its loss) with which no timing can reasonably be associated, or to encounter activities that are several orders of magnitude faster than the activities that are important for the evaluation of certain performance measures. In all of these cases, using a zero duration would be an adequate solution from the modeling standpoint, but this is not permitted by pure Markovian process calculi.

In order to manage zero durations, it is necessary to extend the syntax of Markovian process calculi and, consequently, their underlying CTMC models. In the literature, this has been accomplished in three different ways.

The first one has been to separate action names from time using two distinct prefix operators – one for action names and one for exponentially distributed delays – and to consider the execution of an action name to take zero time [6]. This is the result of the combination of nondeterministic process calculi and CTMCs, which thus yields CTMC models extended with nondeterministic branchings.

The second way has been to introduce a probabilistic choice operator, by means of which it is possible to preselect a certain group of exponentially timed actions that are enabled [10]. As a consequence, this technique yields CTMC models extended with probabilistic branchings. Precisely, the proposed model requires a strict alternation between probabilistic branchings and Markovian branchings, with any probabilistic transition ending in a state having – besides possible exponentially timed transitions – a single probabilistic transition labeled with 1 that goes back to the state itself.

The third way has been to admit immediate actions as first-class citizens in the syntax [3], in the same way as immediate transitions are first-class citizens within generalized stochastic Petri net (GSPN) models [1]. Besides a name and a zero duration, each immediate action has associated with it a priority and a weight, which are used to choose among several immediate actions that are simultaneously enabled. Therefore, this technique yields CTMC models extended with prioritized/probabilistic branchings, which freely alternate with Markovian branchings.

The third technique can thus be viewed as a complementary variant of the first one in which nondeterminism is ruled out by augmenting each action name with a priority and a weight. It can also be regarded as an extension of the second one in which the choice operator is made both prioritized and probabilistic and the alternation constraint is relaxed.

Zero durations are negligible from the performance viewpoint in the same way as internal actions are negligible from the functional viewpoint. As a consequence, in each of the three extended Markovian frameworks mentioned above, any entity that is internal and takes zero time is absolutely unobservable. This should be taken into account when developing behavioral equivalences in those frameworks. Actually, this has already been done both in Ref. 6 and in Ref. 10, where two weak variants of Markovian bisimilarity [7] have been defined.

The problem that we address here is the development of a weak variant of Markovian bisimilarity for a Markovian process calculus – like EMPA$_{gr}$ [4] – extended with immediate actions à la GSPN. The technical difficulty lies in the fact that the objective of abstracting from internal immediate actions is complicated by the need of retaining information about the priorities and the weights of such actions. Moreover, we shall see that it is necessary to distinguish among observable, initially unobservable and fully unobservable process terms, and that congruence and axiomatization can be achieved only for a class of process terms that we shall call well prioritized.

Besides being of theoretical interest, this extension of Markovian bisimilarity would be useful also from a practical viewpoint, as it would increase the number of system models that can be compared/manipulated. As an example, consider a queueing system [8] with two classes of customers. Such customers arrive at the service center according to a Poisson process, then compete for the resources on the basis of their priorities (assume that customers of the second class take precedence over those of the first class). The service center is composed of two buffers – one for each class – and a number of servers that provide a service to the customers of both classes at a certain rate. The activities that are important from the performance viewpoint are the arrivals and the services, while the delivery of a customer from the buffer reserved for its class to one of the servers has a negligible duration. Therefore the delivery activities are the ones that could be abstracted away if viewed as being internal to the service center, so that in the end the queueing system could be viewed as being equivalent to a suitable birth-death process. The point is that the delivery activities necessarily carry over priority information, which cannot be handled with the weak variants of Markovian bisimilarity defined in Refs. 6 and 10.

This paper is organized as follows. In Sect. 2 we revisit EMPA$_{gr}$. In Sect. 3 we define a weak variant of Markovian bisimilarity over EMPA$_{gr}$ and we show that it is a congruence and admits a sound and complete axiomatization for the class of well-prioritized process terms. In Sect. 4 we provide some concluding remarks. The proofs of all results can be found at http://www.sti.uniurb.it/bernardo/.

2. Extended Markovian Process Algebra

In this section we revisit EMPA$_{gr}$ [4], a Markovian process algebra extended with prioritized/weighted immediate actions à la GSPN [1] in which interprocess communication is based on a multiway generative-reactive [5] synchronization mechanism.

In EMPA_{gr} every action is durational, hence it is represented as a pair $<a, \tilde{\lambda}>$, where a is the action name and $\tilde{\lambda}$ is the action rate. There are three kinds of actions: exponentially timed, immediate, and passive.

Exponentially timed actions are of the form $<a, \lambda>$ with $\lambda \in \mathbf{R}_{>0}$. The duration of each such action is exponentially distributed with parameter equal to the action rate (hence its average duration is the inverse of its rate). Whenever several exponentially timed actions are enabled, the race policy is adopted, hence the fastest action is the one that is executed. As a consequence, the execution probability of an exponentially timed action is proportional to its rate.

Immediate actions are of the form $<a, \infty_{l,w}>$, where $l \in \mathbf{N}_{>0}$ is the priority level and $w \in \mathbf{R}_{>0}$ is the weight. Each immediate action has duration zero and takes precedence over exponentially timed actions (which are assumed to have priority level 0). Whenever several immediate actions are enabled, the generative preselection policy is adopted, i.e. each action is given an execution probability proportional to its weight provided that it has the highest priority level within the considered action set.

Passive actions are of the form $<a, *^l_w>$, where $l \in \mathbf{N}$ is the priority constraint and $w \in \mathbf{R}_{>0}$ is the weight. Each passive action with priority constraint l can synchronize only with another passive action having the same name and the same priority constraint, or with a non-passive action having the same name and priority level l. Whenever several passive actions are enabled, the reactive preselection policy is adopted, i.e. within every set of enabled passive actions with the same name and the same priority constraint each action is given an execution probability proportional to its weight. As a consequence, the choice between two passive actions with different names or different priority constraints is nondeterministic.

While in Ref. 4 each passive action had a reactive priority level associated with it, here passive actions are assigned priority constraints. These come into play in the synchronization of a passive action with a non-passive one by forcing the priority level of the latter to be equal to the priority constraint of the former. Priority constraints will be useful to achieve congruence for our weak Markovian bisimilarity, as they allow the interplay of the priorities of actions of different components to be kept under control.

Definition 2.1. Let $Act = Name \times Rate$ be a set of actions, with $Name$ being a set of action names containing a distinguished symbol τ for the invisible action and $Rate = \mathbf{R}_{>0} \cup \{\infty_{l,w} \mid l \in \mathbf{N}_{>0} \wedge w \in \mathbf{R}_{>0}\} \cup \{*^l_w \mid l \in \mathbf{N} \wedge w \in \mathbf{R}_{>0}\}$ being a set of action rates (ranged over by $\tilde{\lambda}$). Let

$Relab = \{\varphi : Name \longrightarrow Name \mid \varphi^{-1}(\tau) = \{\tau\}\}$ be a set of action name relabeling functions that preserve visibility. The set of the process terms of $EMPA_{gr}$ is generated by the following syntax:

$$P ::= \underline{0} \mid <a, \tilde{\lambda}>.P \mid P + P \mid P/L \mid P[\varphi] \mid P \parallel_S P \mid A$$

where $L, S \subseteq Name - \{\tau\}$ and A is a process constant defined through the (possibly recursive) equation $A \overset{\Delta}{=} P$. ∎

The semantics for the set $\mathcal{P}$ of the closed and guarded process terms of $EMPA_{gr}$ is defined in the usual operational style. The behavior of each term P is given by a multitransition system $[\![P]\!]$, whose states correspond to process terms and whose transitions – each of which has a multiplicity equal to the number of proofs of its derivation – are labeled with actions.

The null term $\underline{0}$ cannot execute any action, hence the corresponding labeled multitransition system is just a state with no transitions.

The action prefix term $<a, \tilde{\lambda}>.P$ can execute an action with name a and rate $\tilde{\lambda}$ and then behaves as P:

$$<a, \lambda>.P \xrightarrow{a, \lambda} P \qquad <a, \infty_{l,w}>.P \xrightarrow{a, \infty_{l,w}} P \qquad <a, *^l_w>.P \xrightarrow{a, *^l_w} P$$

The alternative composition $P_1 + P_2$ behaves as either P_1 or P_2 depending on whether P_1 or P_2 executes an action first:

$$\frac{P_1 \xrightarrow{a, \tilde{\lambda}} P'}{P_1 + P_2 \xrightarrow{a, \tilde{\lambda}} P'} \qquad \frac{P_2 \xrightarrow{a, \tilde{\lambda}} P'}{P_1 + P_2 \xrightarrow{a, \tilde{\lambda}} P'}$$

The hiding term P/L behaves as P with the difference that the name of every action executed by P that belongs to L is turned into τ:

$$\frac{P \xrightarrow{a, \tilde{\lambda}} P' \quad a \in L}{P/L \xrightarrow{\tau, \tilde{\lambda}} P'/L} \qquad \frac{P \xrightarrow{a, \tilde{\lambda}} P' \quad a \notin L}{P/L \xrightarrow{a, \tilde{\lambda}} P'/L}$$

The relabeling term $P[\varphi]$ behaves as P with the difference that the name a of every action executed by P is turned into $\varphi(a)$:

$$\frac{P \xrightarrow{a, \tilde{\lambda}} P'}{P[\varphi] \xrightarrow{\varphi(a), \tilde{\lambda}} P'[\varphi]}$$

The parallel composition $P_1 \parallel_S P_2$ behaves as P_1 in parallel with P_2 as long as actions are executed whose name does not belong to S:

$$\frac{P_1 \xrightarrow{a,\tilde{\lambda}} P_1' \quad a \notin S}{P_1 \parallel_S P_2 \xrightarrow{a,\tilde{\lambda}} P_1' \parallel_S P_2} \qquad \frac{P_2 \xrightarrow{a,\tilde{\lambda}} P_2' \quad a \notin S}{P_1 \parallel_S P_2 \xrightarrow{a,\tilde{\lambda}} P_1 \parallel_S P_2'}$$

Synchronizations are forced between any non-passive action executed by one term and any passive action executed by the other term that have the same name belonging to S and the same priority level/constraint:

$$\frac{P_1 \xrightarrow{a,\lambda} P_1' \quad P_2 \xrightarrow{a,*_w^0} P_2' \quad a \in S}{P_1 \parallel_S P_2 \xrightarrow{a,\lambda \cdot \frac{w}{weight(P_2,a,0)}} P_1' \parallel_S P_2'} \qquad \frac{P_1 \xrightarrow{a,*_w^0} P_1' \quad P_2 \xrightarrow{a,\lambda} P_2' \quad a \in S}{P_1 \parallel_S P_2 \xrightarrow{a,\lambda \cdot \frac{w}{weight(P_1,a,0)}} P_1' \parallel_S P_2'}$$

$$\frac{P_1 \xrightarrow{a,\infty_{l,v}} P_1' \quad P_2 \xrightarrow{a,*_w^l} P_2' \quad a \in S}{P_1 \parallel_S P_2 \xrightarrow{a,\infty_{l,v} \cdot \frac{w}{weight(P_2,a,l)}} P_1' \parallel_S P_2'} \qquad \frac{P_1 \xrightarrow{a,*_w^l} P_1' \quad P_2 \xrightarrow{a,\infty_{l,v}} P_2' \quad a \in S}{P_1 \parallel_S P_2 \xrightarrow{a,\infty_{l,v} \cdot \frac{w}{weight(P_1,a,l)}} P_1' \parallel_S P_2'}$$

and between any two passive actions of the two terms that have the same name belonging to S and the same priority constraint:

$$\frac{P_1 \xrightarrow{a,*_{w1}^l} P_1' \quad P_2 \xrightarrow{a,*_{w2}^l} P_2' \quad a \in S}{P_1 \parallel_S P_2 \xrightarrow{a,*_{\frac{w_1}{weight(P_1,a,l)} \cdot \frac{w_2}{weight(P_2,a,l)} \cdot (weight(P_1,a,l)+weight(P_2,a,l))}^l} P_1' \parallel_S P_2'}$$

where $weight(P,a,l) = \sum \{| w \mid \exists P' \in \mathcal{P}. P \xrightarrow{a,*_w^l} P' |\}$.

The process constant A behaves as the right-hand side process term in its defining equation:

$$\frac{P \xrightarrow{a,\tilde{\lambda}} P' \quad A \stackrel{\Delta}{=} P}{A \xrightarrow{a,\tilde{\lambda}} P'}$$

From now on we use the motivating example of Sect. 1 as a running example. Let us formalize with EMPA$_{gr}$ the considered queueing system. The arrival process for customers of class $k \in \{1,2\}$ can be modeled as:

$$A_k \stackrel{\Delta}{=} <a_k,\lambda_k>.A_k$$

where λ_k is the parameter of the Poisson arrival process. The buffer for customers of class $k \in \{1,2\}$ – which we assume to have an unbounded capacity – can be modeled as follows:

$$B_{k,0} \stackrel{\Delta}{=} <a_k,*_w^0>.B_{k,1}$$
$$B_{k,i} \stackrel{\Delta}{=} <a_k,*_w^0>.B_{k,i+1} + <d_k,\infty_{k,w}>.B_{k,i-1} \qquad i \in \mathbf{N}_{\geq 1}$$

Each of the servers can be modeled as follows:

$$S \triangleq <d_1, *_w^1>.S_1' + <d_2, *_w^2>.S_2' \quad S_1' \triangleq <s_1, \mu_1>.S \quad S_2' \triangleq <s_2, \mu_2>.S$$

where μ_k is the service rate for customers of class $k \in \{1, 2\}$. Hence the overall queueing system with $n \in \mathbf{N}_{\geq 1}$ servers can be modeled as follows:

$$QS_n \triangleq (A_1 \parallel_\emptyset A_2) \parallel_{\{a_1, a_2\}} (B_{1,0} \parallel_\emptyset B_{2,0}) \parallel_{\{d_1, d_2\}} (S \parallel_\emptyset S \parallel_\emptyset \cdots \parallel_\emptyset S)$$

If we are interested in evaluating performance properties that are not specific to a single class of customers, a more abstract model can be considered like $QS_n \,/\, L\,[\varphi]$, where $L = \{d_1, d_2\}$ and $\varphi = \{a_1, a_2 \mapsto a, s_1, s_2 \mapsto s\}$. The names d_1, d_2 of the prioritized immediate actions related to the customer delivery have been made internal, while the names a_1, a_2 (resp. s_1, s_2) of the exponentially timed actions related to the customer arrival (resp. service) have been mapped to the same name a (resp. s). Assuming that $\lambda_1 = \lambda_2 \equiv \lambda$ and $\mu_1 = \mu_2 \equiv \mu$, we expect the performance behavior of $QS_n \,/\, L\,[\varphi]$ to be equivalent to the performance behavior of the following simpler birth-death process:

$$BD_{n,0} \triangleq <a, 2 \cdot \lambda>.BD_{n,1}$$
$$BD_{n,j} \triangleq <a, 2 \cdot \lambda>.BD_{n,j+1} + <s, j \cdot \mu>.BD_{n,j-1} \quad 1 \leq j \leq n$$
$$BD_{n,j} \triangleq <a, 2 \cdot \lambda>.BD_{n,j+1} + <s, n \cdot \mu>.BD_{n,j-1} \quad j > n$$

How can we formally establish that $QS_n \,/\, L\,[\varphi]$ is equivalent to $BD_{n,0}$?

3. Weak Extended Markovian Bisimilarity

A behavioral equivalence typically used for reasoning about Markovian process terms is Markovian bisimilarity [7]. In particular, an extension of it has been defined in Refs. 3,4 in order to deal with prioritized/weighted immediate actions. The limitation of extended Markovian bisimilarity is that it does not provide any abstraction mechanism. In fact, actions of the form $<\tau, \infty_{l,w}>$ are invisible and take no time, hence they are unimportant both from the functional viewpoint and from the performance viewpoint. Thus they should not be considered when comparing the behavior of two terms.

After recalling the definition of extended Markovian bisimilarity, we introduce a weak variant of it that abstracts from internal immediate actions. Then we show that this weak variant is a congruence and admits a sound and complete axiomatization for the class of well-prioritized process terms.

3.1. *Extended Markovian Bisimilarity*

The basic idea behind Markovian bisimilarity is to suitably compare the exit rates of the process terms. In order to deal with the various kinds of actions –

exponentially timed, immediate, and passive – the notion of exit rate is further parameterized with respect to a number in $\mathbb{Z}$ representing the priority level of the action, which is 0 if the action is exponentially timed, l if the action rate is $\infty_{l,w}$, $-l - 1$ if the action rate is $*_w^l$.

Definition 3.1. Let $P \in \mathcal{P}$, $a \in Name$, $l \in \mathbb{Z}$, and $C \subseteq \mathcal{P}$. The exit rate of P when executing actions with name a and priority level l that lead to C is defined through the following non-negative real function:

$$
rate(P, a, l, C) = \begin{cases} \sum \{ \lambda \mid \exists P' \in C.\, P \xrightarrow{a, \lambda} P' \} & \text{if } l = 0 \\ \sum \{ w \mid \exists P' \in C.\, P \xrightarrow{a, \infty_{l,w}} P' \} & \text{if } l > 0 \\ \sum \{ w \mid \exists P' \in C.\, P \xrightarrow{a, *_\infty^{-l-1}} P' \} & \text{if } l < 0 \end{cases}
$$

where each sum is taken to be zero whenever its multiset is empty. ∎

Extended Markovian bisimilarity compares the process term exit rates for all possible action names and priority levels, except for those actions that will always be pre-empted by higher priority actions of the form $<\tau, \infty_{l,w}>$. In the following we denote by $pri_\infty^\tau(P)$ the priority level of the highest priority internal immediate action enabled by P, and we set $pri_\infty^\tau(P) = 0$ if P does not enable any internal immediate action. Moreover, given $l \in \mathbb{Z}$, we use $no\text{-}pre(l, P)$ to denote that no action whose priority level is l can be pre-empted in P. Formally, this is the case whenever $l \geq pri_\infty^\tau(P)$ or $-l - 1 \geq pri_\infty^\tau(P)$.

Definition 3.2. An equivalence relation $\mathcal{B} \subseteq \mathcal{P} \times \mathcal{P}$ is an extended Markovian bisimulation iff, whenever $(P_1, P_2) \in \mathcal{B}$, then for all action names $a \in Name$, equivalence classes $C \in \mathcal{P}/\mathcal{B}$, and priority levels $l \in \mathbb{Z}$ such that $no\text{-}pre(l, P_1)$ and $no\text{-}pre(l, P_2)$:

$$
rate(P_1, a, l, C) = rate(P_2, a, l, C)
$$
∎

The definition given in Refs. 3,4 is slightly different from the one above, as the latter includes a concept of pre-emption that embodies the maximal progress of Ref. 6. Note that, in order for $P_1, P_2 \in \mathcal{P}$ to be related by an extended Markovian bisimulation, it is necessary that $pri_\infty^\tau(P_1) = pri_\infty^\tau(P_2)$, from which it follows that $no\text{-}pre(l, P_1)$ iff $no\text{-}pre(l, P_2)$ for all $l \in \mathbb{Z}$.

Definition 3.3. Extended Markovian bisimilarity, denoted by $\sim_{EMB}$, is the union of all the extended Markovian bisimulations. ∎

$\sim_{EMB}$ is a congruence with respect to all the operators of $EMPA_{gr}$. This is because the semantic rules do not prune the transitions labeled with the lower priority actions of a term and these are ignored by $\sim_{EMB}$ only in the presence of alternative higher priority actions of the form $<\tau, \infty_{l,w}>$ (which cannot be disabled by any context into which the term may be plugged).

$\sim_{\text{EMB}}$ admits a sound and complete axiomatization over the set $\mathcal{P}_{\text{nr}}$ of the non-recursive process terms of $\mathcal{P}$. The following six axioms characterize the race policy, the preselection policy, and pre-emption:

$$<a, \lambda_1>.P + <a, \lambda_2>.P = <a, \lambda_1 + \lambda_2>.P$$
$$<a, \infty_{l,w_1}>.P + <a, \infty_{l,w_2}>.P = <a, \infty_{l,w_1+w_2}>.P$$
$$<a, *^l_{w_1}>.P + <a, *^l_{w_2}>.P = <a, *^l_{w_1+w_2}>.P$$
$$<\tau, \infty_{l,w}>.P + <a, \lambda>.Q = <\tau, \infty_{l,w}>.P$$
$$<\tau, \infty_{l,w}>.P + <a, \infty_{l',w'}>.Q = <\tau, \infty_{l,w}>.P \qquad \text{if } l > l'$$
$$<\tau, \infty_{l,w}>.P + <a, *^{l'}_{w'}>.Q = <\tau, \infty_{l,w}>.P \qquad \text{if } l > l'$$

3.2. Abstracting from Internal Immediate Actions

The definition of exit rate can be relaxed by means of a suitable notion of reachability that involves the unobservable actions $<\tau, \infty_{l,w}>$. The idea is that, if a given class of process terms is not reached directly after executing an action with a certain name and priority level, then we have to explore the possibility of reaching that class indirectly via a finite-length unobservable path starting from the term reached after executing the considered action.

Definition 3.4. Let $P \in \mathcal{P}$ and $l \in \mathbb{N}_{>0}$. We say that P is l-unobservable iff $pri^\tau_\infty(P) = l$ and P does not enable any visible action with priority level $l' \in \mathbb{Z}$ such that $l' \geq l$ or $-l' - 1 \geq l$. ∎

Definition 3.5. Let $n \in \mathbb{N}_{>0}$ and $P_1, P_2, \ldots, P_{n+1} \in \mathcal{P}$. A path π of length n:

$$P_1 \xrightarrow{\tau, \infty_{l_1,w_1}} P_2 \xrightarrow{\tau, \infty_{l_2,w_2}} \ldots \xrightarrow{\tau, \infty_{l_n,w_n}} P_{n+1}$$

is unobservable iff for all $i = 1, \ldots, n$ process term P_i is l_i-unobservable. In that case, the probability of executing π is given by:

$$prob(\pi) = \prod_{i=1}^{n} \frac{w_i}{rate(P_i, \tau, l_i, \mathcal{P})}$$ ∎

Definition 3.6. Let $P \in \mathcal{P}$, $a \in Name$, $l \in \mathbb{Z}$, and $C \subseteq \mathcal{P}$. The weak exit rate of P when executing actions with name a and priority level l that lead to C is defined through the following non-negative real function:

$$rate_{\text{w}}(P, a, l, C) = \sum_{P' \in C_{\text{w}}} rate(P, a, l, \{P'\}) \cdot prob_{\text{w}}(P', C)$$

where C_{w} is the weak backward closure of C:

$$C_{\text{w}} = C \cup \{Q \in \mathcal{P} - C \mid Q \text{ can reach } C \text{ via an unobservable path}\}$$

and $prob_{\text{w}}$ is a $\mathbb{R}_{]0,1]}$-valued function representing the sum of the probabilities of all the unobservable paths from a term in C_{w} to C:

$$prob_w(P', C) = \begin{cases} 1 & \text{if } P' \in C \\ \sum\{| prob(\pi) \mid \pi \text{ unobservable path from } P' \text{ to } C |\} \\ & \text{if } P' \in C_w - C \end{cases}$$
∎

The definition of extended Markovian bisimulation can be weakened by using $rate_w$ instead of $rate$ and by skipping the weak exit rate comparison in the case of equivalence classes that are unobservable. More precisely, we distinguish between observable, initially unobservable and fully unobservable sets of states.

An observable state is a state that enables an observable action that cannot be pre-empted by any enabled unobservable action.

An initially unobservable state is a state in which all the enabled observable actions are pre-empted by some enabled unobservable action, but at least one of the paths starting at this state with one of the higher priority enabled unobservable actions reaches an observable state.

A fully unobservable state is a state in which all the enabled observable actions are pre-empted by some enabled unobservable action, and all the paths starting at this state with one of the higher priority enabled unobservable actions are unobservable (note that $\underline{0}$ is fully unobservable).

The weak exit rate comparison must obviously be performed in the case of observable classes, while it is not necessary in the case of initially unobservable classes as each of them can reach an observable class. Besides being not necessary, the weak exit rate comparison with respect to initially unobservable classes may even be counterproductive in terms of abstraction power, as we shall exemplify later on. Thus, the weak exit rate comparison must be skipped in the case of initially unobservable classes. By contrast, the weak exit rate comparison should not be skipped in the case of fully unobservable classes. This is especially true for process terms that conceptually do not behave the same but can reach only fully unobservable states, as in this case the only way we have to distinguish between those process terms is to compare their weak exit rates towards such fully unobservable states. As we shall exemplify later on, in the weak exit rate comparison it is not appropriate to consider the fully unobservable classes one at a time. Instead, the whole set $\mathcal{P}_{fu}$ of fully unobservable process terms of $\mathcal{P}$ has to be considered.

Definition 3.7. An equivalence relation $\mathcal{B} \subseteq \mathcal{P} \times \mathcal{P}$ is a weak extended Markovian bisimulation iff, whenever $(P_1, P_2) \in \mathcal{B}$, then for all action names $a \in Name$ and priority levels $l \in \mathbb{Z}$ such that $no\text{-}pre(l, P_1)$ and $no\text{-}pre(l, P_2)$:

$$rate_w(P_1, a, l, C) = rate_w(P_2, a, l, C) \quad \text{for all observable } C \in \mathcal{P}/\mathcal{B}$$
$$rate_w(P_1, a, l, \mathcal{P}_{fu}) = rate_w(P_2, a, l, \mathcal{P}_{fu})$$
∎

Definition 3.8. Weak extended Markovian bisimilarity, denoted by $\approx_{\mathrm{EMB}}$, is the union of all the weak extended Markovian bisimulations. ∎

Example 3.1. Consider the two following process terms:

$$P_1 \equiv <a, \lambda>.<\tau, \infty_{l,w}>.<b, \mu>.\underline{0}$$
$$P_2 \equiv <a, \lambda>.<b, \mu>.\underline{0}$$

Then $P_1 \approx_{\mathrm{EMB}} P_2$. In fact, denoted by $Id_{\mathcal{P}}$ the identity relation over $\mathcal{P}$, the equivalence relation $\mathcal{B}_{1,2} = \{(P_1, P_2), (P_2, P_1)\} \cup Id_{\mathcal{P}}$ turns out to be a weak extended Markovian bisimulation. In particular:

$$rate_{\mathrm{w}}(P_1, a, 0, [<b, \mu>.\underline{0}]_{\mathcal{B}_{1,2}}) = \lambda \cdot \frac{w}{w} = \lambda \cdot 1 = rate_{\mathrm{w}}(P_2, a, 0, [<b, \mu>.\underline{0}]_{\mathcal{B}_{1,2}})$$

Note that the equivalence class $[<\tau, \infty_{l,w}>.<b, \mu>.\underline{0}]_{\mathcal{B}_{1,2}}$ has not been considered in the $rate_{\mathrm{w}}$-based comparison as it is initially unobservable. If it had been considered, then we would have obtained:

$$rate_{\mathrm{w}}(P_1, a, 0, [<\tau, \infty_{l,w}>.<b, \mu>.\underline{0}]_{\mathcal{B}_{1,2}}) = \lambda \cdot 1 = \lambda$$
$$rate_{\mathrm{w}}(P_2, a, 0, [<\tau, \infty_{l,w}>.<b, \mu>.\underline{0}]_{\mathcal{B}_{1,2}}) = 0$$

which would have led us to the counterintuitive conclusion that P_1 and P_2 are not weakly extended Markovian bisimilar. ∎

Example 3.2. Consider the two following process terms:

$$P_3 \equiv <a, \lambda>.(<\tau, \infty_{l,w_1}>.<b, \mu>.\underline{0} + <\tau, \infty_{l,w_2}>.<c, \gamma>.\underline{0})$$
$$P_4 \equiv <a, \lambda \cdot \frac{w_1}{w_1+w_2}>.<b, \mu>.\underline{0} + <a, \lambda \cdot \frac{w_2}{w_1+w_2}>.<c, \gamma>.\underline{0}$$

Then $P_3 \approx_{\mathrm{EMB}} P_4$. Indeed, $\mathcal{B}_{3,4} = \{(P_3, P_4), (P_4, P_3)\} \cup Id_{\mathcal{P}}$ turns out to be a weak extended Markovian bisimulation. In particular:

$$rate_{\mathrm{w}}(P_3, a, 0, [<b, \mu>.\underline{0}]_{\mathcal{B}_{3,4}}) = \lambda \cdot \frac{w_1}{w_1+w_2} = (\lambda \cdot \frac{w_1}{w_1+w_2}) \cdot 1 =$$
$$= rate_{\mathrm{w}}(P_4, a, 0, [<b, \mu>.\underline{0}]_{\mathcal{B}_{3,4}})$$
$$rate_{\mathrm{w}}(P_3, a, 0, [<c, \gamma>.\underline{0}]_{\mathcal{B}_{3,4}}) = \lambda \cdot \frac{w_2}{w_1+w_2} = (\lambda \cdot \frac{w_2}{w_1+w_2}) \cdot 1 =$$
$$= rate_{\mathrm{w}}(P_4, a, 0, [<c, \gamma>.\underline{0}]_{\mathcal{B}_{3,4}})$$

Note that P_3 and P_4 are also weakly extended Markovian bisimilar to:

$$P_3' \equiv <a, \lambda>.A$$
$$A \stackrel{\Delta}{=} <\tau, \infty_{l,w_1}>.<b, \mu>.\underline{0} + <\tau, \infty_{l,w_2}>.<c, \gamma>.\underline{0} + <\tau, \infty_{l,w_3}>.A$$

In fact, denoted by W the sum $w_1 + w_2 + w_3$, we have:

$$rate_{\mathrm{w}}(P_3', a, 0, [<b, \mu>.\underline{0}]_{\mathcal{B}_{3,4}}) = \lambda \cdot \sum_{i=0}^{\infty} (\frac{w_3}{W})^i \cdot \frac{w_1}{W} = \lambda \cdot \frac{w_1}{W} \cdot \frac{1}{1-w_3/W} =$$
$$= \lambda \cdot \frac{w_1}{W} \cdot \frac{W}{W-w_3} = \lambda \cdot \frac{w_1}{w_1+w_2}$$
$$rate_{\mathrm{w}}(P_3', a, 0, [<c, \gamma>.\underline{0}]_{\mathcal{B}_{3,4}}) = \lambda \cdot \frac{w_2}{w_1+w_2}$$

This means that $\approx_{\mathrm{EMB}}$ can abstract not only from intermediate unobservable actions (see Ex. 3.1) but also from intermediate unobservable self-loops, consistently with the fact that the probability to escape from them is 1. ∎

Example 3.3. Consider the two following process terms:

$$P_5 \equiv <\tau, \infty_{l,w}>.<a, \lambda>.\underline{0}$$
$$P_6 \equiv <a, \lambda>.\underline{0}$$

Although in principle one may view P_5 and P_6 as being equivalent, they are not related by $\approx_{\text{EMB}}$. The reason is that P_5 can reach P_6 after executing an immediate τ-action while P_6 cannot reach itself after executing any action.

However, the fact that $P_5 \not\approx_{\text{EMB}} P_6$ avoids a congruence violation. It is well known that any weak bisimulation equivalence relating a process term that can execute an initial unobservable action with one that cannot breaks compositionality with respect to the alternative composition operator [9].   ■

Example 3.4. Consider the two following process terms:

$$P_7 \equiv <a_1, \lambda_1>.A_1, \quad A_1 \overset{\Delta}{=} <\tau, \infty_{l_1,w_1}>.A_1$$
$$P_8 \equiv <a_2, \lambda_2>.A_2, \quad A_2 \overset{\Delta}{=} <\tau, \infty_{l_2,w_2}>.A_2$$

where $<a_1, \lambda_1> \neq <a_2, \lambda_2>$. Then $P_7 \not\approx_{\text{EMB}} P_8$. In fact, observed that $A_1, A_2 \in \mathcal{P}_{\text{fu}}$, from $<a_1, \lambda_1> \neq <a_2, \lambda_2>$ it follows that for $a_1 \neq a_2$:

$$rate_{\text{w}}(P_7, a_1, 0, \mathcal{P}_{\text{fu}}) = \lambda_1 \cdot 1 \neq 0 = rate_{\text{w}}(P_8, a_1, 0, \mathcal{P}_{\text{fu}})$$

while for $a_1 = a_2$:

$$rate_{\text{w}}(P_7, a_1, 0, \mathcal{P}_{\text{fu}}) = \lambda_1 \cdot 1 \neq \lambda_2 \cdot 1 = rate_{\text{w}}(P_8, a_1, 0, \mathcal{P}_{\text{fu}})$$

If we had not considered $\mathcal{P}_{\text{fu}}$ in Def. 3.7, then there would have been no way to distinguish between P_7 and P_8, as they cannot reach any observable state.   ■

Example 3.5. Consider the two following process terms:

$$P_9 \equiv <a, \lambda>.A_1, \quad A_1 \overset{\Delta}{=} <\tau, \infty_{l_1,w_1}>.A_1$$
$$P_{10} \equiv <a, \lambda>.A_2, \quad A_2 \overset{\Delta}{=} <\tau, \infty_{l_2,w_2}>.A_2$$

where A_1 and A_2 are defined as in the previous example. Then $P_9 \approx_{\text{EMB}} P_{10}$. In fact, the equivalence relation $\mathcal{B}_{9,10} = \{(P_9, P_{10}), (P_{10}, P_9)\} \cup Id_{\mathcal{P}}$ turns out to be a weak extended Markovian bisimulation. In particular, recalled that $A_1, A_2 \in \mathcal{P}_{\text{fu}}$, it holds that:

$$rate_{\text{w}}(P_9, a, 0, \mathcal{P}_{\text{fu}}) = \lambda \cdot 1 = rate_{\text{w}}(P_{10}, a, 0, \mathcal{P}_{\text{fu}})$$

Note that $A_1 \not\approx_{\text{EMB}} A_2$ whenever $<\tau, \infty_{l_1,w_1}> \neq <\tau, \infty_{l_2,w_2}>$. Thus, in this case, if we had considered the two fully unobservable classes $[A_1]_{\mathcal{B}_{9,10}}$ and $[A_2]_{\mathcal{B}_{9,10}}$ separately, then we would have obtained:

$$rate_{\text{w}}(P_9, a, 0, [A_1]_{\mathcal{B}_{9,10}}) = \lambda \cdot 1 \neq 0 = rate_{\text{w}}(P_{10}, a, 0, [A_1]_{\mathcal{B}_{9,10}})$$
$$rate_{\text{w}}(P_9, a, 0, [A_2]_{\mathcal{B}_{9,10}}) = 0 \neq \lambda \cdot 1 = rate_{\text{w}}(P_{10}, a, 0, [A_2]_{\mathcal{B}_{9,10}})$$

which would have led us to the counterintuitive conclusion that P_9 and P_{10} are not weakly extended Markovian bisimilar.

We point out that P_9 and P_{10} are also weakly extended Markovian bisimilar to

$P_6 \equiv <a, \lambda>.\underline{0}$ as from $\underline{0} \in \mathcal{P}_{\text{fu}}$ it follows:

$$rate_w(P_6, a, 0, \mathcal{P}_{\text{fu}}) = \lambda \cdot 1$$

Hence $\approx_{\text{EMB}}$ can abstract not only from intermediate unobservable self-loops (see Ex. 3.2) but also from terminal unobservable self-loops, consistently with the fact that from them it is not possible to escape at all. ∎

Going back to our running example formalized in Sect. 2, it is easy to see that $QS_n / L[\varphi] \approx_{\text{EMB}} BD_{n,0}$. For instance, if we consider the case of $n = 2$ servers, the relation $\mathcal{B}_{QS_2 / L[\varphi], BD_{2,0}}$ given by $Id_{\mathcal{P}}$ plus the following pairs and their symmetrical ones:

$$(((A_1 \|_{\emptyset} A_2) \|_{\{a_1, a_2\}} (B_{1,0} \|_{\emptyset} B_{2,0}) \|_{\{d_1, d_2\}} (S \|_{\emptyset} S)) / L[\varphi], \quad BD_{2,0})$$
$$(((A_1 \|_{\emptyset} A_2) \|_{\{a_1, a_2\}} (B_{1,0} \|_{\emptyset} B_{2,0}) \|_{\{d_1, d_2\}} (S'_l \|_{\emptyset} S)) / L[\varphi], \quad BD_{2,1})$$
$$(((A_1 \|_{\emptyset} A_2) \|_{\{a_1, a_2\}} (B_{1,0} \|_{\emptyset} B_{2,0}) \|_{\{d_1, d_2\}} (S \|_{\emptyset} S'_l)) / L[\varphi], \quad BD_{2,1})$$
$$(((A_1 \|_{\emptyset} A_2) \|_{\{a_1, a_2\}} (B_{1,i_1} \|_{\emptyset} B_{2,i_2}) \|_{\{d_1, d_2\}} (S'_h \|_{\emptyset} S'_k)) / L[\varphi], \quad BD_{2,j})$$

turns out to be a weak extended Markovian bisimulation whenever $l, h, k \in \{1, 2\}$ and $i_1, i_2 \in \mathbf{N}$, $j \in \mathbf{N}_{\geq 2}$ are such that $i_1 + i_2 = j - 2$.

3.3. Congruence Result for Well-Prioritized Terms

We now investigate the congruence property for $\approx_{\text{EMB}}$. We start with the operators of EMPA_{gr} different from parallel composition.

Theorem 3.1. *Let $P_1, P_2 \in \mathcal{P}$. Whenever $P_1 \approx_{\text{EMB}} P_2$, then:*

(1) $<a, \tilde{\lambda}>.P_1 \approx_{\text{EMB}} <a, \tilde{\lambda}>.P_2$ for all $<a, \tilde{\lambda}> \in Act$.
(2) $P_1 + P \approx_{\text{EMB}} P_2 + P$ and $P + P_1 \approx_{\text{EMB}} P + P_2$ for all $P \in \mathcal{P}$.
(3) $P_1/L \approx_{\text{EMB}} P_2/L$ for all $L \subseteq Name - \{\tau\}$.
(4) $P_1[\varphi] \approx_{\text{EMB}} P_2[\varphi]$ for all $\varphi \in Relab$. ∎

When applying the alternative composition operator or the parallel composition operator to two process terms, it may happen that an unobservable state of one term is combined with an observable state of the other term. Given $P_1, P_2 \in \mathcal{P}$ such that $P_1 \approx_{\text{EMB}} P_2$, these hybrid state combinations raise no congruence violation in the case of the alternative compositions $P_1 + P$ and $P_2 + P$ for any $P \in \mathcal{P}$. The reason is that the only combined states are the initial states of the two compositions. Such initial states include the initial states of P_1 and P_2, which must agree on the value of any weak exit rate considered in Def. 3.7.

Unfortunately, problems do arise in the parallel composition case. The first problem is concerned with initially (resp. fully) unobservable states different from the initial one that are combined with observable states, as the comparison of the weak exit rates towards the classes containing such states can no longer be skipped (resp. included into $\mathcal{P}_{fu}$). Consider e.g.:

$$P_1 \equiv <a, \lambda>.<\tau, \infty_{l_1,w_1}>.<b, \mu>.\underline{0}$$
$$P_2 \equiv <a, \lambda>.<\tau, \infty_{l_2,w_2}>.<b, \mu>.\underline{0}$$
$$P \equiv <a, *_w^0>.<c, \infty_{l',w'}>.\underline{0}$$

with $\infty_{l_1,w_1} \neq \infty_{l_2,w_2}$. It is easy to see that $P_1 \approx_{EMB} P_2$. Although the following two states of P_1 and P_2 are initially unobservable:

$$<\tau, \infty_{l_1,w_1}>.<b, \mu>.\underline{0}$$
$$<\tau, \infty_{l_2,w_2}>.<b, \mu>.\underline{0}$$

in $P_1 \parallel_{\{a\}} P$ and $P_2 \parallel_{\{a\}} P$ the two corresponding states:

$$<\tau, \infty_{l_1,w_1}>.<b, \mu>.\underline{0} \parallel_{\{a\}} <c, \infty_{l',w'}>.\underline{0}$$
$$<\tau, \infty_{l_2,w_2}>.<b, \mu>.\underline{0} \parallel_{\{a\}} <c, \infty_{l',w'}>.\underline{0}$$

are observable whenever $c \neq \tau$ and $l' \geq \max(l_1, l_2)$. From $\infty_{l_1,w_1} \neq \infty_{l_2,w_2}$ it follows that the two corresponding observable states are not weakly extended Markovian bisimilar, so we can conclude that $P_1 \parallel_{\{a\}} P \not\approx_{EMB} P_2 \parallel_{\{a\}} P$ as each of them can only reach one of the two new observable states. The same congruence violation would happen in the case that the c-action were passive. A similar violation – in which only one of the two initially unobservable states becomes observable – would happen for $c \neq \tau$ and $\min(l_1, l_2) \leq l' < \max(l_1, l_2)$. Analogous violations would take place in the absence of action $<b, \mu>$ from P_1 and P_2, which would make the two considered original states fully unobservable.

The second congruence-related problem with parallel composition is due to the fact that a different pre-emption scheme may be imposed by unobservable actions of the same process term to initially or fully unobservable states (different from the initial one) of two weakly extended Markovian bisimilar terms. A congruence violation of this kind would happen in the example above in the case that P were replaced by:

$$P' \equiv <a, *_w^0>.<\tau, \infty_{l',w'}>.<c, \infty_{l',w'}>.\underline{0}$$

with $l_1 < l_2 = l'$ and $c \neq \tau$. In fact, after executing $<a, \lambda>$, only $P_2 \parallel_{\{a\}} P'$ would reach via an unobservable path the only observable state in which both $<b, \mu>$ and $<c, \infty_{l',w'}>$ are enabled. An analogous violation would take place in the absence of action $<b, \mu>$ from P_1 and P_2.

In order to overcome these two congruence-related problems, given $P_1 \parallel_S P$ and $P_2 \parallel_S P$ with $P_1 \approx_{EMB} P_2$, we have to restrict ourselves to contexts P that preserve the unobservable states of $[\![P_1]\!]$ and $[\![P_2]\!]$ as well as the pre-emption schemes of their transitions.

The third congruence-related problem with parallel composition is concerned with terminal states – which are fully unobservable states with no outgoing transitions, like $\underline{0}$ – and unescapable paths – which are infinite paths traversing only fully unobservable states. It may happen that a process term with terminal states and a process term with unescapable paths are weakly extended Markovian bisimilar but can be distinguished when placed in parallel with the same process term. This is the case e.g. of terms P_9 and P_6 considered in Ex. 3.5. They are weakly extended Markovian bisimilar, but if we place each of them in the context of $-\|_{\{a\}} <a, *_w^0>.<c, \gamma>.\underline{0}$, after executing $<a, \lambda>$ the first composition gets stuck into an unobservable self-loop while the second composition reaches an observable state in which $<c, \gamma>$ is enabled.

Theorem 3.2. *Let $P_1, P_2 \in \mathcal{P}$ such that both $[\![P_1]\!]$ and $[\![P_2]\!]$ have no unescapable paths or no terminal states. Whenever $P_1 \approx_{\text{EMB}} P_2$, then $P_1 \|_S P \approx_{\text{EMB}} P_2 \|_S P$ and $P \|_S P_1 \approx_{\text{EMB}} P \|_S P_2$ for all $S \subseteq Name - \{\tau\}$ and $P \in \mathcal{P}$ such that any immediate/passive transition of $[\![P]\!]$ has priority level/constraint less than the priority level of any unobservable transition departing from an unobservable state of $[\![P_1]\!]$ or $[\![P_2]\!]$.* ∎

Definition 3.9. The set $\mathcal{P}_{\text{wp}}$ of the well-prioritized process terms is the smallest subset of $\mathcal{P}$ closed with respect to null term, action prefix, alternative composition, hiding, relabeling, recursion and closed with respect to parallel composition in the following sense: If $P_1, P_2 \in \mathcal{P}_{\text{wp}}$ and any immediate/passive transition of each of $[\![P_1]\!]$ and $[\![P_2]\!]$ has priority level/constraint less than the priority level of any unobservable transition departing from an unobservable state of the other one, then $P_1 \|_S P_2 \in \mathcal{P}_{\text{wp}}$. ∎

Corollary 3.1. $\approx_{\text{EMB}}$ *is a congruence with respect to all the operators over the set $\mathcal{P}'_{\text{wp}}$ (resp. $\mathcal{P}''_{\text{wp}}$) of the well-prioritized process terms without unescapable paths (resp. terminal states).* ∎

3.4. Axioms for Non-Recursive Well-Prioritized Terms

The equational laws characterizing $\approx_{\text{EMB}}$ over the set $\mathcal{P}_{\text{wp,nr}}$ of the non-recursive process terms of $\mathcal{P}_{\text{wp}}$ are described by the set $\mathcal{A}$ of axioms shown in Tables 1 and 2. These are the same axioms as for $\sim_{\text{EMB}}$ with in addition the three axiom schemata $\mathcal{A}_{10}$-$\mathcal{A}_{12}$, in each of which the index set I is finite and non-empty. Such axiom schemata express the capability of abstracting from non-initial immediate τ-actions, provided that the weights of these actions are taken into account when setting the rates of the copies of the actions preceding them. As far as the expansion law $\mathcal{A}_{20}$ for parallel composition is concerned, I and J are finite index sets (if empty, the related summations are taken to be $\underline{0}$), "e.t." stands for exponentially timed, "i." stands for immediate, and "p." stands for passive. We observe that $\mathcal{P}_{\text{wp,nr}} \subseteq \mathcal{P}'_{\text{wp}}$ as its process terms are not recursive (hence no unescapable paths).

Table 1.   Axiomatization of $\approx_{\mathrm{EMB}}$ over $\mathcal{P}_{\mathrm{wp,nr}}$ (part I)

$(\mathcal{A}_1)$	$P_1 + P_2 = P_2 + P_1$	
$(\mathcal{A}_2)$	$(P_1 + P_2) + P_3 = P_1 + (P_2 + P_3)$	
$(\mathcal{A}_3)$	$P + \underline{0} = P$	
$(\mathcal{A}_4)$	$<a,\lambda_1>.P + <a,\lambda_2>.P = <a,\lambda_1 + \lambda_2>.P$	
$(\mathcal{A}_5)$	$<a,\infty_{l,w_1}>.P + <a,\infty_{l,w_2}>.P = <a,\infty_{l,w_1+w_2}>.P$	
$(\mathcal{A}_6)$	$<a,*^l_{w_1}>.P + <a,*^l_{w_2}>.P = <a,*^l_{w_1+w_2}>.P$	
$(\mathcal{A}_7)$	$<\tau,\infty_{l,w}>.P + <a,\lambda>.Q = <\tau,\infty_{l,w}>.P$	
$(\mathcal{A}_8)$	$<\tau,\infty_{l,w}>.P + <a,\infty_{l',w'}>.Q = <\tau,\infty_{l,w}>.P$	if $l > l'$
$(\mathcal{A}_9)$	$<\tau,\infty_{l,w}>.P + <a,*^{l'}_{w'}>.Q = <\tau,\infty_{l,w}>.P$	if $l > l'$
$(\mathcal{A}_{10})$	$<a,\lambda>.\sum\limits_{i\in I}<\tau,\infty_{l,w_i}>.P_i = \sum\limits_{i\in I}<a,\lambda \cdot w_i / \Sigma_{k\in I}\, w_k>.P_i$	
$(\mathcal{A}_{11})$	$<a,\infty_{l',w'}>.\sum\limits_{i\in I}<\tau,\infty_{l,w_i}>.P_i = \sum\limits_{i\in I}<a,\infty_{l',w'\cdot w_i / \Sigma_{k\in I}\, w_k}>.P_i$	
$(\mathcal{A}_{12})$	$<a,*^{l'}_{w'}>.\sum\limits_{i\in I}<\tau,\infty_{l,w_i}>.P_i = \sum\limits_{i\in I}<a,*^{l'}_{w'\cdot w_i / \Sigma_{k\in I}\, w_k}>.P_i$	
$(\mathcal{A}_{13})$	$\underline{0}/L = \underline{0}$	
$(\mathcal{A}_{14})$	$(<a,\tilde{\lambda}>.P)/L = <\tau,\tilde{\lambda}>.(P/L)$	if $a \in L$
$(\mathcal{A}_{15})$	$(<a,\tilde{\lambda}>.P)/L = <a,\tilde{\lambda}>.(P/L)$	if $a \notin L$
$(\mathcal{A}_{16})$	$(P_1 + P_2)/L = P_1/L + P_2/L$	
$(\mathcal{A}_{17})$	$\underline{0}[\varphi] = \underline{0}$	
$(\mathcal{A}_{18})$	$(<a,\tilde{\lambda}>.P)[\varphi] = <\varphi(a),\tilde{\lambda}>.(P[\varphi])$	
$(\mathcal{A}_{19})$	$(P_1 + P_2)[\varphi] = P_1[\varphi] + P_2[\varphi]$	

Table 2.   Axiomatization of $\approx_{\mathrm{EMB}}$ over $\mathcal{P}_{\mathrm{wp,nr}}$ (part II – expansion law)

$(\mathcal{A}_{20})$ $\sum\limits_{i\in I}<a_i,\tilde{\lambda}_i>.P_{1,i} \|_S \sum\limits_{j\in J}<b_j,\tilde{\mu}_j>.P_{2,j} =$

$$\sum_{k\in I, a_k \notin S}<a_k,\tilde{\lambda}_k>.\left(P_{1,k} \|_S \sum_{j\in J}<b_j,\tilde{\mu}_j>.P_{2,j}\right) +$$

$$\sum_{h\in J, b_h \notin S}<b_h,\tilde{\mu}_h>.\left(\sum_{i\in I}<a_i,\tilde{\lambda}_i>.P_{1,i} \|_S P_{2,h}\right) +$$

$$\sum_{k\in I, a_k \in S, e.t.}\;\sum_{h\in J, b_h = a_k, p., l_h = 0}<a_k,\lambda_k \cdot \tfrac{w_h}{weight(P_2, b_h, l_h)}>.(P_{1,k} \|_S P_{2,h}) +$$

$$\sum_{k\in I, a_k \in S, p., l_k = 0}\;\sum_{h\in J, b_h = a_k, e.t.}<b_h,\mu_h \cdot \tfrac{v_k}{weight(P_1, a_k, l_k)}>.(P_{1,k} \|_S P_{2,h}) +$$

$$\sum_{k\in I, a_k \in S, i.}\;\sum_{h\in J, b_h = a_k, p., l_h = l_k}<a_k,\infty_{l_k, v_k \cdot \tfrac{w_h}{weight(P_2, b_h, l_h)}}>.(P_{1,k} \|_S P_{2,h}) +$$

$$\sum_{k\in I, a_k \in S, p.}\;\sum_{h\in J, b_h = a_k, i., l_h = l_k}<b_h,\infty_{l_h, w_h \cdot \tfrac{v_k}{weight(P_1, a_k, l_k)}}>.(P_{1,k} \|_S P_{2,h}) +$$

$$\sum_{k\in I, a_k \in S, p.}\;\sum_{h\in J, b_h = a_k, p., l_h = l_k}$$
$$<a_k,*^{l_k}_{\tfrac{v_k}{weight(P_1, a_k, l_k)} \cdot \tfrac{w_h}{weight(P_2, b_h, l_h)} \cdot (weight(P_1, a_k, l_k) + weight(P_2, b_h, l_h))}>.$$
$$(P_{1,k} \|_S P_{2,h})$$

Theorem 3.3. $DED(\mathcal{A})$ *is sound and complete for* $\approx_{\mathrm{EMB}}$ *over* $\mathcal{P}_{\mathrm{wp,nr}}$:
$$\mathcal{A} \vdash P_1 = P_2 \iff P_1 \approx_{\mathrm{EMB}} P_2 \quad \text{for all } P_1, P_2 \in \mathcal{P}_{\mathrm{wp,nr}} \qquad \blacksquare$$

4. Conclusion

Building on Refs. 6,10 in this paper we have defined a weak variant of Markovian bisimilarity, which abstracts from prioritized/weighted actions that are invisible and take zero time. This allows us to cope with expressive calculi like $\mathrm{EMPA}_{\mathrm{gr}}$, in which GSPN-like immediate actions are first-class citizens that freely alternate with exponentially timed actions. On the technical side, besides carefully classifying the states on the basis of their functional and performance observability, we have introduced priority constraints for passive actions together with the class of well-prioritized process terms in order to achieve congruence.

The restriction of compositionality to well-prioritized process terms is an intrinsic limit of $\approx_{\mathrm{EMB}}$, which has nothing to do with the way in which priorities and weights are dealt with. In $\mathrm{EMPA}_{\mathrm{gr}}$ these are associated locally with the immediate actions of the individual components, but can also be used globally to choose among immediate actions enabled in different components. This is the source of a modeling problem known as confusion in the GSPN field, which can be solved by setting the priority levels of the immediate actions in a way that avoids interference among components [11].

On the other hand, separation of concerns can be achieved by considering the priorities and weights associated with the immediate actions of the individual components to be strictly local and – in a way inspired by Ref. 2 – by assigning global priorities and weights to the occurrences of the parallel composition operator, which thus becomes $^{L_1,W_1}\|_S{}^{L_2,W_2}$ and preselects which component is allowed to perform immediate actions. However, even in such a setting the congruence problems with parallel composition mentioned in Sect. 3.3 would persist. As an example, consider the process terms P_1 and P_2 of Ex. 3.1, which are weakly extended Markovian bisimilar, and the process term $P \equiv <a, *_{w'}^0>.<c, \infty_{l',w'}>.\underline{0}$, where $c \neq \tau$. Then $P_1{}^{L_1,W_1}\|_{\{a\}}{}^{L_2,W_2} P \not\approx_{\mathrm{EMB}} P_2{}^{L_1,W_1}\|_{\{a\}}{}^{L_2,W_2} P$ for $L_1 = L_2$ because, after synchronizing on a, the first composed term enables a τ-action and a c-action while the second composed term enables a b-action and a c-action.

The restriction to well-prioritized process terms is not a severe limitation in practice. Compositionality and abstraction of $\approx_{\mathrm{EMB}}$ can in fact be exploited if the parallel subterms composing an arbitrary process term are considered from the most prioritized one to the least prioritized one and the application of the hiding operators is anticipated/postponed accordingly. Consider for instance the following process term:

$$(\ldots((((P_1 \,\|_{S_{1-2}} P_2)/H_{1-2}) \,\|_{S_{1-3}} P_3)/H_{1-3})\ldots \|_{S_{1-n}} P_n)/H_{1-n}$$

If we call priority of a process term P the maximum $l \in \mathbb{Z}$ such that $no\text{-}pre(l, P)$, then the subterms $P_1, P_2, \ldots, P_n$ can be considered in this order if the priority of P_i is greater than the priority of P_{i+1} for all $i = 1, \ldots, n - 1$, otherwise a permutation of the subterms is necessary (together with the adjustment of the synchronization sets and hiding sets). This will be the subject of future work.

References

1. M. Ajmone Marsan, G. Balbo, G. Conte, S. Donatelli, and G. Franceschinis, *Modelling with Generalized Stochastic Petri Nets* (J. Wiley & Sons, 1995).
2. J.C.M. Baeten, J.A. Bergstra, and S.A. Smolka, *Axiomatizing Probabilistic Processes: ACP with Generative Probabilities*, in Information and Computation **121**:234-255 (1995).
3. M. Bernardo, *Theory and Application of Extended Markovian Process Algebra*, Ph.D. Thesis (University of Bologna, Italy, 1999).
4. M. Bernardo and M. Bravetti, *Performance Measure Sensitive Congruences for Markovian Process Algebras*, in Theoretical Computer Science **290**:117-160 (2003).
5. R.J. van Glabbeek, S.A. Smolka, and B. Steffen, *Reactive, Generative and Stratified Models of Probabilistic Processes*, in Information and Computation **121**:59-80 (1995).
6. H. Hermanns, *Interactive Markov Chains*, LNCS 2428 (2002).
7. J. Hillston, *A Compositional Approach to Performance Modelling* (Cambridge University Press, 1996).
8. L. Kleinrock, *Queueing Systems* (J. Wiley & Sons, 1975).
9. R. Milner, *Communication and Concurrency* (Prentice Hall, 1989).
10. M. Rettelbach, *Probabilistic Branching in Markovian Process Algebras*, in Computer Journal **38**:590-599 (1995).
11. E. Teruel, G. Franceschinis, and M. De Pierro, *Well-Defined Generalized Stochastic Petri Nets: A Net-Level Method to Specify Priorities*, in IEEE Trans. on Software Engineering **29**:962-973 (2003).

ANALYZING NON-INTERFERENCE WITH RESPECT TO CLASSES

D. ZANARDINI

CLIP, Universidad Politécnica de Madrid, E-28660 Boadilla del Monte, Madrid, Spain
E-email: damiano@clip.dia.fi.upm.es

The information flow property of Non-Interference was recently relaxed into Abstract Non-Interference (ANI), a weakened version where attackers can only observe properties of data, rather than their exact value. ANI was originally defined on integers: a property models the set of numbers satisfying it. The present work proposes an Object-Oriented, Java-based formulation of ANI, where data take the form of objects, and the observed property comes to be their class. Relevant data are stored in fields; the execution of a program is taken to be the invocation of some (public) method by an external user; a class is *secure* if, for all its public methods, the class of its public data after the execution does not depend on the initial class of its private data. The relation ANI lies in the representation of abstract domains as class hierarchies: upper closure operators map objects into the *smallest* class they belong to. An analyzer for a non-trivial subset of Java is illustrated, which is sound since programs are never misclassified as secure.

Keywords: Verification; Information Flow; Classes as Properties; Abstract Interpretation

1. Introduction

Abstract Non-Interference (ANI) [8] provided a well-founded and parametric framework where the standard notion of Non-Interference (NI) [10,16] can be relaxed. Such a weakening is useful since many programs do not satisfy NI because it requires the separation between public (information every user can observe) and private (to protect from unauthorized users) data to be complete; i.e., the public output must not depend in any way on the private input (there are no *illicit flows* from private to public data). In practice, it is often the case that some flow should be allowed, as long as (i) attackers cannot detect them; or (ii) there is no need to protect some *aspects* of the revealed information. Several techniques have been proposed for weakening NI; existing approaches either limit the observational power of attackers, or declassify the released information. ANI belongs to the first family: it considers attackers which can only observe properties of data (not exact, *concrete* data). Therefore, an illicit flow may not be visible to attackers since the property does not change; such a flow should be considered as harmless, and the program is safely accepted as secure. Properties are described by abstract domains [6].

Abstract Non-Interference originally refers to simple imperative languages with global integer variables. Data properties are sets of values (e.g., *to be even* is the set of even numbers). Our work defines information flow in an Object-Oriented framework, modeled on Java. Values take the form of objects. The main idea is to see a class, which represents a collection of objects with the same structure, as an abstract property: to observe a property amounts to see the class of the object the property refers to. Class hierarchies describe abstract domains, the subclass relation being the partial ordering on abstract values (i.e., abstract properties). It must be pointed out that type/class information has always been very useful in program analysis [5,14,17]; therefore, class-based reasoning in the framework of information flow can be seen as an interesting approach. An analyzer is shown, which checks ANI in method execution, relying on class-based dependencies for a non-trivial subset of Java (exceptions and threads being the main missing features). Its purpose is to check if the output class of non-private fields depends on the initial class of secret fields; in this case, an illicit *information flow* is said to occur. The algorithm is sound (a discussion on soundness is given), i.e., programs are rejected if illicit flows may occur. Examples show methods which are safely detected as secure even though the classical notion of NI is not satisfied.

Information flow security [10,16] relies on *data dependencies* [1,4]. Standard information flow for an OO framework considers data propagation from private to public fields; it is analyzed by means of types [12] or logic [2], the latter being potentially more precise. The foundational work on ANI provided a set-theoretic definition of secrecy in a simple imperative language. Attempts have been made to make ANI algorithmically verifiable; a compositional proof system was proposed [9], which checks ANI by inferring secrecy assertions via Hoare triples. Assertions are combined syntactically to derive safety proofs; it is also shown how to derive attackers which do not violate a security policy. ANI was recently extended to functional languages [18]; in this work, some ideas for an analysis algorithm were provided as a type system. Data are equipped with *security types* describing the behavior w.r.t. the private-public boundary. Type/class inference for OO languages [14,17] aims at verifying that data cannot belong, at runtime, to the wrong class. The link between type information and data properties has been underlined [5] in Abstract Interpretation. Since information flow and dependencies are closely related, ANI involves a notion of *abstract data dependency* [15], whose computation in the general case is part of ongoing work [11].

Introductory example Consider the recruitment unit of an enterprise (Fig. 1). People applying for a job should fill in their personal data in a questionnaire; in order to avoid discriminating candidates on sex, race etc., only a subset of data (experience, skills, spoken languages) can be used in the (non-automatic) evaluation process. Let personal information be stored in objects of class Candidate; some data in this class are sex-dependent, and are going to be used for bureaucratic reasons *after* the candidates have been evaluated; this means that this information exists in the database from the beginning, yet should be kept invisible to evaluators. In the spirit of OO programming, it makes sense to define two subclasses FemaleCandidate and MaleCandidate of Candidate in order to consistently store sex-dependent data. The information which should be used in the evaluation process can be fetched by calling the method getEvalData(CandidateID id)EvalData [a], which accesses a *private* Candidate object by its id and returns an EvalData object containing data to be evaluated. In the same spirit, the system, possibly coming from previous uses, may implement two subclasses FemaleEvalData and MaleEvalData of EvalData, and private methods (to be invoked by getEvalData(id)) Candidate.ReleaseEvalData()EvalData in the superclass, and the redefined FemaleCandidate.ReleaseEvalData()FemaleEvalData and MaleCandidate.ReleaseEvalData()MaleEvalData. Yet, in this case, the class of the result of getEvalData(id) would reveal information about sex. Such a code is not ill-designed w.r.t. the OO programming style; yet, it is not adequate if security requirements include forbidding the sex of candidates to be revealed.

Figure 1. The introductory example

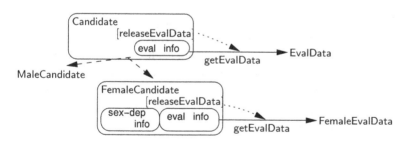

---

[a]In this example and in the rest of the paper, the full notation for method signatures will take the form methodName(Param1class param1, ..., ParamKclass paramK)ReturnClass.

2. Preliminaries

Abstract Interpretation   Abstract Interpretation (AI) [6] is a theory for systematically deriving non-standard, approximated program semantics. *Abstract domains* can be formulated either in terms of Galois connections or closure operators [7]. An *upper closure operator* (uco) on a poset $\langle \mathcal{C}, \leq \rangle$ is a function $\rho : \mathcal{C} \mapsto \mathcal{C}$ monotone, idempotent and extensive. The set of all ucos on $\mathcal{C}$ is UCO $(\mathcal{C})$. A closure operator is uniquely determined by the set of its fixpoints (called *abstract values*); this set is (isomorphic to) the abstract domain $\mathcal{A}$ approximating the concrete domain $\mathcal{C}$. A set $X \subseteq \mathcal{C}$ is the set of fixpoints of a uco iff it is a *Moore-family*, i.e., $X = \mathcal{M}(X) = \{ \wedge S \mid S \subseteq X \}$. In the following, $\rho(v)$ will stand for $\rho(\{v\})$ whenever $\{v\} \in \mathcal{C}$. Abstraction formalizes the idea that $\mathcal{A}$ is simpler than $\mathcal{C}$, being a subset. On the other hand, a computation $f_{\mathcal{A}}$ on $\mathcal{A}$ can be less precise than $f_{\mathcal{C}}$ since values $V \in \mathcal{C} \setminus \mathcal{A}$ cannot be used. $f_{\mathcal{A}}$ approximates $f_{\mathcal{C}}$ by providing the abstract version of constants and operators. It is a *sound* abstraction if the abstract result is always a correct approximation of the concrete result: $\forall x.\ f_{\mathcal{C}}(x) \leq f_{\mathcal{A}}(x)$ (read $\leq$ as *more concrete* or *more precise*). If $\langle \mathcal{C}, \top, \bot, \vee, \wedge \rangle$ is a complete lattice, then $\langle \text{UCO}\,(\mathcal{C}), \text{TOP}, \text{ID}, \vee', \wedge' \rangle$, ordered pointwise, is also a complete lattice where $\text{ID} = \lambda V.V$ describes the identity abstraction ($\mathcal{A} = \mathcal{C}$, no loss of information) and $\text{TOP} = \lambda V.\top$ is the trivial abstraction mapping $\mathcal{C}$ into a singleton $\mathcal{A} = \{\top\}$. The *reduced product* $\sqcap$ [7] of a set $\{\mathcal{A}_i\}$ is the most abstract among the domains which are more concrete than each $\mathcal{A}_i$: formally, $\sqcap_i \mathcal{A}_i = \mathcal{M}(\cup_i \mathcal{A}_i)$. Notation will be often abused by referring to ρ as the set of its fixpoints; i.e., $V \in \rho$ if V belongs to the domain $\mathcal{A}$ generated by ρ. In the present work, AI plays two roles: (i) providing the basis for defining the security property; (ii) giving the background for developing the static analyzer.

Information Flow   If a user wants to keep some data confidential, (s)he can take as a requirement that information cannot go from private to public data. An untrusted user, which can only see public data, should not be able to guess anything about what is protected (private). Such a policy allows programs to use private data as long as the visible output does not reveal information about it. In *Non-Interference* (NI) [10], a program $\mathcal{P}$ is *secure* if any two runs only differing in their *private* input (i.e., indistinguishable by an untrusted user) cannot be distinguished by only observing the *public* output. Formally,

$$\forall h_1, h_2, l_1, l_2.\quad l_1 = l_2 \implies [\![\mathcal{P}]\!]^{\mathsf{L}}(h_1, l_1) = [\![\mathcal{P}]\!]^{\mathsf{L}}(h_2, l_2)$$

where $[\![\mathcal{P}]\!]^{\mathsf{L}}(h, l)$ is the public (*low-security*, L) part of $[\![\mathcal{P}]\!]$ on the input (h, l), divided into a private (*high-security*, H) part h and a public part l. In other words, there must be no *information flow* from h to l: h and l do not interfere.

Abstract Non-Interference Non-Interference can be weakened by modeling secrecy relatively to some observable property. The observational power of an attacker is limited, and a *secure* program preserves secrecy only as regards the information the attacker can observe. Let the concrete domain be the set of all properties (e.g., $\wp(\mathbb{N})$ for integers, where a property is identified with the set $P \subseteq \mathbb{N}$ of values satisfying it), representing which values can be distinguished by attackers. Ucos describe the ability of an attacker: if one has precision ρ, then (s)he cannot distinguish v_1 and v_2 if $\rho(v_1) = \rho(v_2)$ (i.e., values having the same property w.r.t. ρ). $\mathcal{P}$ is secure for domains η and ρ (written $[\eta]\mathcal{P}(\rho)$) if no flows are detected by observing public input (resp. output) data only up to a precision η (resp. ρ):

$$\forall h_i, l_i. \quad \eta(l_1) = \eta(l_2) \implies \rho(\llbracket \mathcal{P} \rrbracket^{\mathsf{L}} (h_1, l_1)) = \rho(\llbracket \mathcal{P} \rrbracket^{\mathsf{L}} (h_2, l_2))$$

If l_1 and l_2 cannot be distinguished, then it is not possible to guess h from the (abstracted) output. Standard NI is a special case of ANI, equivalent to $[\text{ID}]\mathcal{P}(\text{ID})$ (no abstraction). Unfortunately, flows may be detected, which are caused by a change in the public instead of the private input. These flows are called *deceptive* since they are not really dangerous. A more general version of ANI, (η, ϕ, ρ)-secrecy[b], rules out deceptive flows by computing $\llbracket \mathcal{P} \rrbracket$ on an abstraction of the input:

$$\forall h_i, l_i. \quad \eta(l_1) = \eta(l_2) \implies \rho(\llbracket \mathcal{P} \rrbracket^{\mathsf{L}} (\phi(h_1), \eta(l_1))) = \rho(\llbracket \mathcal{P} \rrbracket^{\mathsf{L}} (\phi(h_2), \eta(l_2)))$$

In the following, we deal with (ρ, ρ, ρ)-secrecy: the class hierarchy will identify the abstract domain to be considered.

Figure 2. The program and the attacker

A realistic approach to OO Information Flow Most information flow properties were originally defined on simple languages. Yet, advanced features in present-day OO languages make a correct definition much more difficult to obtain. Particularly, in order to reasonably adapt the NI notion *what an attacker can see at the output does not allow him or her to acquire (abstract) information about secret input* to Java, we must clarify (i) what a running program is; (ii) what an attacker is and can do; (iii) which data we want to protect (see Fig. 2 for a picture).

---

[b]This version is called *abstract*, opposed to the *narrow* version in the previous definition.

Running programs. A Java program is a collection of cooperating classes; we are interested in detecting if the legal interaction with a class C may disclose its protected data. The *program execution* takes the form of the invocation of a public method m of C; a class is secure if all its public methods are secure, i.e., it is not possible to access its private data by interacting with its public part.

Attackers. We see attackers as programs which can interact with external classes C and aim at breaking their secrets by calling public methods. An attacker cannot observe auxiliary information as the amount of allocated memory or the execution time of, which would involve additional flows.

Public and private data. Java comes with field modifiers **public, private** and **protected**, which model security requirements by regulating data access. However, NI analysis does not only deal with *direct* access: secret information should not *propagate* through the computation, as shown in the following code:

```
public class D {
    public C l;    private C h;    public C m() { return h; } }
```

This declaration is legal; yet, the private h is propagated via the return value of m (public); this means that NI may be violated without breaking the access policy. Our security policy requires that there be no (abstract) flow from **private** to **public** fields or return values. If f is declared as private in D, then all the objects stored in the field f of D objects are considered as private; if we want some object $o : D$ not to protect its field f, then it must be an instance of $D' \sqsubset D$, where f is public.

3. Class-Oriented Abstract Non-Interference

ANI is parametric on the degree of precision attackers have in reading public information. Given a universe of values, properties are sets of values sharing some common behavior. In an OO framework, classes have a similar purpose: they identify objects with the same internal structure. Therefore, modeling properties with classes is quite natural. In our setting, program classes are the properties attackers can observe. Identifying properties with classes reduces property checking to a class-directed program analysis [14]. Classes are ordered by the subclass relation: a class is a superset of any subclass; a subclass models a sub-property, i.e., more precise since it is satisfied by less values. Names C, D etc. will denote either sets of semantic values, classes or properties; o stands for objects or values. The subclass relation $C' \sqsubset C$ is basically $C' \subseteq C$ if C' and C are considered as sets of values. The predicate $o : C$ (or $o \in C$) holds if o has class C, while $o :: C$ holds iff $o : C$ and there is no $D \sqsubset C$ s.t. $o : D$. Finally, $C_\downarrow = \{D | D \sqsubseteq C\}$.

Class hierarchies as abstract domains Consider an object set C and a concrete domain $\mathcal{C} = \wp(C)$. A class hierarchy rooted at C^c identifies a subset of properties $D \in \mathcal{C}$, i.e., an abstract domain ρ; $\rho(D)$, for $D \in \wp(C)$, is the smallest class $D' \in \rho$ s.t. $D \sqsubseteq D'$. Since *multiple inheritance* is not allowed in Java, generally there is no subclass C of both C_1 and C_2 which models $C_1 \cap C_2$ (unless $C_1 \sqsubset C_2$ or $C_2 \sqsubset C_1$). Therefore, to have ρ closed under intersection, as required by ucos, the Bot_ρ empty class is supposed to exist for every hierarchy ρ. As a consequence, representable domains are those where classes are either related by $\sqsubset$ or disjoint; languages allowing multiple inheritance do not suffer from this limitation.

The link to the Abstract Non-Interference theory The program $\mathcal{P}$ whose secrets are to be broken takes the form, at runtime, of a collection $\mathcal{O}$ of objects and $\mathcal{C}$ of classes. $\mathcal{E}$ denotes the set of *execution states*. The visible part of $\varepsilon \in \mathcal{E}$ consists of public instance fields of $\mathcal{O}$ objects, and public static fields of $\mathcal{C}$ classes. Let $\varepsilon_1, \varepsilon_2 \in \mathcal{E}$; the *indistinguishability condition* IC $(\varepsilon_1, \varepsilon_2)$ holds if (i) for every $C, o_1, o_2 : C$ (note the :) and public field f, the value $o_1.f$ in ε_1 and $o_2.f$ in ε_2 belongs to the same class $(\exists D. \ \varepsilon_1(o_1.f) :: D \wedge \varepsilon_2(o_2.f) :: D)$; (ii) for every D and public static field g, $D.g$ belongs to the same class in both states.

Given two sequences of values $\overline{v}_1$ and $\overline{v}_2$, IC $(\overline{v}_1, \overline{v}_2)$ is taken to be class equality for every two corresponding elements. The meaning of the condition is that two states cannot be distinguished by someone who can only check the class of public data. An attacker may try to break $\mathcal{P}$ secrets by running $o.m$ of $o \in \mathcal{O}$, or a static $C.m$ of $C \in \mathcal{C}$. The *Abstract Non-Interference condition* ANI (m) holds for m if IC $(\varepsilon_1, \varepsilon_2) \wedge$ IC $(\overline{v}_1, \overline{v}_2)$ implies IC $([\![o.m \, (\overline{v}_1)]\!]_{\varepsilon_1}, [\![o.m \, (\overline{v}_2)]\!]_{\varepsilon_2})$, where $[\![o.m \, (\overline{v})]\!]_\varepsilon$ is the state obtained by executing $o.m$ with parameters $\overline{v}$ in ε (return value included). This means that, after executing m in two states only differing (in the abstract sense) in their private part, we cannot distinguish the output states. The attacked program $\mathcal{P}$ is secure (written ANI $(\mathcal{P})$) if this condition holds for every public method. It is easy to see that this definition of Abstract Non-Interference is quite close to the original one; in fact, it is an adaptation to our OO framework.

4. ANI Analysis for Class Information

This section describes the *class-flow* analyzer in its main features. It is basically an AI-based tool, implemented in the `Ciao` [3] system, which performs an *abstract execution* of a method and tries to detect illicit abstract flows from private fields to public fields or the returned value. Apart from some minor simplifica-

---

[c]That is, with C as the greatest class. Usually, we may want to ignore the Object superclass, thus obtaining a set of hierarchies instead of a single hierarchy rooted at Object.

tions, Java is supported in its main features, including static fields and methods, abstract classes and polymorphism. Exceptions are the most important direction of future work. Analysis relies on *abstract states* $\sigma \in \mathcal{E}$, which consist of a global part (the fixed set of class fields) and the framestack storing local environments. We note that, due to how private and public data are defined (Sec. 2), there is no need to keep an abstract *heap*. $\sigma(C.f)$ is the class of the field f of C in σ, while $\sigma(x)$ refers to the class of x in the active frame of σ. Abstract states map fields and variables to *abstract values* $V = \mathcal{C}_\phi \in \mathcal{V}$, where $\mathcal{C}$ is a set of classes and $\phi \in \{H, L\}$ is a *security flag* indicating the security level of data. Private fields are initially $(C_\downarrow)_H$, where C is the declared class. *Least upper bound* $\sqcup$ is $\mathcal{C}'_{\phi'} \sqcup \mathcal{C}''_{\phi''} = (\mathcal{C}' \cup \mathcal{C}'')_{\phi' \sqcup \phi''}$, where $L \sqcup L = L$ and $\phi' \sqcup \phi'' = H$ otherwise. In type theory, types are a partial order, a type being an abstraction of a set of values [5]; when x has type τ, information about which $\tau' \leq \tau$ it can belong to is lost. Using class sets is more precise, and allows exploiting abstract declarations (Sec. 5). For example, let D be abstract, $D_1, D_2 \sqsubseteq D$. In our setting, $\{D_1, D_2\}_\phi$ may be computed for o declared as D; this is more precise than $(D_\downarrow)_\phi = \{D, D_1, D_2\}_\phi$, but still correct since it describes the same set (D has no instances).

In Java, illicit flows come as (i) assignment of a private value to a public variable or field (*explicit flows*); or (ii) execution of conditional statements or loop whose guard depends on private data (*implicit flows*). In detecting explicit flows, the main point is computing abstract values for expressions; a flow is soundly assumed to exist if a private value is computed for an expression assigned to a public v. Implicit flows are dealt with by means of a global analysis which remembers the security level under which a command is executed: if an assignment to public depends on a private guard, then its effect may cause an illicit flow.

Abstract values In $x = e$, e may be quite complicated: e.g., a method call with side effects. Therefore, computing the security content ϕ_e is non-trivial. Fig. 3 shows how abstract values are computed (ANALYZE is shown below). The *expression semantics* $[\![]\!]^\sharp$ takes e, $\sigma \in \mathcal{E}$ and ϕ, and gives a pair (value, resulting state).

The operator $[\![]\!]^\phi$ *raises* the security level of a value: $(\mathcal{C}_{\phi'})^{\phi''} = \mathcal{C}_{\phi' \sqcup \phi''}$. The flag ϕ in $[\![e]\!]^\sharp_\phi(\sigma)$ means that e is computed under a level ϕ (see implicit flows).

The function LS is only applied to the first element of the pair (i.e., the abstract value); it lowers the flag of a value if the class set is a singleton: LS $(\langle \mathcal{C}_\phi, \sigma \rangle)$ is $\langle \mathcal{C}_L, \sigma \rangle$ if $\mathcal{C}$ is a singleton, $\langle \mathcal{C}_\phi, \sigma \rangle$ otherwise. This function is very important since it shows how abstract data dependencies may differ w.r.t. their concrete counterpart. Let $\{C\}_\phi$ be $[\![e]\!]^\sharp_{\phi'}(\sigma)$, and o be the object computed by runtime (concrete) execution. Thus, $o :: C$ certainly holds (soundness). Even if e contains private data, it can be considered as L; in fact, illicit flows do not occur since the class of

o is constant. Typically, $\mathcal{C}$ is a singleton $\{C\}$ if C has no subclasses; however, it can be the case, as in new $C()$, that the class is unique although C has subclasses.

Methods and statements The function $\text{ANALYZE}_\sigma\left(V.m(\ldots)\right)^\phi$, already used above, performs the security analysis of methods. A method can be invoked as a command (when there is no return value, or it is ignored), or inside expressions. Let V and $V_1..V_k$ be abstract values obtained by previous computations. The result of $\text{ANALYZE}_\sigma\left(V.m(V_1..V_k)\right)^{\phi'}$ is obtained by (thelub of) the abstract execution in σ of each instance $C.m$ such that $V = \mathcal{C}_\phi$ and $C \in \mathcal{C}$. More formally:

$$\text{ANALYZE}_\sigma\left(\mathcal{C}_\phi.m(V_1,..,V_k)\right)^{\phi'} = \sqcup_{C \in \mathcal{C}}\left(\text{ANALYZE}_\sigma\left(C_\phi.m(V_1,..,V_k)\right)^{\phi'}\right)$$

where $\sqcup$ works on both the return value and the final state. The notation C_ϕ means that the flag of the caller is kept in the analysis of each C method instance (it is copied in this). This is another difference with respect to standard information flow analysis, and it is also applied to field access: usually, the analysis of $o.f$ or $o.m(\ldots)$ leads to an H flag whenever o is H. In our formulation, the H content of o is not a sufficient condition to consider $o.f$ or $o.m(\ldots)$ as private. For example, let $o : C$ be private, and $C_\downarrow = \{C, C_1, C_2\}$. In all classes, f has class D, and $D_\downarrow = \{D\}$ (i.e., no subclasses). In this case, regardless of whether f is declared as public or private, $o.f$ is considered as L since its class is unique.

The analysis of a method body computes (abstract) commands and expressions. $\sigma\left[x \leftarrow V\right]$ (resp. $\sigma\left[C.f \leftarrow V\right]$) is the *updated* state obtained by storing the abstract value V in x (resp. $C.f$); $\sigma\left[C.f \leftarrow V\right]$ is the set extension for each $C \in \mathcal{C}$. The *upgraded* state $\sigma' = \sigma\left[v \leftarrow V\right]$ satisfies $\sigma'(v) = \sigma(v) \sqcup V$.

Upgrading (instead of updating) is used since it is not known which instances $C.f$ will be actually assigned; therefore, the initial value cannot be forgotten.

$$[\![x]\!]_\phi^\sharp(\sigma) = \left\langle\sigma(x)^\phi,\ \sigma\right\rangle$$

$$[\![o.f]\!]_\phi^\sharp(\sigma) = \text{LS}\left(\left\langle\sqcup\left\{\sigma'(C.f) \mid C \in \mathcal{C}^o\right\},\ \sigma'\right\rangle^\phi\right)$$

$$\text{where}\quad \left\langle\mathcal{C}^o{}_{\phi_o},\ \sigma'\right\rangle = [\![o]\!]_\phi^\sharp(\sigma)$$

$$[\![C.f]\!]_\phi^\sharp(\sigma) = \text{LS}\left(\left\langle\sigma(C.f),\ \sigma\right\rangle^\phi\right)$$

$$[\![o.m(p_1,..,p_k)]\!]_\phi^\sharp(\sigma) = \text{LS}\left(\text{ANALYZE}_{\sigma_k}\left(V_o.m(V_1,..,V_k)\right)^\phi\right)$$

$$\text{where}\quad \left\langle V_o, \sigma_0\right\rangle = [\![o]\!]_\phi^\sharp(\sigma)\quad\text{and}\quad\left\langle V_i, \sigma_i\right\rangle = [\![p_i]\!]_\phi^\sharp(\sigma_{i-1})$$

$$[\![C.m(p_1,..,p_k)]\!]_\phi^\sharp(\sigma_0) = \text{LS}\left(\text{ANALYZE}_{\sigma_k}\left((\{C\}_\downarrow).m(V_1,..,V_k)\right)^\phi\right)$$

$$\text{where}\quad\sigma_0 = \sigma\quad\text{and}\quad\left\langle V_i, \sigma_i\right\rangle = [\![p_i]\!]_\phi^\sharp(\sigma_{i-1})$$

Figure 3. Rules for analyzing expressions

$$\text{EXEC}_\sigma \left(x = e \right)^\phi = \sigma' \left[x \leftarrow \mathcal{C}_{\phi'} \right]$$
$$\text{where} \quad \langle \mathcal{C}_{\phi'}, \sigma' \rangle = \llbracket e \rrbracket_\phi^\sharp (\sigma)$$
$$\text{EXEC}_\sigma \left(o.f = e \right)^\phi = \sigma'' \left[\mathcal{C}.f \leftarrow \mathcal{C}'_{\phi'} \right]$$
$$\text{where} \quad \langle \mathcal{C}_\phi, \sigma' \rangle = \llbracket o \rrbracket_\phi^\sharp (\sigma) \text{ and } \langle \mathcal{C}'_{\phi'}, \sigma'' \rangle = \llbracket e \rrbracket_\phi^\sharp (\sigma')$$
$$\text{EXEC}_\sigma \left(\text{if}(b) \ s_1 \text{ else } s_2 \right)^\phi = \text{EXEC}_{\sigma_1} (s_1)^{\phi \sqcup \phi_b} \sqcup \text{EXEC}_{\sigma_2} (s_2)^{\phi \sqcup \phi_b}$$
$$\text{where} \quad (\phi_b, \sigma_1, \sigma_2) = \llbracket b \rrbracket_g^\sharp (\sigma)$$

Example 4.1. Let o be given $\{D, D_1\}$, and $D_1 \sqsubseteq D$. Let $o.f$ be H before $o.f = e$, and e be L. *Updating* the state would result in a final L flag for both $D.f$ and $D_1.f$, which is unsound if the runtime class of o is D_1, since $D.f$ would be harmfully considered as L. Yet, *upgrading* is sound since H is kept for $D.f$ by lub.

The function $\llbracket b \rrbracket_g^\sharp (\sigma)$ computes, for a guard b, its flag ϕ in σ. States σ_1 and σ_2 are only different when we can infer something from the truth value: e.g., if b is x instanceof C, assuming $\neg b$ means that its class is not a subclass of C. $\text{EXEC}_\sigma (s)^\phi$ means that the effects of s on σ will be raised by ϕ (see def. of $\llbracket \rrbracket^\sharp$): when V is computed in σ, its flag ϕ_V is raised to $\phi_V \sqcup \phi$. This is important in dealing with implicit flows, originating from non-public guards (i.e., $\phi = $ H).

Global analysis and soundness The analyzer has a *global* part, dealing with method invocation and the problems arising from mutual recursion; a *security signature* is maintained for every method instance; it is updated whenever the method is successfully analyzed. If an instance is invoked when another activation is already in the framestack, then the current security signature is used instead of re-analyzing the method. A global fixpoint is performed; its adherence to the usual AI-based techniques for designing program analyzers ensures soundness. As for the intra-body part of the analyzer, the main non-standard issue about soundness is the correctness of LS, argued above: the flag L only if the class is a constant. Because of this, $\llbracket \rrbracket^\sharp$ computes an over approximation $\mathcal{C}_\phi$ of the *optimal* (the one obtained by directly abstracting the concrete result) abstract value, i.e., $\mathcal{C}$ is a superset of the set of possible runtime classes, and ϕ is L only if indeed no flows are possible. Soundness of the use of state upgrading is also motivated above.

5. An Example

The code in Fig. 4 shows the main features of the analysis; it is possible to accept programs which would be rejected by a standard NI analyzer. We focus on A.flow(D, D1)E. It computes an expression by calling three methods; we study whether the return value depends on private information when d1 and d2 are pri-

```
class A { E flow(D d1,D1 d2) { return ((d1.m()).n(d2)).met(); } }

class C { public E f1 ;   private E f2 ;   E n(D d) { return f2 ; } }
class C1 extends C { private E f2 ;
  E n(D d) { if(d instanceof D1){ return new E2(d) } else { return f2 }}}
class C2 extends C { private E f2 ;   E n(D d) { return new E2(d); } }
class C3 extends C { private E f2 ;
  E nn(E e) { return new E(); }
  E n() { return nn(f2); } }

abstract class D { abstract C m(); }
class D1 extends D { C m() { return new C1(); } }
class D3,D4 extends D1 {}
class D2 extends D { C m() { return new C2(); } }
abstract class D5 extends D2 {}
class D6,D7 extends D5 { C m() { return new C2(); } }

class E { private C fpr ;   public C fpb ;   C met() { return fpb ; } }
class E1,E2 extends E {}
class E3 extends E2 { C met() { return fpr ; } }
```

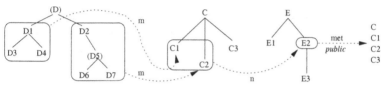

Figure 4.   The Java code (with abuse of syntax) and the abstract behavior of methods

vate. We note that d1 may belong to any of the Dx classes, but the *abstract* D and D5. Therefore, m() must be evaluated for all non-abstract instances. The key point in m() is that, although the declared return class be C, it can be statically inferred to be C1 or C2. By lub, d1.m() yields $\{C1, C2\}_L$. This was possible since D is abstract, thus C (i.e., the return of D.m) is not to be dealt with. Here, using sets of classes can indeed make a difference: excluding C.n() allows to get rid of C.n, which returns E. On the other hand, both C1.n() and C2.n() return E2 (in the first, guard analysis was used to exclude *else*). Finally, E2.met() is the only met instance to consider. This shows another use of using class sets: we do not need to consider the closure of E2, which would have involved a flow from the private fpr via E3.met(). Instead, no illicit flows occur because the public fpb is returned by the E2 instance of met(); the final value comes to be $\{C, C1, C2, C3\}_L$.

6. Conclusions and Future Work

The present work introduces a reformulation of Abstract Non-Interference for a non-trivial subset of Java. By defining abstract properties as classes, detecting illicit information flows can be reduced to finding low security data whose class after a method run depends on the initial class of some high security data. This is a sort of type-based dependency analysis, tracking how class information propagates. The result is substantially different from standard NI verification, since (i) it models a weaker property, i.e., it does not distinguish between values of the same class; and (ii) it is not completely syntax-based, so that data can be considered as public even if they have private syntactic sub-parts (e.g., o and f in $o.f$).

The main direction of future work is towards the implementation of a real analyzer; the current tool is a prototype which can be improved and optimized in several ways. This would lead to a more efficient and possibly more precise analysis, capable of soundly accept a wider set of programs. Moreover, a larger subset of Java would be worth considering, in particular the use of exceptions. Finally, this framework could be part of a *Proof-Carrying code* [13] architecture. In a PCC Java framework, the code user wants to be sure that the bytecode program (s)he receives is safe. The program is not executed unless the producer provides a correctness proof for the desired security property. The inclusion into PCC would involve the translation of the analysis (or of its results, by means of soundness of the compiling process) to the bytecode level, since the consumer is interested in verifying low-level programs.

References

1. M. Abadi, A. Banerjee, N. Heintze, and J. Riecke. A core calculus of dependency. In *POPL*, 1999.
2. T. Amtoft, S. Bandhakavi, and A. Banerjee. A logic for information flow in object-oriented programs. In *POPL*, 2006.
3. F. Bueno, D. Cabeza, M. Carro, M. Hermenegildo, P. López, and G. Puebla. The Ciao System. Reference Manual (v1.13). Technical report, UPM, 2006.
4. I. Cartwright and M. Felleisen. The semantics of program dependence. In *PLDI*, 1989.
5. P. Cousot. Types as abstract interpretations, invited paper. In *POPL*, 1997.
6. P. Cousot and R. Cousot. Abstract interpretation: a unified lattice model for static analysis of programs by construction or approximation of fixpoints. In *POPL*, 1977.
7. P. Cousot and R. Cousot. Systematic design of program analysis frameworks. In *POPL*, 1979.
8. R. Giacobazzi and I. Mastroeni. Abstract non-interference: Parameterizing non-interference by abstract interpretation. In *POPL*, 2004.
9. R. Giacobazzi and I. Mastroeni. Proving abstract non-interference. In *CSL*, 2004.
10. J. Goguen and J. Meseguer. Security policies and security models. In *SSP*, 1982.
11. I. Mastroeni and D. Zanardini. The calculus of Abstract Dependencies. unpbl., 2007.
12. A. Myers. JFlow: practical mostly-static information flow control. In *POPL*, 1999.
13. G. Necula. Proof-Carrying Code. In *POPL*, 1997.
14. J. Palsberg and M. Schwartzbach. Object-oriented type inference. In *OOPSLA*, 1991.
15. X. Rival. Abstract dependences for alarm diagnosis. In *APLAS*, 2005.
16. A. Sabelfeld and A. Myers. Language-based information-flow security. *IEEE Journal on Selected Areas in Communications*, (1), 2003.

17. F. Spoto and T. Jensen. Class Analyses as Abstract Interpretations of Trace Semantics. *ACM TOPLAS*, (5), 2003.

18. D. Zanardini. Higher-Order Abstract Non-Interference. In *TLCA*, 2005.

COMPUTING MINIMUM DIRECTED FEEDBACK VERTEX SET IN $O^*(1.9977^n)$

IGOR RAZGON *

i.razgon@cs.ucc.ie

Computer Science Department, University College Cork, Ireland

In this paper we propose an algorithm which, given a directed graph G, finds the minimum directed feedback vertex set (FVS) of G in $O^*(1.9977^n)$ time and polynomial space. To the best of our knowledge, this is the first algorithm computing the minimum directed FVS faster than in $O(2^n)$. The algorithm is based on the branch-and-prune principle. The minimum directed FVS is obtained through computing of the complement, i.e. the maximum induced directed acyclic graph. To evaluate the time complexity, we use the measure-and-conquer strategy according to which the vertices are assigned with weights and the size of the problem is measured in the sum of weights of vertices of the given graph rather than in the number of the vertices.

1. Introduction

In this paper we consider the following problem: given a directed graph G, find the maximum acyclic subset (MAS) of G i.e. the largest subset of vertices of G inducing a directed acyclic graph (DAG). We propose an algorithm solving this problem in $O^*(1.9977^n)$ time and polynomial space. The complement of MAS is the minimum directed Feedback Vertex Set (FVS). The directed FVS problem is one of the "canonical" NP-hard optimization problems whose NP-complete version is mentioned in [8]. Thus the proposed algorithm solves the directed FVS problems as well. To the best of our knowledge, this is the first algorithm solving this problem faster than in $O(2^n)$. For the undirected version of the FVS problem, the $O(2^n)$ barrier has been broken by Razgon [9].

The proposed algorithm belongs to the area of exact exponential algorithms whose subject is design of algorithms solving intractable problems faster than brute-force enumeration of all the possibilities (see a tutorial of Woeginger [10] for introduction to the field). However, the directed FVS problem is considered

---

*I dedicate this paper to my son Gabriel Razgon who was born on 14/04/2007, just one day before the ICTCS 2007 abstract submission deadline.

challenging and interesting in other areas of Theoretical Computer Science, especially Parameterized Complexity and Approximation Algorithms. Therefore, the proposed result may be interesting to a broader audience of researchers as providing a new insight into the nature of the directed FVS problem.

The proposed algorithm is based on the branch-and-prune approach. That is, the algorithm selects a vertex v of the given graph G, finds the largest acyclic subset of G containing v and the largest one without v, and returns the larger of the above two. These two subsets are found by recursive application of the algorithm to the corresponding *residual* graphs. The $O(2^n)$ barrier can be easily broken if one shows that selection or removal of v necessarily causes removal of additional vertices from the respective residual graph. For example, for the Maximum Independent Set (MIS) problem that can be easily seen since selection of a non-isolated vertex causes removal of its neighbors. In our case, this is not always possible. For example, if graph G is strongly connected (that is, the problem cannot be divided into a number of independent subproblems) and has no cycles of size 2 (that is, selection of vertex v does not cause removal of an additional vertex) then many vertices may be selected or removed before at least one additional vertex can be eliminated from the residual graph. To overcome, the difficulty, we associate vertices with weights and measure the size of the problem as the sum of weights of the vertices rather than the number of vertices. If the given branching decision does not cause *real* elimination of additional vertices, the weights of the vertices which are likely to be removed in the future are decreased. This updating of weights "amortizes" the effect of vertex elimination among a number of iterations so that each branching decision gets "a small bit" of the effect sufficient for breaking the $O(2^n)$ barrier.

The above methodology of complexity analysis called *Measure-and-Conquer* is quite recent [1,2,4] but proved very successful in the last two years: it served as a basis of design and analysis of algorithms for such problems as Dominating Set [7], MIS [5], undirected FVS [3,9], connected Dominating Set [6].

The rest of the paper is structured as follows. Section 2 introduces the necessary terminology. Section 3 presents the algorithm, proves its correctness, and describes intuitively why the algorithm breaks the $O(2^n)$ barrier. Section 4 presents complexity analysis of the algorithm which is, essentially, formalization of the intuitive description given in Section 3. Due to the space constraints, some proofs or parts of them are omitted. [†]

[†]The preliminary (unpolished) version of the paper which contains all the proofs is available at http://www.cs.ucc.ie/ ir2/papers/mas1203.pdf

2. Preliminaries

All graphs considered in the paper are directed graphs without loops and multiple arcs. Let G be a directed graph with the set of vertices $V(G)$ and the set of arcs $A(G)$. Let $v, w \in V(G)$. If $(w, v) \in A(G)$, we say that w is an *entering* neighbour of v and v is a *leaving* neighbour of w.

A subset S of $V(G)$ is a directed Feedback Vertex Set (FVS), if every directed cycle of G contains at least one vertex of S. We call the complement $V(G) \backslash S$ of S an *acyclic subset* of G because it induces an acyclic subgraph of G. A Maximum Acyclic Subset (MAS) is the complement of a minimum directed FVS.

Let $v \in V(G)$. Graph $G^C(v)$ is obtained from $G \setminus v$ as follows. For each entering neighbour u of v and for each leaving neighbour w of v, an edge from u to w is added (if there is no such edge in G). If u is both an entering and a leaving neighbour of v then u becomes a *loop vertex*. All loop vertices are removed from the resulting graph.

Let D be a subset of vertices of G. The graph $G^C(D)$ is defined recursively as follows. If $D = \emptyset$ then $G^C(D) = G$. Otherwise, $G^C(D) = (G^C(v))^C(D \setminus \{v\})$ for some $v \in D$. Observe that the definition of $G^C(D)$ makes sense only if D is acyclic in G: otherwise one of the vertices of D will be eventually removed as a loop vertex and there will be no possibility to finish up the recursive construction. We say that $G^C(D)$ is obtained from G as a result of *contraction* of vertices of D.

The complexity of the algorithm proposed in the paper is measured in terms of O^* notation [10], which suppresses polynomial factors. For example, $O(n^2 * 2^n)$ is transformed into $O^*(2^n)$.

3. The Algorithm

We present the algorithm for computing the MAS of G as a recursive procedure $GetMAS(G, R)$.

The parameter R is the function on $V(G)$ such that for $v \in V(G)$, $R(v)$ is the *role* of v. Initially, the role of each vertex is *UNMARKED (UM)*. During the run of the algorithm, a vertex can change its role to *LEFT MARKED (LM)*, *RIGHT MARKED (RM)*, *WEAKLY LEFT MARKED (WLM)*, *WEAKLY RIGHT MARKED (WRM)*, *LEFT MARKED DISCONNECTED (LMD)*, and *RIGHT MARKED DISCONNECTED (RMD)*. The notion of roles is crucial for the complexity analysis because the vertices are assigned with weights according to their roles. As well, the roles guide the branching decisions made by the algorithm.

Let us denote by $V_X(G, R)$ the set of vertices v of G such that $R(v) = X$. In the further description of the algorithm, we frequently refer to the sets $V_{LM}(G, R) \cup V_{LMD}(G, R)$ and $V_{RM}(G, R) \cup V_{RMD}(G, R)$. For the

sake of succinctness we denote these sets by $VL(G, R)$ and $VR(G, R)$, respectively. We refer to the vertices whose roles are *UM* as *unmarked* vertices and to the rest of the vertices as *marked* ones. Also, the vertices of
$VL(G, R) \cup V_{WLM}(G, R)$, $VR(G, R) \cup V_{WRM}(G, R)$, $VL(G, R) \cup VR(G, R)$,
$V_{WLM}(G, R) \cup V_{WRM}(G, R)$ are referred as *left-marked, right-marked, strongly
marked,* and *weakly marked,* respectively.

Below we present the algorithm in the form of a list of items. Each item be-
gins with the condition written in bold and associated with a short name in square
brackets for easier reference. The condition is followed by the description of operations to be performed, if this condition is satisfied. The conditions are presented
in the order they are checked by the algorithm. For each condition but the first
one, it is assumed that this condition is checked only if all the previous conditions
are not satisfied. The formal description is followed by intuitive explanation why
the algorithm breaks the $O(2^n)$ barrier.

We assume that the first operation performed by $GetMAS(G, R)$ (prior to the
operations described below) is the *balancing operation* ensuring that $|VL(G, R)|$
and $|VR(G, R)|$ differ by at most 3. In particular if $|VR(G, R)| - |VL(G, R)| > 3$
then arbitrary $|VR(G, R)| - (|VL(G, R)| + 3)$ vertices of $VR(G, R)$ are selected
and their roles in R are changed to WRM. Symmetrically, if $|VL(G, R)| -
|VR(G, R)| > 3$ then arbitrary $|VL(G, R)| - (|VR(G, R)| + 3)$ vertices of
$VL(G, R)$ are selected an their roles in R are changed to WLM.

(1) **[C1] Graph G has at most 3 vertices.** Find a MAS of G efficiently and
    return it.
(2) **[C2] Graph G has a cycle of length 2.** Let v be a vertex participating in
    such a cycle. Return the largest set among $\{v\} \cup GetMAS(G^C(v), R')$ and
    $GetMAS(G \setminus v, R)$. ‡, where R' is computed as follows. If v is unmarked
    then $R' = R$. If v is left-marked then R' is obtained from R by setting to
    WLM the roles of all unmarked entering neighbors of v. Finally, if v is right-
    marked then R' is obtained from setting to WRM the roles of all unmarked
    leaving neighbors of v.
(3) **[C3] Graph G has two or more strongly connected components.** Let v_1
    and v_2 be vertices of different strongly connected components G_1 and G_2
    that *preferably* belong to $V_{LMD}(G, R) \cup V_{RMD}(G, R)$. Let $T_1 = \{v_1, v_2\} \cup
    GetMAS(G^C(\{v_1, v_2\}), R)$, $T_2 = GetMAS(G \setminus \{v_1, v_2\}, R)$. Return
    $max(T_1 \cap V(G_1), T_2 \cap V(G_1)) \cup max(T_1 \cap V(G_2), T_2 \cap V(G_2)) \cup (T_1 \setminus
    (V(G_1) \cup V(G_2)))$, where $max(S_1, S_2)$ means the larger set of S_1 and S_2.

---

‡We assume that R is projected to the vertices of the graph given as the first parameter.

(4) **[C4]** $VL(G,R) = \emptyset$ **or** $VR(G,R) = \emptyset$. We identify the following two subcases.

- **[C41] There is an *unmarked* or *weakly marked* vertex v with the in-degree at most 3 or the out-degree at most 3.** Let $v_1,\ldots,v_l$ $(l \leq 3)$ be the set of all entering (or leaving) neighbors of v. The algorithm branches on selection of $v, v_1,\ldots,v_l$. In particular, $GetMAS(G,R)$ selects the largest set among $\{v\} \cup GetMAS(G^C(v),R), \{v_1\} \cup GetMAS((G\setminus v)^C(v_1),R),\ldots,\{v_l\} \cup GetMAS((G\setminus\{v,v_1,v_{l-1}\})^C(v_l),R)$.

- **[C42] The condition C41 is not satisfied** Select a vertex v *preferably* unmarked or weakly marked. Return the larger set of $\{v\} \cup GetMAS(G^C(v),R')$ and $GetMAS(G\setminus v,R)$ where $R' = R$ if $v \in VL(G,R) \cup VR(G,R)$ [§], otherwise R' is constructed as follows. Set the roles of all vertices of $G^C(v)$ to *UM*. Let $u_1,\ldots,u_4$ be any 4 entering neighbours of v and let $w_1,\ldots w_4$ be any 4 leaving neighbours of G. These neighbours necessarily exist because the condition **C41** is not satisfied. Set the roles of $u_1\ldots u_4$ in R' to be *LM* and the roles of $w_1,\ldots w_4$ to be *RM*. If v has entering neighbours other than $\{u_1,\ldots,u_4\}$ set their roles in R' to *WLM*. If there are leaving neighbours of v other than $\{w_1,\ldots w_4\}$, set their roles to *WRM*.

(5) **[C5] The conditions C1 to C4 are not satisfied.** We describe the case assuming that $|VL(G,R)| \leq |VR(G,R)|$. If $|VL(G,R)| > |VR(G,R)|$ then the behavior of $GetMAS(G,R)$ is symmetric with the difference that the vertices with roles RMD, RM, and WRM are considered instead the vertices with roles LMD, LM, and WLM, respectively. As well, in the places where **entering** neighbors of **left-marked** vertices are mentioned, the **leaving neighbors** of the respective vertices are considered in the symmetric "right-marked" case. We consider three subcases of the given condition.

- **[C51] All the vertices of $VL(G,R)$ have role LMD or no vertex of $VL(G,R)$ has an unmarked entering neighbor.** [¶] Let v be an arbitrary vertex of $VL(G,R)$. Return the largest set among $\{v\} \cup GetMAS(G^C(v),R)$ and $GetMAS(G\setminus v,R)$.

- **[C52] There is a left-marked vertex v which does not belong to $V_{LMD}(G,R)$ and has at least 4 unmarked entering neighbors.**

[§] In the complexity analysis, we show that the case where $v \in VL(G,R) \cup VR(G,R)$ never happens. We provide it here for the sake of completeness of the description.

[¶] Again, this case is provided for the sake of completeness only. In the next section we rule out the possibility of its appearance.

Let $v_1, \ldots, v_4$ be arbitrarily selected unmarked entering neighbors of v. Return the largest set among $\{v\} \cup GetMAS(G^C(v), R')$ and $GetMAS(G \setminus v, R)$ where R' differs from R in that the roles of $v_1, \ldots v_4$ are set to LM and the roles of the rest unmarked entering neighbors of v are set to WLM.

- **[C53] Conditions C51 and C52 are not satisfied.** Select a left-marked vertex v with the largest number of unmarked entering neighbors. Let X be the set of unmarked entering neighbors of v. For each acyclic subset $Y \subseteq X$, let $G_Y = (G \setminus (X \setminus Y))^C(Y)$ and return the largest set among $T_Y = Y \cup GetMAS(G_Y, R'(Y))$, where $R'(Y) = R$ if Y is non-empty. Otherwise, $R'(Y)$ is obtained from R by setting the role of v to LMD.

Theorem 3.1. *Given a directed graph* G *and a function* R *assigning roles to the vertices of* G, *$GetMAS(G, R)$ finds a MAS of* G *taking a finite time and polynomial space.*

Now we shall describe intuitively why the algorithm breaks the $O(2^n)$ barrier. The branching rules corresponding to conditions **C2**, **C3**, and **C41** result in *immediate* pruning effect. In particular, the branching rule corresponding to **C2** removes from the residual graph at least one additional vertex on the selection branch, the branching rule corresponding to **C3** removes 2 vertices on both branches, the branching rule corresponding to condition **C41** selects a subset of $k + 1$ vertices ($k \leq 3$) to be included to the returned MAS, spending only $k + 1$ branches instead of 2^{k+1} ones.

The pruning effect of branching rules corresponding to conditions **C42** and **C52** is based on our setting that vertices with roles LM or RM have smaller weight than unmarked vertices (the weakly marked vertices have the same weight as unmarked). As a result of the selection branch of the considered branching rules, some unmarked vertices acquire roles LM or RM reducing the size of the problem which is the sum of weights of vertices of the underlying graph. To be useful in decreasing of the overall complexity, this weight reduction should be compensated by the *real* pruning effect occurring later on during the processing. The idea of the compensation is based on the invariant stating that for any pair (G, R) to which $GetMAS$ is applied recursively during the processing, each left-marked vertex is an entering neighbor of each right-marked vertex (we prove this invariant in the next section). To understand why it is helpful, consider a sequence of vertex selection branches, with the first branch corresponding to condition **C42** and the rest corresponding to condition **C52**. Each of these vertex selection branches increases the number of left-marked and right-marked vertices so, if the sequence is long enough, the underlying graph can be partitioned into the left-marked and right-marked vertices. From this moment and until one of the partition classes wipes out, either condition **C2** or **C3** is satisfied which results in a *real* pruning effect. Really if there is an edge from a right-marked vertex to a left-marked vertex then the above invariant guarantees that the underlying graph has a directed cycle of length 2 satisfying condition **C2**. Otherwise, left-marked and right-marked vertices belong to different strongly connected components, that is condition **C3** is satisfied.

The above strategy has two major obstacles. The first obstacle occurs if, for example, there are no left-marked vertices and there are many vertices with roles RM. The most undesired event in this situation is applying the branching rule corresponding to condition **C42**. On the vertex selection branch all the vertices with roles RM are unmarked. Since there are many such vertices, this results in massive increase of the problem size which neutralizes the effect of previous weight reductions. To avoid this obstacle, we apply the balancing operation which guarantees that the size of $VL(G, R)$ and $VR(G, R)$ differ by at most 3. However this balancing operation turns out to be helpless if there are many consecutive calls of the vertex selection branch corresponding to condition **C52** applied to *the same* side, say to the left-marked vertices. In this case the pruning effect of weight reduction might be diminished by the subsequent balancing operation. To avoid this undesired effect, the vertex selection branch is applied to the *smaller side*, i.e. if $|VL(G, R)| \leq |VR(G, R)|$ then new left-marked vertices are created otherwise new right-marked ones appear. Combining this "alternating" application of the vertex selection branch with the balancing operation has the desired effect of avoiding the considered obstacle.

The second obstacle that may occur is satisfaction of condition **C53**. In this case the weight reduction produced by the vertex selection rule of condition **C52** is insufficient for the complexity improvement. To avoid this obstacle the algorithm performs an ordinary branching on all combinations of unmarked entering (or leaving) neighbors of the specified vertex v and changes the role of v to LMD or RMD on the branch where all the considered neighbors are removed. This results in weight reduction on that branch due to our setting that vertices with roles LMD or RMD have the lowest weight. We prove in the next section that if all the left-marked vertices of (G, R) have roles LMD (or all right-marked vertices have role RMD) then left-marked vertices and right-marked ones belong to different strongly connected components, i.e. condition **C3** is satisfied. This ensures that multiple application of the above branching rule eventually result in a *real* pruning effect.

4. Analysis

We start the analysis from introducing additional terminology. Let G_{IN} be the input graph whose MAS we are interested to compute. Let R_{IN} be the function assigning role UM to each vertex of G_{IN}. Recall that $GetMAS(G_{IN}, R_{IN})$ is the initial application of the considered algorithm. The set of *legal pairs* explored by $GetMAS(G_{IN}, R_{IN})$ includes (G_{IN}, R_{IN}) and all pairs (G, R) to which $GetMAS$ is recursively applied during the run of $GetMAS(G_{IN}, R_{IN})$.

Let (G', R') be a legal pair. Recall that the first operation performed by $GetMAS(G', R')$ is the balancing of (G', R') producing as a result the pair (G, R) for which $|VL(G, R)|$ and $|VR(G, R)|$ differ by at most 3 (if the condition is true regarding (G', R') then $(G', R') = (G, R)$). Then the appropriate type of recursive branching is selected regarding (G, R). We call (G, R) a *balanced pair* (BP). Note that $GetMAS(G', R') = GetMAS(G, R)$. If (G, R) satisfies condition **C1**, we call (G, R) an *atomic balanced pair*.

The set of BPs explored by $GetMAS(G_{IN}, R_{IN})$ can be naturally represented as a search tree. The root of the tree is (G_{IN}, R_{IN}) (this is a BP since all the vertices of G_{IN} are unmarked in R_{IN}). Let (G, R) be a node of the tree. If (G, R) is atomic then this node is a leaf. Otherwise, depending on the condition satisfied by (G, R), $GetMAS(G, R)$ produces legal pairs $(G'_1, R'_1), \ldots, (G'_k, R'_k)$ to which $GetMAS$ is recursively applied. (For example, if (G, R) satisfies condition **C2** then the produced pairs are $(G^C(v), R')$ and $(G \setminus v, R)$, where v and R' are as shown in the description of the algorithm.) The pairs $(G_1, R_1), \ldots, (G_k, R_k)$ obtained as a result of balancing of $(G'_1, R'_1), \ldots, (G'_k, R'_k)$, respectively, are the *children* of (G, R). Accordingly, (G, R) is the *parent* of $(G_1, R_1), \ldots, (G_k, R_k)$. Now, we recursively define the notion of *descendants*. If (G, R) is atomic, it is the only descendant of itself. Otherwise, the set of descendants of (G, R) include (G, R) and the union of descendants of the children of (G, R). ‖ If a descendant of (G, R) is an atomic BP, we call it an *atomic descendant* of (G, R).

The crucial step of the analysis is ruling out the possibility of application of the branching rule corresponding to condition **C51**.

Theorem 4.1. *No BP (G, R) satisfies condition **C51** and causes $GetMAS(G, R)$ to check this condition.*

In order to prove the theorem, we need two additional lemmas.

Lemma 4.1. *For each BP, each left-marked vertex is an entering neighbor of each*

‖ We admit that a node is a descendant of itself in order to ensure that an atomic node has exactly one descendant which will be convenient for the complexity computation.

right-marked vertex.

Lemma 4.2. *Let (G, R) be any BP such that both $VL(G, R)$ and $VR(G, R)$ are nonempty. Let $v \in V_{LMD}(G, R)$, let u be an entering neighbor of v such that u and v belong to the same strongly connected component. Then u is a left marked vertex of (G, R). Analogously, if $v \in V_{RMD}(G, R)$ and u is a leaving neighbor of v in the same strongly connected component then u is a right-marked vertex of (G, R).*

Proof of theorem 4.1. Assume by contradiction that there is a BP (G, R) that satisfies condition **C51** and causes $GetMAS(G, R)$ to check this condition. We assume that condition **C51** is satisfied regarding the left-marked vertices of (G, R), the case with right-marked vertices is symmetric. Since $GetMAS(G, R)$ checks condition **C51**, the earlier conditions **C1** ... **C4** are not satisfied regarding (G, R). That is, both $VL(G, R)$ and $VR(G, R)$ are nonempty and G is a strongly connected graph. In particular, there is a path in G from a right-marked vertex to a left-marked vertex. This path necessarily contains an edge (u, v) such that v is left-marked and u is not. If u is right-marked then by Lemma 4.1, u and v constitute a cycle of size 2, which satisfied condition **C2**, a contradiction. If u is unmarked then the second part of condition **C51** is not satisfied regarding left-marked vertices (v has an unmarked entering neighbor of u). It remains to assume that $v \in V_{LMD}(G, R)$ but this contradicts Lemma 4.2. $\square$

Let w, wm, wmd be 3 real numbers so that $w > wm > wmd$. Let (G, R) be a BP. We assign each vertex v of G a weight $W_R(v)$ according to the role of v in (G, R). In particular, if $v \in V_{UM}(G, R) \cup V_{WLM}(G, R) \cup V_{WRM}(G, R)$ then $W_R(v) = w$. If $v \in V_{LM}(G, R) \cup V_{RM}(G, R)$ then $W_R(v) = wm$. Finally, if $v \in V_{LMD} \cup V_{RMD}(v)$ then $W_R(v) = wmd$. The weight $W_R(G)$ of G is the sum of weights of its vertices. The following theorem provides an upper bound on the number of atomic descendants of (G, R) depending on $W_R(G)$.

Theorem 4.2. *Let (G, R) be a BP. Assume that $w = 1, wm = 0.925, wmd = 0.884.$ [**] Let $m = W_R(G)$. Then the number of atomic descendants of (G, R) is at most 1.9977^m.*

Proof. The proof is by induction on the sequence of balanced pairs sorted in the reverse chronological order (we are allowed to consider this sequence due to the finite number of generated BPs as verified by Theorem 3.1). The first BP in this

---

[**]The values are obtained by a computer program which guessed all the triplets of values from 0 to 1 with interval 0.001 with the objective to minimize c where c is the resulting constant, 1.9977 in the considered case.

sequence is atomic, hence the theorem trivially holds for that pair (this pair is the only atomic descendant of itself). Consider a BP which is not the first in the sequence assuming that the theorem holds for all the previous pairs. Since the theorem trivially holds for all atomic BPs, we may assume that (G, R) is not atomic. In this case the number of atomic descendants of (G, R) is the sum of the numbers of atomic descendants of the children of (G, R). Let $(G_1, R_1), \ldots, (G_k, R_k)$ be the children of (G, R). Denote $W_{R_1}(G_1), \ldots, W_{R_k}(G_k)$ by $m_1, \ldots, m_k$, respectively. By the induction assumption, the number of atomic descendants of each (G_i, R_i) is at most 1.9977^{m_i}. We are going to show that $1.9977^{m_1} + \cdots + 1.9977^{m_k} \leq 1.9977^m$ which will finish the proof of the theorem. The rest of the proof follows all the conditions checked by the algorithm and shows that the theorem holds regarding (G, R) if it satisfies the given conditions. All these conditions are analyzed in a similar manner. Due to the space constraints, we cannot provide the analysis of all the conditions. Hence, we prove the analysis of the most nontrivial condition, which occurs when conditions **C1**, ..., **C4** are not satisfied and condition **C52** is satisfied. According to Theorem 4.1, the condition **C51** cannot be satisfied in the considered case, hence the algorithm performs the operations associated with condition **C52**. Then (G, R) has two children (G_1, R_1) and (G_2, R_2) corresponding to selection and non-selection of the specified vertex v. Due to our agreement that $|VL(G, R)| \leq |VR(G, R)|$, v is a left-marked vertex in (G, R). Condition **C52** explicitly forbids v to have role LMD, hence v has role LM or WLM in (G, R). We prove these two subcases separately.

Assume first that $R(v) = LM$ The transformation from (G, R) removes v contributing wm to the decreasing of m_1. Next, 4 unmarked entering neighbors of v change their roles to LM which contributes $4(w - wm)$ to the decreasing of m_1. Observe that the subsequent balancing operation does not change roles of the vertices. Really, (G, R) is balanced and, by our agreement, $|VL(G, R)|$ is not greater than $|VR(G, R)|$. As a result of this transformation one strongly marked vertex (namely, v) is removed and four new ones appear. Clearly, the resulting difference between the number of strongly left-marked vertices and the strongly right-marked ones is not greater than 3. Thus $m_1 = m - wm - 4(w - wm) = m - 4w + 3wm$. The transformation from (G, R) to (G_2, R_2) removes v decreasing m_2 by wm. Since v is strongly marked, at most one vertex is made weakly marked by the subsequent balancing operation, which increases m_2 by at most $w - wmd$. In total $m_2 \leq m - wm + (w - wmd) = m - wm - wmd + w$. We obtain that $1.9977^{m_1} + 1.9977^{m_2} \leq 1.9977^{m-4w+3wm} + 1.9977^{m-wm-wmd+w} = 1.9977^m * (1.9977^{-4w+3wm} + 1.9977^{-wm-wmd+w}) < 1.9977^m * 0.9998$, getting the last inequality by the substitution of w, wm, and wmd with their values guessed by the statement of the theorem.

Assume now that $R(v) = WLM$. This time the removal of v and making 4 unmarked entering neighbors of v to have roles LM decreases m_1 by $w + 4(w - wm)$. However, the resulting number of strongly left-marked vertices may be greater by 4 than the number of strongly right-marked vertices (if initially $|VL(G, R)| = |VR(G, R)|$). Consequently, at most one strongly right-marked vertex can be made weakly marked by the subsequent balancing operation which increases m_1 by at most $w - wmd$. In total $m_1 \leq m - w - 4(w - wm) + w - wmd = m - 4w + 4wm - wmd$. The transformation from (G, R) to (G_2, R_2) removes v thus decreasing m_2 by w. Since w is a weakly marked vertex, its removal does not violate the difference between the number of strongly left-marked and strongly right-marked vertices in (G, R), hence the subsequent balancing operation does not change the roles of the vertices. That is, $m_2 = m - w$. Consequently, $1.9977^{m_1} + 1.9977^{m_2} \leq 1.9977^{m - 4w + 4wm - wmd} + 1.9977^{m - w} = 1.9977^m * (1.9977^{-4w + 4wm - wmd} + 1.9977^{-w}) < 1.9977^m * 0.968$. Thus we have verified that the theorem holds for both subcases of the considered case. $\square$

Corollary 4.1. *There is an algorithm that finds the largest acyclic subset of the given graph G_{IN} in time $O^*(1.9977^n)$, where $n = |V(G_{IN})|$ and space polynomial in n.*

Acknowledgements

This work was supported by Science Foundation Ireland (Grant Number 05/IN/I886).

I would like to thank the reviewers for their very useful comments that allowed me to essentially improve the presentation of the final version of the paper.

References

1. D. Eppstein. Quasiconvex analysis of backtracking algorithms. In *SODA*, pages 788–797, 2004.
2. D. Eppstein. Improved algorithms for 3-coloring, 3-edge-coloring, and constraint satisfaction. In *SODA*, pages 329–337, 2001.
3. F. Fomin, S. Gaspers, and A. Pyatkin. Finding a Minimum Feedback Vertex Set in time $O(1.7548^n)$. In *IWPEC 2006*, pages 184–191, 2006.
4. F. Fomin, F. Grandoni, and D. Kratsch. Some new techniques in design and analysis of exact (exponential) algorithms. *Bulletin of the EATCS*, 87:47–77, 2005.
5. F. Fomin, F. Grandoni, and D. Kratsch. Measure and conquer: a simple $O(2^{0.288})$ independent set algorithm. In *SODA*, pages 18–25, 2006.
6. F. Fomin, F. Grandoni, and D. Kratsch. Solving Connected Dominating Set faster than 2^n. In *FSTTCS*, pages 152–163, 2006.
7. F. Fomin, F. Grandoni, and D. Kratsch. Measure and conquer: Domination - a case study. In *ICALP*, pages 191–203, 2005.

8. M. Held and R. Karp. A dynamic programming approach to sequencing problems. *Journal of SIAM*, 10:196–210, 1962.
9. I. Razgon. Exact Computation of Maximum Induced Forest. In *SWAT 2006, LNCS 4059*, pages 160–171, 2006.
10. G. Woeginger. Exact algorithms for NP-hard problems: A survey. In *Combinatorial Optimization*, pages 185–208, 2001.

SEEING THE TREES AND THEIR BRANCHES
IN THE NETWORK IS HARD

I. A. KANJ

School of Computer Science, Telecommunications, and Information Systems,
DePaul University, Chicago, IL 60604-2301, USA
E-mail: ikanj@cs.depaul.edu

L. NAKHLEH* and C. THAN†

Department of Computer Science, Rice University,
Houston, TX 77005-1892, USA
*E-mail: nakhleh@cs.rice.edu †E-mail: cvthan@cs.rice.edu

G. XIA

Department of Computer Science, Acopian Engineering Center, Lafayette College,
Easton, PA 18042, USA
E-mail: gexia@cs.lafayette.edu

Phylogenetic networks are a restricted class of directed acyclic graphs that model evolutionary histories in the presence of *reticulate* evolutionary events, such as horizontal gene transfer, hybrid speciation, and recombination. Characterizing a phylogenetic network as a collection of trees and their branches has long been the basis for several methods of reconstructing and evaluating phylogenetic networks. Further, these characterizations have been used to understand molecular sequence evolution on phylogenetic networks.

In this paper, we address theoretical questions with regard to phylogenetic networks, their characterizations, and sequence evolution on them. In particular, we prove that the problem of deciding whether a given tree is contained inside a network is NP-complete. Further, we prove that the problem of deciding whether a branch of a given tree is also a branch of a given network is polynomially equivalent to that of deciding whether the evolution of a molecular character (site) on a network is governed by the *infinite site model*. Exploiting this equivalence, we establish the NP-completeness of both problems, and provide a parameterized algorithm that runs in time $O(2^{k/2}n^2)$, where n is the total number of nodes and k is the number of recombination nodes in the network, which significantly improves upon the trivial brute-force $O(2^k n)$ time algorithm for the problem. This reduction in time is significant, particularly when analyzing recombination hotspots.

Keywords: Phylogenies; Networks; Complexity; Parameterized algorithms.

1. Introduction

Phylogenies, i.e., evolutionary histories, play a major role in representing the relationships among biological entities. Their pervasiveness has led biologists, mathematicians, and computer scientists to design a variety of methods for their reconstruction. Until recently, most of these methods were designed to construct trees. Yet, biologists have long recognized that trees oversimplify our view of evolution in certain cases, since they cannot model events such as hybrid speciation, horizontal gene transfer (HGT), and recombination. These events, which are collectively referred to as *reticulation events* or *reticulate evolutionary events*, give rise to non-treelike evolutionary histories which are best modeled by *phylogenetic networks*. Reconstructing and evaluating the quality of phylogenetic networks is very important, given the emerging evidence of the ubiquity of reticulation events and the evolutionary roles they play.

Relationships between phylogenetic networks on one hand, and the trees and their branches on the other, have great significance. From the computational perspective, these relationships form the basis for the wide array of methods that have been devised for reconstructing phylogenetic networks [8,10]. From the biological perspective, these relationships shed light on how molecular sequences evolve down these networks. Events such as recombination, hybrid speciation, and lateral gene transfer break up the genomic history into many small pieces, each of which has a strictly treelike pattern of descent [9]. Identifying these trees and reconciling their discordance is the basis for several phylogenetic network reconstruction methods. [3,13] Understanding the relationship between a phylogenetic network and its branches, particularly in terms of the *clusters* (or *splits*) of taxa that they induce, has been the basis for another category of reconstruction methods [1,4]. Very recently, Nakhleh and colleagues introduced new approaches for augmenting a tree into a phylogenetic network to fit the evolution of a set of sequences based on parsimony [6] and likelihood [5] criteria.

Almost all of the aforementioned methods are based on understanding relationships among networks, trees, and clusters of taxa. Further, some of them rely on analysis of the evolution of sequences on networks. In this paper, we provide a theoretical treatment of the computational complexity of establishing some of these relationships. Nakhleh and Wang [14] devised efficient algorithms for restricted cases of some of these problems, while leaving the computational complexity of the general cases as open questions. In this paper, we prove that the problem of deciding whether a given tree is contained inside a network is NP-complete. Further, we prove that the problem of deciding whether a branch of a given tree is also a branch of a given network is polynomially equivalent to that of deciding whether the evolution of a molecular character (site) on a network is governed by the *infinite site model*. Exploiting this equivalence, we establish the NP-completeness of both problems, and provide a parameterized algorithm that runs in time $O(2^{k/2}n^2)$, where n is the total number of nodes and k is the number of recombination nodes in the network, which significantly improves upon the trivial brute-force $O(2^k n)$ time algorithm for the problem. This improvement is very significant in practice [12]. Kanj *et al.* [7] considered the problem of character compatibility on a different model of phylogenetic networks that is used in historical linguistics. Whereas the NP-hardness result from that work is modified and used here, that is not the case, however, for the new parameterized algorithm that we present here. The algorithmic techniques do not carry over to the biologically-motivated model of phylogenetic networks that we consider here. Due to the lack of space, many proofs have been omitted.

2. Phylogenetic Networks, Trees, and the Infinite Site Model

Let $T = (V, E)$ be a tree, where V and E are the *tree nodes* and *tree edges*, respectively, and let $L(T)$ denote its leaf set. Further, let $\mathcal{X}$ be a set of taxa (species). Then, T is a phylogenetic tree over $\mathcal{X}$ if there is a bijection between $\mathcal{X}$ and $L(T)$. A tree T is said to be *rooted* if the set of edges E is directed and there is a single distinguished internal node r with in-degree 0.

A character c labeling the leaves of T is a function $c : L(T) \to \{0, 1\}$. Biologically, such character corresponds to a single SNP, and the two states it takes are the two possible *alleles* that the SNP may exhibit.[a] The commonly assumed model of evolution of SNPs is the *infinite site model*, which states that when a character (site) mutates, it changes its state to a new one that is not observed anywhere else in the tree. We denote by $c(v)$ the state of character c for node v. A *haplotype* of length k is a sequence of such characters $c_1 \cdots c_k$. A *full labeling*, or labeling for short, for character c on the tree is an extension, $\hat{c}$, of character c to label all the nodes of T; i.e., $\hat{c} : V(T) \to \{0, 1\}$ and $\hat{c}(v) = c(v)$ for every $v \in L(T)$. In this paper, we focus on characters that exhibit *exactly* two states.

Definition 2.1. A character c is *compatible* on tree T if there is a labeling $\hat{c}$ which extends c such that there exists exactly one edge $e = (u, v) \in E(T)$ where $\hat{c}(u) \neq \hat{c}(v)$, and for all other edges $e' = (u', v') \neq e$, $\hat{c}(u') = \hat{c}(v')$.

Notice that if SNP c evolves under the infinite site model, then there is a tree on which it is compatible. Hence, the compatibility criterion reflects this model of evolution. A sequence of characters $c_1 \cdots c_k$ is compatible on tree T if every

---

[a]Even though SNPs may exhibit all four states (A, C, T, and G), bi-allelic SNPs, i.e., SNPs that exhibit two states, are the most common.

character c_i, $1 \le i \le k$, is compatible on T. By this definition of compatibility, it suffices to establish the computational complexity of and develop algorithms for testing the compatibility of single characters. Therefore, from this point on, we focus on the case of a single character. Testing whether a character is compatible on a tree T with n leaves can be done in $O(n)$ time [11].

As explained in Section 1, when reticulation events occur, the evolutionary history of a set of sequences is best modeled by a phylogenetic network. A phylogenetic network $N = (V, E)$ is a rooted directed acyclic graph, with set $L(N)$ of leaves, such that there is a bijection between a set of taxa $\mathcal{X}$ and $L(N)$. A network N has three types of nodes: (1) one node r with in-degree 0, which corresponds to the root; (2) nodes with in-degree 1, which correspond to *coalescence* events; and (3) nodes with in-degree 2, which correspond to recombination. Fig. 1 shows an example of a phylogenetic network on four taxa A, B, C, and D. A

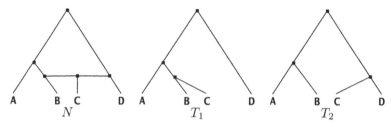

Figure 1. A phylogenetic network N on four taxa A, B, C, and D, and the two trees T_1 and T_2 it contains. Character c_1, where $c_1(A) = c_1(D) = 0$ and $c_1(B) = c_1(C) = 1$ is compatible on tree T_1, but not compatible on tree T_2. Character c_2, where $c_2(A) = c_2(B) = 0$ and $c_2(C) = c_2(D) = 1$ is compatible on T_2 but not on T_1. It can be easily checked that there does not exist any tree T on which both characters are compatible. However, both characters are compatible on network N. The two horizontal edges in N are directed towards the parent of C.

phylogenetic network N induces, or contains, a set of trees; these trees model the evolutionary histories of sets of non-recombining segments (or, genes) in the genomic sequences. We denote by $\mathcal{T}(N)$ the set of all trees contained inside network N. Each such tree is obtained by the following two steps: (1) for each node of in-degree 2, remove one of the incoming edges, and then (2) for every node x of in-degree and out-degree 1, whose parent is u and child is v, remove node x and its two adjacent edges, and add a new edge from u to v. If node x is the root and its out-degree is 1, remove x and make its only child the new root for the tree. Figure 1 shows the two trees contained inside network N. The membership problem of trees and networks, which is heavily used in network reconstruction methods, is formulated as follows.

Problem 2.1. *Tree Containment (TC)*

    Input: *A phylogenetic network N and tree T over the same set $\mathcal{X}$ of taxa.*
    Question: *Is $T \in \mathcal{T}(N)$?*

In the next section, we prove that the TC problem is NP-complete. The notion of character compatibility is extended to phylogenetic networks so as to reflect the biological fact that the evolutionary history of a character is modeled by one of the trees inside the network.

Definition 2.2. A character c is *compatible* on network N if c is compatible on at least one tree $T \in \mathcal{T}(N)$.

The problem of testing the infinite site model on a phylogenetic network can be defined as follows.

Problem 2.2. *Infinite Site on Phylogenetic Networks (ISPN)*

    Input: *Phylogenetic network N and a binary character c labeling the leaves of N.*
    Question: *Is c compatible on N?*

Given a network N with k nodes of in-degree 2, the size of $\mathcal{T}(N)$ is $O(2^k)$. Therefore, The ISPN problem is solvable in $O(2^k n)$ time, given the algorithm for solving the problem when N is a tree [11]. In the next sections, we prove that ISPN is NP-complete and introduce a more efficient algorithm for solving it.

    Further, we establish equivalence between the ISPN problem and another problem from phylogenetics, namely the Cluster Containment problem [14]. Let T be a phylogenetic tree on a set $\mathcal{X}$ of taxa. We say that edge e induces, or defines, cluster $X \subseteq \mathcal{X}$, where X is the set of all leaves reachable from the root of T through edge e. We denote by $\mathcal{C}(T)$ the set of all clusters defined by tree T. This notion is extended to networks by $\mathcal{C}(N) = \cup_{T \in \mathcal{T}(N)} \mathcal{C}(T)$. The Cluster Containment problem is defined as follows.

Problem 2.3. *Cluster Containment (CC)*

    Input: *A phylogenetic Network N and set X of taxa.*
    Question: *Is $X \in \mathcal{C}(N)$?*

Nakhleh and Wang [14] devised a polynomial time algorithm for a restricted version of the CC problem, yet its complexity in the general case was left open. We show that CC and ISPN are polynomially equivalent, thus establishing NP-completeness of the former problem as well.

3. Computational Complexity of the TC Problem

A straightforward way to answer this question is to generate all possible trees from the network and compare them with T. Checking if two trees are identical can be done in polynomial time. However, for a network N with k recombination nodes, the number of trees induced by the network is $O(2^k)$, and therefore checking if a tree is contained in a network using this brute-force approach takes exponential time.

Theorem 3.1. *The problem TC is NP-complete.*

4. The ISPN Problem: Complexity and a Parameterized Algorithm

4.1. *NP-completeness of* ISPN

Kanj *et al.* [7] proved the NP-completeness for the problem of character compatibility on phylogenetic networks when the network edges are bi-directional. We modify their proof to make it work for the ISPN problem and present the theorem.

Theorem 4.1. ISPN *is NP-complete.*

4.2. *A Parameterized Algorithm for* ISPN

A Prelude to the Algorithm

An instance of a parameterized problem is a pair consisting of an input instance x of size n and a parameter k. A parameterized problem is *fixed-parameter tractable* if it can be solved in time $f(k)n^{O(1)}$, where f is a computable function of the parameter k [2].

Naturally, the ISPN problem can be parameterized by the number of *recombination nodes* (nodes of in-degree 2) k in the phylogenetic network, which is usually much smaller than the total number of nodes in the network [12]. Every recombination node in N has two incoming edges, and hence two possible parents. Deciding the parent of each recombination node in N *induces* a tree from N, and N is compatible if and only if there exists an induced tree from N that is compatible. Since there are $O(2^k)$ such induced trees, the ISPN problem can be solved in $O(2^k n)$ time, where n is the number of nodes in N, by enumerating all possible induced trees then checking whether any of them is compatible using the linear time algorithm [11]. We shall improve on this trivial upper bound next by presenting a simple branch-and-search algorithm that runs in $O(2^{k/2} n^2)$ time.

For two nodes u and v in N, we denote by the ordered pair (u, v) the directed edge from u to v (in case the edge exists in N). A node u in N is an *internal* node if u is not a leaf in N, that is, if the out-degree of u is greater than 0.

Definition 4.1. For a node $u \in N$ we define the *weight* of u, denoted $wt(u)$, to be the in-degree of u minus 1 if u is not the root of N, and to be 0 if u is the root of N.

Definition 4.2. A node u in N is a said to be a *recombination node* if it is weight is greater or equal to 1, otherwise, u is said to be a *non-recombination node*.

Definition 4.3. Let N be a network. A node p in N is said to be a *partition node* if there exists an induced compatible tree T from N such that there is a valid labeling for the nodes in T with all the nodes in the subtree rooted at p in T labeled with the same label, and all the other nodes in T labeled with the other label.

While applying the branch-and-search process, the algorithm will label some of the internal nodes in the network. Therefore, the network will get partially labeled as the algorithm progresses. In many cases the (resulting) network can be simplified, or even, its compatibility can be inferred easily. We describe next some of the scenarios in which the compatibility of the network can be directly decided. We also describe some operations that simplify the network. The algorithm will make use of these operations and simplifications.

Proposition 4.1. *If there is at most one leaf of label 0 (similarly 1) in N then N is compatible.*

Proposition 4.2. *Let $u \in N$ be a node. Suppose that u has two children that are non-recombination nodes. Suppose further that these two children have different labels and none of them is a partition node. Then N is not compatible.*

Proposition 4.3. *If a labeled node $u \in N$ has a non-recombination child v such that $label(v) \neq label(u)$ and v is not a partition node, then N is not compatible.*

Proposition 4.4. *Let u be a recombination node in N and let (u', u) be an incoming edge to u. Suppose that $label(u) \neq label(u')$. Let N' be the network resulting from N by removing the edge (u', u). Then N is compatible if and only if N' is. Moreover, if p is a partition node in N then p is also a partition node in N'.*

Proposition 4.5. *Let u be a labeled non-recombination node in N with the incoming edge (u', u). Suppose that u' is unlabeled. Let N' be the network obtained from N by setting $label(u') = label(u)$ if u is not the partition node, and $label(u') = 1 - label(u)$ if u is the partition node. Then N is compatible and p is a partition node in N if and only if N' is compatible and p is a partition node in N'.*

Proposition 4.6. *Let u be a node in N and let (u', u) be an incoming edge to u. Suppose that $label(u) = label(u')$. Suppose further that u is a recombination node and let (u'', u) be another incoming edge to u. Let N' be the network resulting from N by removing the edge (u'', u). Then N is compatible with a partition node p if and only if N' is compatible with a partition node p.*

Proposition 4.7. *Let w be a node in N such that all its children are leaves labeled with the same label. Let N' be the network obtained from N by: (1) replacing w and its children with a leaf w' labeled with the same label as the children of w, (2) making every incoming edge to w an incoming edge to w', and (3) making every incoming edge to a child of w an incoming edge to w'. Then N is compatible if and only if N' is. Moreover, if p is a partition node of N then p is also a partition node of N', unless p is either w or one of its children and in which case w' is a partition node in N'.*

We describe below a procedure that simplifies the network according to the operations and simplifications described in the previous propositions.

Simplify(N)

1. **while** there is a node $u \in N$ of out-degree 0 **do** remove u from N;
2. **if** there is only one leaf in N with label 0 (or 1) **then return** (TRUE);
3. **if** the partition node p is a leaf **then return** (FALSE);
4. **if** there exists a node $u \in N$ that has two children with different labels that are non-recombination nodes and such that none of them is a partition node **then return** (FALSE);
5. **if** there exists a labeled node $u \in N$ that has a non-recombination child v such that $label(v) \neq label(u)$ and v is not a partition node **then return** (FALSE);
6. **if** there exists a recombination node $u \in N$ and an edge $(u', u) \in N$ such that $label(u') \neq label(u)$ **then** remove (u', u) and decrease $wt(u)$ by 1;
7. **if** u' is unlabeled and has a labeled child u such that u is a non-recombination node **then**
   if u is designated as the partition node **then** set $label(u') = 1 - label(u)$;
   else set $label(u') = label(u)$;
8. **if** there exists a recombination node $u \in N$ and an edge $(u', u) \in N$ such that $label(u') = label(u)$ **then**
   for every edge $(u'', u) \in N$ where $u'' \neq u$ **do**
   remove (u'', u) and decrease $wt(u)$ by 1;
9. **if** there exists a node $w \in N$ such that all the children of w are leaves labeled with the same label **then**
   9.1. remove w and its children and replace them with a leaf w';
   9.2. label w' with the same label as the children of w;
   9.3. make all incoming edges to w and its children incoming edges to w' and set $wt(w')$ to be $wt(w)$ plus the sum of the weights of the children of w;
   9.4. **if** w is designated as the partition node **then** designate w' as the partition node in the resulting network;

Figure 2. The procedure **Simplify**.

Proposition 4.8. *Let N be a network with a given partition node p. If the procedure* **Simplify** *decides the instance N, then its decision is correct, and if it applies an operation to N to obtain a network N′ with a partition node p′, then N is compatible with p as a partition node if and only if N′ is compatible with p′ as a partition node.*

Lemma 4.1. *Let N be a network with a partition node p and suppose that the procedure* **Simplify** *if applied to N does not decide N nor does it perform any operation to N. Then there exists a node w ∈ N satisfying the following properties: (1) w has at least two children and all the children of w are leaves; (2) there are at least two children of w with different labels; (3) w is unlabeled; and (4) every child of w is a recombination node.*

Proof. *Let ℓ be a leaf in N such that the root-leaf path P to ℓ has maximum length. Note that ℓ must exist by step 1 of* **Simplify** *(every path starting at the root of N must lead to a leaf). Let w be the parent of ℓ on the path P. By the maximality of P, all the children of w must be leaves. If all the children of w are labeled with the same label, then step 9 of* **Simplify** *would apply to w. This shows that w has at least two children labeled with different labels, and properties (1) and (2) about w have been established.*

Suppose, to get a contradiction, that w is labeled. Let u be a child of w such that label(u) ≠ label(w). By step 6 of **Simplify**, *u must be a non-recombination node otherwise the edge (w, u) would be removed. By step 5 of* **Simplify**, *v must be a partition node. But then by step 3 of* **Simplify** *the procedure would have rejected the instance, contradicting the statement of the lemma. It follows that w is unlabeled establishing property (3) about w.*

Finally, if w had a child that is a non-recombination node, then by step 7 of **Simplify**, *w would have been labeled contradicting property (3) shown above. This establishes property (4) about w and completes the proof.* □

The Algorithm

The algorithm **ISPN-Solver** is given in Figure 3. The algorithm implicitly assumes that the partition node p is given. This assumption can be removed by trying every node in N as the partition node, then calling the algorithm with that node as the partition node. This will increase the running time of the algorithm by an $O(n)$ factor. If the algorithm **ISPN-Solver** returns TRUE on any of these calls then N must be compatible. To keep the presentation of the algorithm concise, we will not enumerate the partition nodes, but we will compensate for that by multiplying the running time of the algorithm by a linear factor at the end.

The algorithm **ISPN-Solver** is a branch-and-search process. Each stage of the algorithm starts with an instance (N, k) of the problem, where k is the total weight of all the nodes in N, and then tries to reduce k either by branching or by simplifying the network. Then the algorithm recursively works on the reduced instances. We implicitly assume that after each step, the network N and the parameter k are updated accordingly.

ISPN-Solver (N, k)
$\{ * \ k$ is the total weight of all the nodes in N $*\}$
1. **if** $k = 0$ and N is not compatible **then** reject;
2. **while** the procedure **Simplify** is applicable to N **do** apply it;
3. let w be a node satisfying the statement of Lemma 4.1; branch as follows:
    first side of the branch: set $label(w) = 1$;
    second side of the branch: set $label(w) = 0$;

Figure 3. The algorithm **ISPN-Solver**.

Theorem 4.2. *The algorithm **ISPN-Solver** correctly decides in time $O(2^{k/2}n)$ whether a phylogenetic network with a given partition node is compatible or not.*

Proof.

*The correctness of the algorithm can be easily checked. To analyze the running time of the algorithm **ISPN-Solver**, notice that the algorithm is a branch-and-bound process and its execution can be depicted by a search tree. The running time of the algorithm is proportional to the number of root-to-leaf paths, or equivalently the number of leaves in the search tree, multiplied by the time spent along each such path. Therefore, the main step in the analysis of the algorithm is deriving an upper bound on the number of leaves in the search tree. Let $\mathcal{T}$ be the search tree for the algorithm **ISPN-Solver** on an input instance (N, k), and let $T(k)$ be the number of leaves in $\mathcal{T}$. Let w be a node that the algorithm **ISPN-Solver** branches on in step 3.*

*Since all the children of w are leaves, the children of w are all labeled. Since all the children of w are recombination nodes by property (3) of Lemma 4.1, when the algorithm labels w in each of the two branches, at least one incoming edge to each child of w having the same label as w will be removed by step 8 of **Simplify** when applied next to the network. On the other hand, an incoming edge to every child of w whose label is different from w will be removed by step 6 of **Simplify**. Therefore, for every child of w, the weight of the child will be decreased by at least 1 in the next call to **Simplify**. Since w has at least two children by property (2) of Lemma 4.1, the total weight k of all the nodes in N is reduced by at least 2 in* *every side of the branch. It follows that the number of leaves $T(k)$ of the search tree $\mathcal{T}$ satisfies the recurrence relation $T(k) \leq 2T(k-2)$, and $T(k) = O(2^{k/2})$.*

Now consider a root-leaf path in the search tree $\mathcal{T}$. On every node of this path the algorithm might need to call the procedure **Simplify**, *which could take $O(n)$ time since the size of N is $O(n)$. However this need not be the case with a careful implementation of this procedure. Instead of calling this procedure at each node of N, we only call it on the nodes on which the operation is applicable. The time spent by the procedure in each such call is proportional to the number of nodes/edges removed plus the number of nodes labeled in the call. Since we can only have $O(n)$ nodes/edges, the total time spent by the procedure on a root-leaf path of $\mathcal{T}$ is proportional to the size of the network, which is $O(n)$. It follows that the running time of the algorithm is $O(2^{k/2}n)$.* □

Corollary 4.1. *The ISPN problem can be solved in time $O(2^{k/2}n^2)$, where n is the number of nodes and k is the number of recombination nodes, respectively, in the phylogenetic network.*

5. The Cluster Containment Problem

Let T be phylogenetic tree on set $\mathcal{X}$ of taxa and rooted at node r. Each edge $e = (u, v)$ induces a cluster c_e of taxa, which is the set of leaves reachable from root r only through v. It is easy to see that the leaves in c_e are exactly the leaves of the subtree rooted at v. A cluster c_e is contained in a network N if it is a cluster in a tree induced from N.

We can easily determine if a cluster c is in a tree by finding the least common ancestor $lca(c)$ of leaves in c, and then comparing the leaf set under $lca(c)$ and c. The CC problem is hard because there are many different trees that can be induced from the network N. The NP-hardness of CC is a byproduct of the following theorem.

Theorem 5.1. *The problems CC and ISPN are polynomially equivalent.*

Corollary 5.1. *The problem CC is NP-hard.*

Corollary 5.2. *The CC problem when parameterized by the number of recombination nodes k in the network is solvable in time $O(2^{k/2}n^2)$, where n is the number of nodes in the network.*

Bibliography

1. D. Bryant and V. Moulton. NeighborNet: An agglomerative method for the construction of planar phylogenetic networks. In R. Guigo and D. Gusfield, editors, *Proc. 2nd*

Workshop Algorithms in Bioinformatics (WABI'02), volume 2452 of *Lecture Notes in Computer Science*, pages 375–391. Springer Verlag, 2002.

2. R. Downey and M. Fellows. *Parameterized Complexity*. Springer, New York, 1999.

3. M.T. Hallett and J. Lagergren. Efficient algorithms for lateral gene transfer problems. In *Proc. 5th Ann. Int'l Conf. Comput. Mol. Biol. (RECOMB01)*, pages 149–156, New York, 2001. ACM Press.

4. D.H. Huson. SplitsTree: A program for analyzing and visualizing evolutionary data. *Bioinformatics*, 14(1):68–73, 1998.

5. G. Jin, L. Nakhleh, S. Snir, and T. Tuller. Maximum likelihood of phylogenetic networks. *Bioinformatics*, 22(21):2604–2611, 2006.

6. G. Jin, L. Nakhleh, S. Snir, and T. Tuller. Inferring phylogenetic networks by the maximum parsimony criterion: a case study. *Molecular Biology and Evolution*, 24(1):324–337, 2007.

7. I. Kanj, L. Nakhleh, and G. Xia. Reconstructing evolution of natural languages: Complexity and parameterized algorithms. In *12th Annual International Computing and Combinatorics Conference*, volume 4112 of *Lecture Notes in Computer Science*, pages 299–308. Springer, 2006.

8. C.R. Linder, B.M.E. Moret, L. Nakhleh, and T. Warnow. Network (reticulate) evolution: biology, models, and algorithms. In *The Ninth Pacific Symposium on Biocomputing (PSB)*, 2004. A tutorial.

9. W.P. Maddison. Gene trees in species trees. *Systematic Biology*, 46(3):523–536, 1997.

10. V. Makarenkov, D. Kevorkov, and P. Legendre. Phylogenetic network reconstruction approaches. *Genes, Genomics, and Bioinformatics*, 6, 2005.

11. L. Nakhleh. *Phylogenetic Networks*. PhD thesis, The University of Texas at Austin, 2004.

12. L. Nakhleh, D. Ringe, and T. Warnow. Perfect phylogenetic networks: A new methodology for reconstructing the evolutionary history of natural languages. *LANGUAGE*, 2005. In press.

13. L. Nakhleh, D. Ruths, and L.S. Wang. RIATA-HGT: A fast and accurate heuristic for reconstructing horizontal gene transfer. In L. Wang, editor, *Proceedings of the Eleventh International Computing and Combinatorics Conference (COCOON 05)*, pages 84–93, 2005. LNCS #3595.

14. L. Nakhleh and L.S. Wang. Phylogenetic networks, trees, and clusters. In *Proceedings of the 2005 International Workshop on Bioinformatics Research and Applications (IW-BRA 05)*, pages 919–926, 2005. LNCS #3515.

MODELING FUZZY BEHAVIOURS IN CONCURRENT SYSTEMS

LILIANA D'ERRICO and MICHELE LORETI

Dipartimento di Sistemi e Informatica
Università di Firenze
Viale Morgagni, 65 – Firenze
E-mail: loreti@dsi.unifi.it

The behaviour of concurrent systems has been classically specified by means of Labelled Transition Systems. Uncertainty can be modeled in LTS by means of *non-determinism* that can be used for modeling systems whose behaviour is not completely specified or for specifying unpredictable behaviours like, for instance, errors. However, such approach is not completely satisfactory. Indeed, it is not able to give a *measure* of such uncertainty. In this paper we propose a new variant of LTS, named *Fuzzy Labelled Transition Systems* (FLTS), where fuzziness is used for modeling uncertainty in concurrent systems. In FLTS, transition relation is defined in term of a *L-Fuzzy Set* that gives the membership degree of a given transition/computation. To reason about FLTS, a variant of Hennessy-Milner Logic is also proposed. The proposed logic will be used for specifying behavioural properties of systems for which a measure of the satisfaction is defined.

Keywords: Concurrency, Fuzzy Sets, Modal Logics

1. Introduction

A concurrent system, can be thought of as a set of autonomous components (hardware or software) that communicate and interact with each other and with the environment where they are executed. The behaviour of concurrent systems has been classically specified by means of Labelled Transition Systems, introduced by Keller [6] to strictly describe parallel programs and used by Plotkin [11], to give an operational structural semantic for programming languages.

A *Labelled Transition System* (LTS) consists of a set of states Q, a set of transition labels A and a transition relation $\rightarrow \subseteq Q \times A \times Q$. *States* correspond to the configurations systems can reach. *Labels* describe the actions systems can perform to interact with the environment. *Transition relations* describe systems evolutions as determined by the execution of specific actions.

LTS may be considered a generalization of finite state automata: they can have an initial state, but not a final one and can contain an infinite number of states.

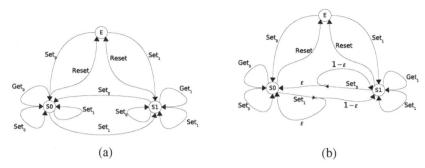

Figure 1.   LTS and PLTS of a memory cell with errors

Consequently, if automata are used to describe behavior of a system from the initial state to the final one, LTS permits describing behavior and interactions in concurrent systems that may evolve in time without reaching a final state.

An LTS may be represented graphically by a graph (said transition graph) whose nodes correspond to states in Q and whose arcs, labelled by actions in A, represent transitions $\longrightarrow$.

Uncertainty can be modeled in LTS by means of *non-determinism*, for instance, when a system is in a given state can evolve to two different configurations by executing the same action. Non-determinism can be used for modeling systems whose behaviour is not completely specified or for specifying unpredictable behaviours like, for instance, errors. In Figure 1 (a) is presented a LTS representing a memory cell where an error can occur when a value is stored. However, such an approach is not completely satisfactory. Indeed, it is not able to give a *measure* of such uncertainty. For instance, for the memory cell of Figure 1 (a) there is no way to distinguish between the correct behaviour and the erroneous one.

A solution for this problem is the one of Segala and Lynch [12]. They proposed a natural evolution toward probability of LTS. In such a model non-deterministic and probabilistic choices are differentiated: in each state a non-deterministic choice happens to select the outgoing transition, the consequent action is the one represented by the transition label. The next state is the one resulting by a probabilistic law (formally a distribution on the set of states).

A *Probabilistic Labelled Transition System* (PLTS) is defined as a triple $(Q, A, Steps)$: Q is a countable set of states; A is a countable set of actions; and $Steps \subseteq Q \times A \times Dist(Q)$ is a transition relation, where $Dist(Q)$ denotes probabilistic distributions on Q. Please notice that a LTS may be seen as a generalization of a PLTS. In fact, system $(Q, A, \longrightarrow)$ corresponds to a probabilistic system $(Q, A, Steps)$ where $Steps = \left\{(q, a, \delta_t)|s \xrightarrow{a} t\right\}$[a].

In Figure 1 (b) is an example of PLTS representing the same memory cell described by the LTS in Figure 1 (a) comprehensive of actions representing errors. PLTS has a more realistic behavior in comparison to the LTS. Indeed, when a value is stored in the cell, an error can occur only with a probability ϵ while with probability $1 - \epsilon$ the correct value is stored in the cell.

Even if PLTSs permit defining a measure of uncertainty in concurrent systems, this is not related to non-determinism. Indeed, the next state is chosen making use of the (non-deterministically selected) distribution of probability corresponding to the expected transition. Larsen and Skou [8] define the model for *Probabilistic Reactive Systems*. A reactive system is a PLTS whose states are *deterministic*: for each state s and action a exists at most one distribution controlling the selection of next state. In this model the "internal choice" is governed by a probabilistic law while the "external choice" depends by interactions with environment, i.e. by expected actions. Consequently actions are not selected probabilistically. Reactive Systems can be analysed by means of well known formal techniques like Markov chains [2–4].

In this paper we propose a new variant of LTS, named *Fuzzy Labelled Transition Systems* (FLTS), where features and properties of fuzzy sets [7,16] are used for modeling uncertainty in concurrent systems. Consequently each action is enriched by an information about *uncertainty measurement*. Indeed, transition relation in a FLTS is defined by means of a *L-Fuzzy Set* [5] describing the membership degree of each transition to the behaviour of the described system.

To reason about FLTS, a variant of Hennessy-Milner Logic is also proposed. The proposed logic will be used for specifying behavioural properties of systems for which a measure of the satisfaction is defined.

The rest of the paper is organised as follows. In Section 2 the basic notions related to Fuzzy Sets (and in particular to L-Fuzzy Sets) are introduced. In Section 3 Fuzzy Labelled Transition Systems are introduced while Fuzzy Hennessy-Milner Logic is described in Section 4. Finally, Section 5 concludes the paper.

2. Fuzzy Sets

Human perception of real world abounds with concepts without strictly defined constraints (example given by *tall, fat, very, more, slowly, old, familiar, considerable, largest than, kind*, etc. . .). Such concepts can be described by means of Fuzzy Sets: classes of objects in which transit from membership to not member-

---

[a]Where $\delta_t(q)$ is 1 if $t = q$ 0 otherwise

ship gradually takes place. A fuzzy set is a simple and intuitive generalization of the classical *crisp*[b] one.

Fuzzy sets are denoted by means of a generalised *membership function* that gives the *membership degree* of each element of the *universe*. This degree usually takes values in $[0, 1]$, the interval of real numbers from 0 to 1 inclusive. Although above range is the one most commonly used for representing membership degrees, any arbitrary set with some natural full or partial ordering can be used. Elements of this set are not required to be numbers as long as the ordering among them can be interpreted as representing various strengths of membership degree [18].

Let U be a universal set and L be a *complete lattice*, a *L-Fuzzy Set* [5,7] A is denoted by a membership function $\mu_A : U \rightarrow L$.

Standard operations on sets and lattices L, like complement, intersection and union, can be generalised to L-Fuzzy Sets. These operations rely on the use of three function $c\,(\cdot)$, $i\,(\cdot, \cdot)$ and $u\,(\cdot, \cdot)$ that, respectively, give the measure of complement, intersection and union of fuzzy degrees.

The complement of a L-Fuzzy Set A, denoted by $\overline{A}$, is specified by a function $c : L \rightarrow L$ which assigns a value $\mu_{\overline{A}}(x) = c\,(\mu_A(x))$ to each membership degree $\mu_A(x)$. This assigned value is interpreted as the membership degree of the element x in the L-Fuzzy Set representing the negation of the concept represented by A.

Intersection and union of two L-Fuzzy Sets A and B are defined using functions $i : L \times L \rightarrow L$ and $u : L \times L \rightarrow L$. For each element a in the universal set U, these functions take as argument the pair consisting of the membership degrees of a in A and B. Function i, also named *t-norm*, yields the membership degree of a in $A \cap B$, while u, also named *t-conorm*, returns the membership degree of a in $A \cup B$. Thus, $\mu_{A \cap B}(a) = i\,(\mu_A(a), \mu_B(a))$ while $\mu_{A \cup B}(a) = u\,(\mu_A(a), \mu_B(a))$.

Function c, i and u operating on L-Fuzzy Sets must be *continuous* on L and satisfy all axioms in Table 1, where 0 and 1 denote respectively the least and the greatest element in L while $\leq$ denotes the partial ordering on L. In the rest of this paper we will use $\mathcal{L}$ to denote a tuple $\langle L, c, i, u \rangle$ containing a complete lattice L together with its complement, intersection and union functions used for defining a family of L-Fuzzy Sets.

Example 2.1. Fuzzy set theory was initially formulated by considering the complete lattice $[0, 1]$, denoting the interval of real numbers from 0 to 1 (inclusive), and the following complement, intersection and union functions:

$$c\,(x) = 1 - x \qquad i\,(x, y) = \min[x, y] \qquad u\,(x, y) = \max[x, y]$$

---

[b]Crisp set is defined to split individuals belonging to a certain universe into two group: members (who surely belong to the set) and not members (who surely don't belong).

Table 1.   Axioms of fuzzy operations

Axioms for $c(\cdot)$

$$c(1) = 0 \qquad c(0) = 1 \qquad \dfrac{x \leq y}{c(y) \leq c(x)} \qquad c(c(x)) = x$$

Axioms for $i(\cdot, \cdot)$

$$i(1,1) = 1 \qquad i(0,x) = 0 \qquad i(1,x) = x \qquad \dfrac{x_1 \leq x_2 \quad y_1 \leq y_2}{i(x_1, y_1) \leq i(x_2, y_2)}$$

$$i(i(x,y), z) = i(x, i(y,z)) \qquad\qquad i(x,y) = i(y,x)$$

Axioms for $u(\cdot, \cdot)$

$$u(0,0) = 0 \qquad u(0,x) = x \qquad u(1,x) = 1 \qquad \dfrac{x_1 \leq x_2 \quad y_1 \leq y_2}{u(x_1, y_1) \leq u(x_2, y_2)}$$

$$u(u(x,y), z) = u(x, u(y,z)) \qquad\qquad u(x,y) = u(y,x)$$

It is easy to prove that these functions are continuous on $[0,1]$ and satisfy the axioms of Table 1.

Example 2.2. Other lattices can be considered for defining the membership degree of L-Fuzzy sets. For instance, the lattice L defined as follows can be considered:

$$never \leq rarely \leq sometimes \leq frequently \leq always$$

This can be used for describing how frequently an event occurs without providing an exact value. This could be obtained after the execution of a statistical analysis performed after a set of examinations. For lattice L we can consider functions i and u defined as in Example 2.1, while complement function c defined as follows:

	never	rarely	sometimes	frequently	always
$c(\cdot)$	always	frequently	sometimes	rarely	never

3. Fuzzy Labelled Transition Systems

In this section we introduce an extension of LTS that permits reasoning about the fuzziness of concurrent systems. We let a Fuzzy LTS be an LTS where the transition relation is defined in term of a L-Fuzzy Set. Following this approach we aim at modeling situations like: "the transition takes place *rarely*" or "the transition occurs *frequently*" which may be distinguished and treated as a consequence.

Definition 3.1 ($\mathcal{L}$-FLTS). Let $\mathcal{L} = \langle L, c, i, u \rangle$, a *Fuzzy Labelled Transition System for $\mathcal{L}$ ($\mathcal{L}$-FLTS) $\mathcal{F}$ is a tuple $\langle Q, A, \chi_{\rightarrow} \rangle$ where:*

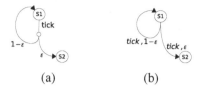

(a)   (b)

Figure 2.   Comparing PLTS and FLTS

- Q *is a set whose elements are said states*
- A *is a finite set whose elements represent actions*
- $\chi_{\rightarrow} : (Q \times A \times Q) \rightarrow L$ *is the total membership function.*

We will write $q_0 \xrightarrow{\alpha}_\varepsilon q_1$ to denote that a transition from state q_0 to state q_1 by action α has a membership degree ε to the automaton. Note that a transition $q_0 \xrightarrow{\alpha}_\varepsilon q_1$ happens (i.e. belongs to the system) with degree ε and, at the same time, does not happen with degree $c(\varepsilon)$.

Differently from a PLTS, where the sum of outgoing arcs for each state can be less than or equal to 1, in a FLTS we do not require any kind of constraints concerning the total degree of outgoing arcs of a state. In fact, each behavior of the system can be represented by a transition which happens *rarely, frequently* etc. only concerning itself without considering the degree of other possible transitions.

In PLTS probability distributions are used for selecting possible next states. This permits defining an *exact* probability measure that is associated to *computations*. On the contrary, in FLTS next states are selected nondeterministically. The membership degree associated to each transition is used to give a measure to computations. This measure is not *exact* as the probability one induced by PLTS, but can be used as the base for *approximate* reasoning in the spirit of Fuzzy Logic.

For instance, if we consider the PLTS of Figure 2 (a) we have that the total probability of computations leading to state s_2 is 1. On the contrary, when considering the similar system specified in $\mathcal{L}$-FLTS, Figure 2 (b), we have that the membership degree of the computations leading to state s_2, when considering lattice $\mathcal{L}$ of Example 2.1, is ε. This intuitively means that state s_2 is reachable by performing a transition whose membership degree is ε.

Example 3.1. In Figure 3 is depicted the $\mathcal{L}$-FLTS for the memory cell with errors (where $\mathcal{L}$ is the one defined in Example 2.2) where the transition degree is omitted when it is *always* and transitions with degree *never* are not drawn. When the system is in state $S1$ (resp. $S0$), it can non-deterministically evolve with degree *rarely* (resp. *sometimes*), executing action Set_0 (resp. Set_1), to state $S1$ (resp. $S0$). Thus the wrong value is stored in the cell. The same transition *does not belong* to the system behaviour with degree $c(rarely)$ (resp. $c(sometimes)$).

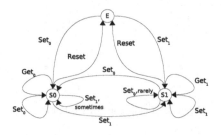

Figure 3.   A FLTS for the memory cell with errors

Hence, *frequently* (resp. *sometimes*) the cell behaves correctly.

4. Fuzzy Hennessy-Milner Logic

In this section we introduce a modal logic that can be used for *measuring* system behaviours. Indeed, the semantic of the formulas is defined in term of L-Fuzzy Sets describing the satisfaction/unsatisfaction degree of a state.

Fuzzy Hennessy-Milner Logic (FHML) is an extension of HML, which aims at specifying properties of concurrent systems whose behavior is detailed by means of FLTS. Let $\mathcal{L} = \langle L, c, i, u \rangle$, $\Phi_{\mathcal{L}}$ be the set of formulas φ defined by the following syntax:

$$\varphi ::= tt \mid ff \mid \neg \varphi \mid \varphi_1 \wedge \varphi_2 \mid \langle \alpha \rangle \varphi \mid \varphi \bowtie \varepsilon$$

where $\varepsilon \in L$.

Fuzzy Hennessy-Milner Logic extends HML by considering new operator $\varphi \bowtie \varepsilon$ ($\bowtie \in \{<, >\}$) that states about the satisfaction degree of a given formula in a given state. Such operator makes possible to describe the satisfaction degree of a formula in terms of an upper or a lower bound[c].

The semantic of FHML is defined in term of functions $\mathcal{M}_{\mathcal{L},\mathcal{F}}$ and $\mathcal{M}^{\smile}_{\mathcal{L},\mathcal{F}}$ that for each formula φ yield the L-Fuzzy Sets that respectively give the measure of satisfaction and unsatisfaction of φ. This approach permits defining semantics of FHML in a general way without considering any special constraint on the underlying L-Fuzzy Sets. Indeed, in general, standard properties of sets do not hold in the case of L-Fuzzy Sets. For instance, the intersection between a L-fuzzy set and its complement could be not empty. Notice that, in general, $\mathcal{M}_{\mathcal{L},\mathcal{F}}[\![\neg\varphi]\!] \neq c\,(\mathcal{M}_{\mathcal{L},\mathcal{F}}[\![\varphi]\!])$.

Interpretation functions are parameterized with respect to $\mathcal{L}$, used for defining the underlying L-Fuzzy Sets and the relative operations, and with respect

---

[c]This is somehow reminiscent of operator $[\varphi]_p$ proposed by Parma and Segala [10]

Table 2.   Formulae Semantics

$$\mathcal{M}_{\mathcal{L},\mathcal{F}}[\![tt]\!](p) = 1 \quad \mathcal{M}_{\mathcal{L},\mathcal{F}}[\![ff]\!](p) = 0 \quad \mathcal{M}_{\mathcal{L},\mathcal{F}}[\![\neg\,\varphi]\!](p) = \mathcal{M}^{\curvearrowright}_{\mathcal{L},\mathcal{F}}[\![\varphi]\!](p)$$

$$\mathcal{M}_{\mathcal{L},\mathcal{F}}[\![\varphi_1 \wedge \varphi_2]\!](p) = i\left(\mathcal{M}_{\mathcal{L},\mathcal{F}}[\![\varphi_1]\!](p), \mathcal{M}_{\mathcal{L},\mathcal{F}}[\![\varphi_2]\!](p)\right)$$

$$\mathcal{M}_{\mathcal{L},\mathcal{F}}[\![\varphi \bowtie \varepsilon]\!](p) = \begin{cases} 1 \ if \ \mathcal{M}_{\mathcal{L},\mathcal{F}}[\![\varphi]\!](p) \bowtie \varepsilon \\ 0 \ else \end{cases}$$

$$\mathcal{M}_{\mathcal{L},\mathcal{F}}[\![\langle\alpha\rangle\varphi\,]\!](p) = u_{q\in Q}\left(i\left(\chi_{\rightarrow}(p,\alpha,q), \mathcal{M}_{\mathcal{L},\mathcal{F}}[\![\varphi]\!](q)\right)\right)$$

$$\mathcal{M}^{\curvearrowright}_{\mathcal{L},\mathcal{F}}[\![tt]\!](p) = 0 \quad \mathcal{M}^{\curvearrowright}_{\mathcal{L},\mathcal{F}}[\![ff]\!](p) = 1 \quad \mathcal{M}^{\curvearrowright}_{\mathcal{L},\mathcal{F}}[\![\neg\,\varphi]\!](p) = \mathcal{M}_{\mathcal{L},\mathcal{F}}[\![\varphi]\!](p)$$

$$\mathcal{M}^{\curvearrowright}_{\mathcal{L},\mathcal{F}}[\![\varphi_1 \wedge \varphi_2]\!](p) = u\left(\mathcal{M}^{\curvearrowright}_{\mathcal{L},\mathcal{F}}[\![\varphi_1]\!](p), \mathcal{M}^{\curvearrowright}_{\mathcal{L},\mathcal{F}}[\![\varphi_2]\!](p)\right)$$

$$\mathcal{M}^{\curvearrowright}_{\mathcal{L},\mathcal{F}}[\![\varphi \bowtie \varepsilon]\!](p) = \begin{cases} 1 \ if \ \mathcal{M}_{\mathcal{L},\mathcal{F}}[\![\varphi]\!](p) \not\bowtie \varepsilon \\ 0 \ else \end{cases}$$

$$\mathcal{M}^{\curvearrowright}_{\mathcal{L},\mathcal{F}}[\![\langle\alpha\rangle\varphi\,]\!](p) = i_{q\in Q}\left(u\left(i\left(\chi_{\rightarrow}(p,\alpha,q), \mathcal{M}^{\curvearrowright}_{\mathcal{L},\mathcal{F}}[\![\varphi]\!](q)\right), c\left(\chi_{\rightarrow}(p,\alpha,q)\right)\right)\right)$$

to the $\mathcal{L}$-FLTS $\mathcal{F}$ used for interpreting the formulae. Note that, interpretation of FHML coincides with the standard interpretation of HML when considering standard Boolean lattices.

Definition 4.1 (Formulae Semantics). *Let* $\mathcal{L} = \langle L, c, i, u\rangle$ *and* $\mathcal{F}_{\mathcal{L}} = \langle Q, A, \chi_{\rightarrow}\rangle$. *Functions* $\mathcal{M}_{\mathcal{L},\mathcal{F}} : \Phi_{\mathcal{L}} \to Q \to L$ *and* $\mathcal{M}^{\curvearrowright}_{\mathcal{L},\mathcal{F}} : \Phi_{\mathcal{L}} \to Q \to L$ *are inductively defined in Table 2.*

Formulae tt and ff are satisfied by every state with degree 1 and 0 respectively. A state p satisfies $\neg\varphi$ with degree ε if and only if p *does not satisfies* φ with degree ε. Fuzzy set $\mathcal{M}_{\mathcal{L},\mathcal{F}}[\![\varphi_1 \wedge \varphi_2]\!]$ is defined as the intersection between $\mathcal{M}_{\mathcal{L},\mathcal{F}}[\![\varphi_1]\!]$ and $\mathcal{M}_{\mathcal{L},\mathcal{F}}[\![\varphi_2]\!]$. If a state p satisfies φ with a degree that is $<$ (resp. $>$) of ε then p satisfies $\varphi < \varepsilon$ (resp. $\varphi > \varepsilon$) with degree 1 (resp. 0). Finally, $\mathcal{M}_{\mathcal{L},\mathcal{F}}[\![\langle\alpha\rangle\varphi]\!](p)$, which gives a measure of how p can reach with a transition labelled α a state satisfying φ, is defined as the disjunction, for each q, of $i(\chi_{\rightarrow}(p,\alpha,q), \mathcal{M}_{\mathcal{L},\mathcal{F}}[\![\varphi]\!](q))$. Where $\chi_{\rightarrow}(p,\alpha,q)$ gives membership degree of the transition from p to q with label α to the behaviour of the system. $\mathcal{M}_{\mathcal{L},\mathcal{F}}[\![\varphi]\!](q)$ indicates the satisfaction degree of formula φ by q.

The definition of function $\mathcal{M}^{\curvearrowright}_{\mathcal{L},\mathcal{F}}$ is similar and straightforward. However, more attention has to be paid for $\mathcal{M}^{\curvearrowright}_{\mathcal{L},\mathcal{F}}[\![\langle\alpha\rangle\varphi]\!]$. Each state q, contributes to the unsatisfaction of $\langle\alpha\rangle\varphi$ by p as a factor that depends on the degree of the transition α from p to q and on the unsatisfaction degree of formula φ by q. This value is obtained as a disjunction of: $c\left(\chi_{\rightarrow}(p,\alpha,q)\right)$ and $i\left(\chi_{\rightarrow}(p,\alpha,q), \mathcal{M}^{\curvearrowright}_{\mathcal{L},\mathcal{F}}[\![\varphi]\!](q)\right)$. The former indicates how much the transition from p to q with label α *does not belong* to the behaviour of the system. The latter, gives the measure of the unsatisfaction of φ when the action is executed.

Example 4.1. Using FHML we can specify properties for the Memory Cell described in Figure 3. In particular we could be interested in verifying occurrences of errors. An error is experienced whenever after the execution of action Set_0 (resp. value Set_1), the system can perform action Get_1 (resp. Get_0).

This behaviour can be specified by using the following formulae:

$$\varphi_1 = \langle Set_0 \rangle \langle Get_1 \rangle tt \qquad\qquad \varphi_2 = \langle Set_1 \rangle \langle Get_0 \rangle tt$$

Both φ_1 and φ_2 are never satisfied in state E. Indeed, in such a state an error never occurs. On the contrary, errors can be experienced in states $S0$ and $S1$. Indeed, formula φ_1 is *rarely* satisfied in state $S1$ while formula φ_2 is *sometimes* satisfied in $S0$.

4.1. *FHML with recursion*

FHML (as HML) does not permit specifying properties involving infinite behaviors. For this reason we extend the logic by considering maximum ($\nu X.\varphi$) and minimum ($\mu X.\varphi$) fixed point operators and logical variables (X).

Syntax of FHML is now denoted by the following grammar:

$$\varphi ::= tt \mid ff \mid \neg\varphi \mid \varphi \bowtie \varepsilon \mid \varphi_1 \wedge \varphi_2 \mid \langle \alpha \rangle \varphi \mid X \mid \nu X.\varphi$$

The following definitions are used for guaranteeing well-definedness of interpretation formulae.

Definition 4.2 (Positive and negative variables). *Let φ be a FHML formula, variable X is positive in φ if:*

- $\varphi = tt$ *or* $\varphi = X$;
- $\varphi = \varphi_1 \wedge \varphi_2$ *and X is positive in φ_1 and in φ_2;*
- $\varphi = \neg\varphi'$, $\varphi = \varphi' > \varepsilon$ *or* $\varphi = \langle \alpha \rangle \varphi'$ *and X is positive in φ';*
- $\varphi = \varphi' < \varepsilon$ *and X is negative in φ';*
- $\varphi = \nu Y.\varphi'$, $Y \neq X$ *and X is positive in φ'.*

Variable X is negative in φ if

- $\varphi = \varphi_1 \wedge \varphi_2$ *and X is negative in φ_1 and in φ_2;*
- $\varphi = \neg\varphi'$, $\varphi = \varphi' > \varepsilon$ *or* $\varphi = \langle \alpha \rangle \varphi'$ *and X is negative in φ';*
- $\varphi = \varphi' < \varepsilon$ *and X is positive in φ';*
- $\varphi = \nu Y.\varphi'$, $Y \neq X$ *and X is negative in φ'.*

Definition 4.3 (Well formed formula). *A formula is said to be well formed if in each subformula of the form $\nu X.\varphi$, variable X is positive.*

The functions of Table 2 are extended to consider an extra parameter δ that associates to each logical variable X a L-fuzzy set, i.e. a function $Q \to L$. Moreover the following clauses are considered:

$$\mathcal{M}_{\mathcal{L},\mathcal{F}}[\![X]\!]\delta = \delta(X) \qquad \mathcal{M}_{\mathcal{L},\mathcal{F}}[\![\nu X.\varphi]\!]\delta = \cup \left\{ \chi \mid \chi \leq \mathfrak{F}_X^{\delta,\varphi}(\chi) \right\}$$

$$\mathcal{M}_{\mathcal{L},\mathcal{F}}^{\curvearrowright}[\![X]\!]\delta = \delta(X) \qquad \mathcal{M}_{\mathcal{L},\mathcal{F}}^{\curvearrowright}[\![\nu X.\varphi]\!]\delta = \cap \left\{ \chi \mid \chi \geq^{\curvearrowright} \mathfrak{F}_X^{\delta,\varphi}(\chi) \right\}$$

where $\mathfrak{F}_X^{\delta,\varphi}$ and $^{\curvearrowright}\mathfrak{F}_X^{\delta,\varphi}$ are defined as follows:

$$\mathfrak{F}_X^{\delta,\varphi} = \mathcal{M}_{\mathcal{L},\mathcal{F}}[\![\varphi]\!]\delta[\chi/X] \qquad ^{\curvearrowright}\mathfrak{F}_X^{\delta,\varphi} = \mathcal{M}_{\mathcal{L},\mathcal{F}}^{\curvearrowright}[\![\varphi]\!]\delta[\chi/X]$$

Note that if one considers only well-formed formulae, functions $\mathfrak{F}_X^{\delta,\varphi}$ and $^{\curvearrowright}\mathfrak{F}_X^{\delta,\varphi}$ are monotone in the complete lattice of Q L-Fuzzy Sets. This, thanks to the Tarski's fixed point theorem [13], guarantees the well-definedness of functions $\mathcal{M}_{\mathcal{L},\mathcal{F}}$ and $\mathcal{M}_{\mathcal{L},\mathcal{F}}^{\curvearrowright}$.

Example 4.2. In Example 4.1 formulae φ_1 and φ_2 have been defined for specifying the states where an error can be experienced. One could also be interested in studying the satisfaction degree of property: "an error can eventually occur". This property is specified by means of the following formula:

$$\varphi = \mu X.\varphi_1 \vee \varphi_2 \vee \langle Set_1 \rangle X \vee \langle Set_0 \rangle X$$

where $\mu X.\varphi = \neg \nu X.\neg \varphi[\neg X/X]$.

This formula is satisfied by all the states composing the Fuzzy Memory Cell (Figure 3) with degree *sometimes*.

The following property states that a state where an error can be experienced *frequently* is never reached:

$$\neg \mu X.(\varphi > sometimes) \vee \langle Set_0 \rangle X \vee \langle Set_1 \rangle X$$

5. Conclusions and Future Works

In this paper we have proposed a new variant of LTS, named *Fuzzy Labelled Transition Systems* (FLTS), where fuzziness has been used for modeling uncertainty in concurrent systems. The underlying idea of the proposed work is to use features and properties of fuzzy sets in the area of concurrent systems.

Even if the proposed approach seems to be interesting, it is not yet used for specifying *real* systems. In literature there are examples [9,14,17] where Fuzzy Theory is used for modeling the behaviour of "systems", like for instance those involving human interactions, where uncertainty is a central feature. Indeed, the membership degree associated to each transition is used to give a measure to computations. This measure is not *exact* as the probability one induced by PLTS, but can be used as the base for *approximate* reasoning in the spirit of Fuzzy Logic.

To reason about FLTS, a variant of Hennessy-Milner Logic has been also proposed. The proposed logic can be used for specifying behavioural properties of systems for which a measure of the satisfaction is defined.

We also plan to use a standard local model checking technique [15] for defining a proof system for FHML. This will permit simplifying the verification of properties for FLTS.

A similar approach was proposed by Chechik et al. [1] for reasoning on systems with inconsistence and uncertainty. This approach relies on multi-valued logics that are used for characterizing properties of system states. An extension of CTL is used for describing properties of system computations. Differently from the approach proposed in this paper, Chechik et al. restrict the considered multivalued logics on those based on *quasi-boolean* lattices. Moreover, *multi-valued* logics are used only for describing state properties without informations about the satisfaction degree of temporal properties that are satisfied or not.

Bibliography

1. M. Chechik, S. Easterbrook, and V. Petrovykh. Model-checking over multi-valued logics. In *FME '01: Proceedings of the International Symposium of Formal Methods Europe on Formal Methods for Increasing Software Productivity*, pages 72–98, London, UK, 2001. Springer-Verlag.
2. J. Desharnais. Logical characterization of simulation for Markov chains. In M. Kwiatkowska, editor, *Probmiv99, Proceedings of the second international workshop on probabilistic methods in verification*, pages 33–48. The University of Birmingham, 1999.
3. J. Desharnais, Abbas Edalat, and Prakash Panangaden. Bisimulation for labelled Markov processes. *Inf. Comput.*, 179(2):163–193, 2002.
4. J. Desharnais, Vineet Gupta, Radha Jagadeesan, and Prakash Panangaden. Metrics for labelled Markov processes. *Theor. Comput. Sci.*, 318(3):323–354, 2004.
5. J. A. Goguen. L-fuzzy sets. *J. Math. Anal. Appl.*, 18:145–174, 1967.
6. R. M. Keller. Formal verification of parallel programs. *Commun. ACM*, 19(7):371–384, 1976.
7. G.J. Klir and T.A. Folger. *Fuzzy sets, uncertainty, and information*. Prentice-Hall International, Inc, 1988.
8. K. G. Larsen and A. Skou. Bisimulation through probabilistic testing. *Inf. Comput.*, 94(1):1–28, 1991.
9. B. Möller, W. Graf, and S. Nguyen. Modeling the life cycle of a structure using fuzzy processes. *Computer-Aided Civil and Infrastructure Engineering*, 2004.
10. A. Parma and R. Segala. Logical characterizations of bisimulations for discrete probabilistic systems. In Springer-Verlag, editor, *FOSSACS 2007, LNCS*, volume 4423,

pages 287–301, 2007.

11. G. D. Plotkin. A Structural Approach to Operational Semantics. Technical Report DAIMI FN-19, University of Aarhus, 1981.

12. R. Segala and N. Lynch. Probabilistic simulations for probabilistic processes. *Nordic J. of Computing*, 2(2):250–273, 1995.

13. A. Tarski. A lattice-teoretichal fixpoint theorem and its applications. *Pacific J. Math.*, 5:285–309, 1955.

14. E. Tron and M. Margaliot. Mathematical modeling of observed natural behavior: a fuzzy logic approach. *Fuzzy Sets and Systems*, 2004.

15. G. Winskel. Topics in concurrency. Technical report, 2005.

16. L. A. Zadeh. Fuzzy sets. *Information and Control*, 8:338–353, 1965.

17. L. A. Zadeh. Commonsense reasoning based on fuzzy logic. In *WSC '86: Proceedings of the 18th conference on Winter simulation*, pages 445–447, New York, NY, USA, 1986. ACM Press.

18. L. A. Zadeh. Fuzzy logic = computing with words. *IEEE Transactions on Fuzzy Systems*, 4(2):103–111, 1996.

A FORMAL FRAMEWORK FOR COMPOSITIONAL COMPILATION
(extended abstract)

DAVIDE ANCONA* and ELENA ZUCCA

DISI, Università di Genova,
Italy
* E-mail: davide@disi.unige.it
www.disi.unige.it

We define a general framework for *compositional compilation*, meant as the ability of building an executable application by separate compilation and linking of single fragments, opposed to *global compilation* of the complete source application code. More precisely, compilation of a source code fragment in isolation generates a corresponding binary fragment equipped with type information, formally modeled as a *typing*, allowing type safe linking of fragments without re-inspecting code.

We formally define a notion of soundness and completeness of compositional compilation w.r.t. global compilation, and show how linking can be in practice expressed by an *entailment* relation on typings. Then, we provide a sufficient condition on such entailment to ensure soundness and completeness of compositional compilation, and compare this condition with the *principal typings* property. Furthermore, we show that this entailment relation can often be modularly expressed by an entailment relation on type environments and a subtyping relation.

Keywords: Type systems; Separate compilation.

1. Introduction

Modern software systems, besides allowing global compilation, support also *separate compilation*: open code fragments can be compiled in isolation, provided that type information on the needed external definitions are available in some form, and can then be linked in a type safe way. In this way, *smart recompilation*, also known as *selective recompilation* [1,7–9], is promoted, since a fragment can be reused in many different applications, without re-inspecting its source code, provided that mutual compatibility requirements among fragments are verified. More importantly, separate compilation is essential for developing applications in modern systems where fragments can be distributed and loaded/linked dynamically, as happens in Java and C#.

Despite this, there has been little work on formal models for separate compilation and linking, except for the seminal paper [5], which formalized *intra-checking* (separate compilation simplified to typechecking of fragments in isolation) and *inter-checking* of *linksets* (collection of successfully compiled fragments equipped with mutual type assumptions) on simply typed lambda-calculus, and some other papers [2,3], where Cardelli's ideas are further developed, by formally defining *compositional compilation* for Java-like languages as the combination of separate compilation and linking steps. Our approach here, instead, is to abstract away from language-specific problems, aiming at providing an abstract framework in order to capture the main general properties needed by compilation to be compositional.

To this end, we extend (in Sect.2) the simple framework in [5] in many respects. First, we define an *abstract* framework which can be instantiated on an arbitrary type system providing some ingredients. In particular, we abstract from the form of type assumptions, rather than just considering assumptions $x : \tau$ meaning that the fragment named x should have type τ. Moreover, we model *linking* rather than just inter-checking, that is, a well-formed linkset is obtained not only by checking that mutual assumptions are satisfied, but also by a non-trivial manipulation of the original fragments. In other words, the framework supports *code specialization*. Finally, we expect linking to satisfy some properties which ensure that it can actually replace global compilation: it should be at least *sound* (if linking succeeds, then compiling altogether the fragments we would succeed as well and get the same binaries); furthermore, if linking is *complete*, then when it fails we would get a failure as well by compiling altogether the fragments.

In Sect.3, we show that compositional compilation is sound and complete if linking can be expressed by an *entailment* relation on typings such that each composable fragment has a typing which entails all and only other typings, and separate compilation always produces typings of this kind. Indeed, in this way failure of linking cannot be caused by the fact that for some fragment we have selected a typing which is not adequate in that particular linkset. In Sect.4, we formally compare this property with the *principal typings* property [6], formalized in a system-independent way by Wells [10].

In Sect.5 we show that an entailment relation on typings can often be modularly expressed by an entailment relation on type environments and a subtyping relation which should in turn satisfy appropriate conditions of soundness and completeness.

This is an extended abstract, where due to space limitations we focus on presenting basic ideas and the formal abstract frameworks with their properties. We recommend the interested reader to look at the full paper [4], available at ftp://ftp.disi.unige.it/pub/person/AnconaD/FFCClong.pdf, for proofs and, even more importantly, for three rather different examples of instantiations: simply typed lambda-calculus, Featherweight Java, and Featherweight Java extended with a boxing/unboxing mechanism, showing how the framework also supports code specialization in a broader sense.

2. An abstract framework

In this section, we define a schema formalizing both global and compositional compilation on top of a given *type system* $\mathcal{T}$, consisting of the following ingredients.

Terms s, modeling *source fragments*, defined over a given numerable infinite set of variables $x \in Var$. Let S range over mappings from names into source fragments, written $S = [x_i \mapsto s_i^{i \in 1..n}]$.

Types τ, modeling *binary fragments*, since our notion of typechecking also includes binary code generation. Let T range over mappings from names into binary fragments, written $T = [x_i \mapsto \tau_i^{i \in 1..n}]$.

Type assumptions γ, which always include those of the form $x{:}\tau$, but possibly also other kinds, as shown in the examples in [4].

Type environments Γ, which are possibly empty sequences of type assumptions. We denote by Γ, Γ' the concatenation of Γ and Γ', when it is defined (because the concatenation operator might be partial), and by $\emptyset$ the empty type environment.

Type judgments $\Gamma \vdash s{:}\tau$ with meaning: term s has type τ in the type environment Γ.

Typings $t = (\Gamma, \tau) \in Typing$, modeling binary fragments equipped with type assumptions. If $\Gamma \vdash s{:}\tau$ is a valid judgment, then we say that (Γ, τ) is a *typing of* s; we denote by $typings(s)$ the set of all the typings of a term s, and by $terms(t)$ the set of all terms which have typing t. A term s is *typable* if $typings(s) \neq \emptyset$.

Separate compilation judgments $\Gamma \vdash_C s{:}\tau$, which are a subset of type judgments, since typechecking a term in isolation we fix some type assumptions on missing entities.

Linking judgments $\vdash_C L{:}T$, where $L = [x_i \mapsto (\Gamma_i, \tau_i)^{i \in 1..n}]$ is a *linkset*, that is, a mapping from names into typings. This judgment models an effective procedure for linking together a collection of binary fragments equipped with type assumptions, each one obtained by separate compilation of a term. Note that this check does *not* depend on the source code.

On top of $\mathcal{T}$ we can model two different approaches to compilation, which we will call *global* and *compositional*, respectively.

Global compilation In the first approach, a collection of named source fragments can be compiled only if it is self-contained, that is, if all terms typecheck in the context of full type information about each other. This is formalized by the judgment $\vdash_G$S:T, defined by the rule in Fig.1.

$$(glob)\frac{x_i : \tau_i^{i\in 1..n} \vdash s_j : \tau_j, j \in 1..n}{\vdash_G [x_i \mapsto s_i^{i\in 1..n}] : [x_i \mapsto \tau_i^{i\in 1..n}]}$$

Figure 1. Global compilation

Compositional compilation In the second approach, instead, single source fragments can be compiled in isolation, generating binary fragments which are equipped with type assumptions on the missing entities, and which can then be linked together provided that mutual assumptions are satisfied. This is formalized by the judgment $\vdash_C$S:T, defined by the rule in Fig.2.

$$(comp)\frac{\Gamma_i \vdash_C s_i : \tau_i', i \in 1..n \quad \vdash_C [x_i \mapsto (\Gamma_i, \tau_i')^{i\in 1..n}] : [x_i \mapsto \tau_i^{i\in 1..n}]}{\vdash_C [x_i \mapsto s_i^{i\in 1..n}] : [x_i \mapsto \tau_i^{i\in 1..n}]}$$

Figure 2. Compositional compilation

A simple example of instantiation of the framework is the simply typed λ-calculus, where terms, types, type environments, type judgments, typings are defined in the standard way (code generation is not significant in this case), type assumptions are of the form $x{:}\tau$, separate compilation judgments are type judgments where typings are *principal* [10], and linking succeeds if there exists an instantiation of type variables such that mutual assumptions are satisfied. For instance, let us consider the collection of source fragments S $= [f \mapsto \lambda x.(g\ (g\ x)), g \mapsto \lambda x.(h\ (h\ c)), h \mapsto \lambda x.c\lambda x.(q\ c)]$, where c is a constant of type κ. By separate compilation we can derive the following typings for the three terms named f, g and h, respectively:

- $t_f = (g : \alpha \to \alpha, \alpha \to \alpha)$ for $\lambda x.(g\ (g\ x))$

- $t_g = (h : \kappa \rightarrow \kappa, \alpha \rightarrow \kappa)$ for $\lambda x.(h \ (h \ c))$
- $t_h = (\emptyset, \alpha \rightarrow \kappa)$ for $\lambda x.c$

Linking succeeds on the linkset $L = [f \mapsto t_f, g \mapsto t_g, h \mapsto t_h]$, that is,

$$\vdash_C L:[f \mapsto \kappa \rightarrow \kappa, g \mapsto \kappa \rightarrow \kappa, h \mapsto \kappa \rightarrow \kappa].$$

Clearly, if we compile the three functions globally we get the same result, that is, $\vdash_G S:[f \mapsto \kappa \rightarrow \kappa, g \mapsto \kappa \rightarrow \kappa, h \mapsto \kappa \rightarrow \kappa]$.

The advantages of compositional compilation (that is, separate compilation plus linking) w.r.t. global compilation are clear. Each fragment can be compiled without inspecting the fragments it depends on; then, a collection of fragments can be put together without re-inspecting source code. However, in order to really offer these advantages, compositional compilation should satisfy some properties which ensure that it can actually replace global compilation. This issue was not considered in [5].

Definition 2.1. Compositional compilation $\vdash_C$ is *sound and complete (w.r.t. global compilation)* iff for all S, T, $\vdash_C S:T \iff \vdash_G S:T$.

The $\Rightarrow$ implication corresponds to soundness of linking and, thus, can be considered as the minimal requirement to be met by a linking procedure. Indeed, it ensures that, in case of successful linking, global (re)compilation would succeed as well and generate the same binaries. On the other hand, we would like to be sure that, if linking fails, then we would get failure by global (re)compilation as well. This is expressed by the $\Leftarrow$ implication which corresponds to completeness of linking. Note that soundness and completeness of linking allow optimal selective recompilation: we *never* need to recompile a source fragment when we put it together with others, hence, even more, we never need to have source code available. Note that, even though desirable, completeness is not as fundamental as soundness. Indeed, as shown in the examples in [4], in general linking is not complete if in separate compilation we select arbitrary judgments (e.g., all valid judgments); the intuition suggests that, in order to achieve completeness, linksets should only contain those typings that better represent a given source. As we will see in the next sections, the intuitive notion of best representative typing is intimately connected with that of principal typing. On the other hand, soundness can be reasonably extended to all valid judgments.

3. Linking by entailment

We introduce now a more concrete model where linking is expressed by a relation $\preceq$ on typings (expected to be computable). We call this relation *entailment* since we will see later that in reasonable cases it is expected to preserve typability of terms. However, in principle there are no requirements on this relation. We show that a necessary and sufficient condition for soundness and completeness of compositional compilation is that each *composable* term has a $\preceq$-principal typing, where a composable term s is a source fragment for which there exists an S which contains s and which can be globally compiled. This means that, for each composable term s, it is possible to select a typing t of s which entails all and only all the typings of s, hence can be considered a "representative" of the typings of s.

In the following, an *entailment relation* is a relation on *Typing*. Moreover, if $\preceq$ is an entailment relation and $t \preceq t'$, then we say that t *entails* t'.

Definition 3.1. A typing t of s is a $\preceq$-*principal typing* of s iff it entails all and only all the typings of s; that is, $\forall t' \in$ *Typing* $t \preceq t' \Leftrightarrow$ s $\in$ *terms*(t').

A type system $\mathcal{T}$ *has* $\preceq$-*principal typings* if each typable term has a $\preceq$-principal typing.

Definition 3.2. A term s is *composable* iff there exists S $= [x_i \mapsto \mathsf{s}_i^{i \in 1..n}]$ s.t.

(1) s is in S, that is, there exists $k \in 1..n$ s.t. s $= \mathsf{s}_k$;
(2) S is globally compilable, that is, there exists T s.t. $\vdash_G$ S:T.

Note that the notion of composable is in general stricter than that of typable. Indeed, by definition of composable term and of global compilation, a composable term is always typable, whereas the converse might not hold. This happens in type systems where deciding whether the type assumptions of a given type environment are satisfiable is so hard that in practice it is better to allow typings with unsatisfiable type environments, with the drawback that some type error can be detected only at linking time rather than at (separate) compilation time (for a concrete example, see FJP as defined in [4]).

Definition 3.3. Let $\preceq$ be an entailment relation. We denote by $\vdash^{\preceq}$ the *separate compilation and linking induced by* $\preceq$, defined as follows:

- $\Gamma \vdash^{\preceq}$ s:τ iff (Γ, τ) is a $\preceq$-principal typing of s;
- $\vdash^{\preceq}[x_i \mapsto (\Gamma_i, \tau_i')^{i \in 1..n}] : [x_i \mapsto \tau_i^{i \in 1..n}]$ iff
  for all $i \in 1..n, ((\Gamma_i, \tau_i')) \preceq ((x_j : \tau_j^{j \in 1..n}, \tau_i))$.

We denote by $\vdash_C^{\preceq}$ the *compositional compilation induced by* $\preceq$, defined by the rule *(comp)* in Fig.2 on top of the separate compilation and linking $\vdash^{\preceq}$.

Theorem 3.1. *Let $\preceq$ be an entailment relation. Then, the compositional compilation induced by $\preceq$ is sound and complete iff each composable term has a $\preceq$-principal typing.*

4. Compositional compilation and principal typings

In this section we investigate the relation between the notion of $\preceq$-principal typing and that of principal typing introduced, in its general formulation, by Wells [10], which is based on a fixed semantic relation on typings (a typing is stronger than another iff it is a typing of less terms). We show that the latter notion is a specialization of the former which is obtained when the entailment relation is sound. In this case, besides soundness and completeness, compositional compilation satisfies an *extended soundness property* (Theorem 4.2), which amounts to saying that linking is sound (but not necessarily complete) for all linksets, not only those which are formed by principal typings.

Definition 4.1. For all typings t, t', we say that t is *stronger* than t', and write $t \leq t'$, iff $terms(t) \subseteq terms(t')$.

A typing t is *principal* for s iff it is a typing of s which is stronger than all typings of s. A term s *has a principal typing* iff there exists a typing principal for s; conversely, a typing *is principal* iff it is principal for some s. A type system $\mathcal{T}$ *has principal typings* if each typable term has a principal typing.

Proposition 4.1. *The following facts hold:*

(1) If a type system $\mathcal{T}$ has principal typings, then it has $\preceq$-principal typings for some entailment relation $\preceq$.

(2) The opposite implication does not hold.

A counterexample proving the second fact is given below (Example 4.1).

Definition 4.2. An entailment relation $\preceq$ is *sound* iff, for all typings t, t', $t \preceq t' \Rightarrow terms(t) \subseteq terms(t')$.

Theorem 4.1. *A type system $\mathcal{T}$ has principal typings iff it has $\preceq$-principal typings for some sound entailment relation $\preceq$.*

Remark 4.1. Note that if a type system $\mathcal{T}$ has $\preceq$-principal typings for a sound entailment relation $\preceq$, such relation does not necessarily coincide with $\leq$. Indeed, by soundness trivially $\preceq \subseteq \leq$, but the converse inclusion does not hold in general. For instance, if there exists a term with two different principal typings t and t', then $\mathcal{T}$ has $\preceq$-principal typings for the sound entailment $\preceq$ defined by $\leq \setminus \{(t', t)\} \subsetneq \leq$.

Theorem 4.2. *Let $\preceq$ be a sound entailment relation and $\vdash_C$ the separate compilation defined by $\Gamma \vdash_C s{:}\tau \iff \Gamma \vdash s{:}\tau$. Then the compositional compilation $\vdash_C$ defined by rule (comp) in Fig.2 on top of the separate compilation $\vdash_C$ and of the linking $\vdash^{\preceq}$ is sound, that is, for all S, T, $\vdash_C S{:}T \Rightarrow \vdash_G S{:}T$.*

Example 4.1. Given a $\mathcal{T}$ which does not have principal typings, we show how it is possible to define a relation $\preceq$ so that each typable term s has a $\preceq$-principal typing.

Let us consider, for instance, system F in Curry style, which is known [10] not to have principal typings[a]:

$$s ::= x \mid (s_1 s_2) \mid (\lambda x.s)$$
$$\tau ::= \alpha \mid \tau_1 \to \tau_2 \mid (\forall \alpha.\tau)$$

Without any loss of generality, we may assume that there exists a bijection η between type and term variables. Then any λ-term can be encoded into a type in the following way:

$$enc(x) = \eta(x)$$
$$enc(s_1 s_2) = enc(s_1) \to enc(s_2)$$
$$enc(\lambda x.s) = (\forall \eta(x).enc(s))$$

Let dec denote the inverse function of enc; then $\preceq$ is the relation on F typings defined as follows:

$$(\Gamma, x : \tau_1, \tau_2) \preceq (\Gamma', \tau') \text{ iff } \Gamma' \vdash dec(\tau_1) : \tau' \text{ is valid in } \mathsf{F}.$$

Note that in the definition x is a meta-variable (not a fixed variable) corresponding to the rightmost type assumption in the environment (recall that we assume that type environments are sequences of type assumptions). We claim that any typable term s in F has a $\preceq$-principal typing. Indeed, if s is typable in F, then we can choose a typing (Γ, τ) of s and derive from it another typing $t = (\Gamma, x : enc(s), \tau)$ (where x is a term variable not defined in Γ). By weakening t is a typing of s, and, by definition, for all t', $t \preceq t'$ iff t' is a typing of $dec(enc(s)) = s$.

As one would expect $\preceq$ fails to be sound; for instance, if $t_1 = (x : \forall \alpha.\alpha \to \alpha, \forall \alpha.\alpha \to \alpha)$ and $t_2 = (\emptyset, \forall \alpha.\alpha \to \alpha)$, then $t_1 \preceq t_2$, t_1 is a typing of x, but not t_2.

5. Linking by environment entailment and subtyping

In Sect.3 we have shown that compositional compilation can be expressed in terms of an entailment relation $\preceq$ between typings, and in Sect. 4 that such a relation is expected to be sound, and, therefore, a subset of the semantic relation $\leq$ defined in Def. 4.1.

---

[a]In particular, $(x\ x)$ does not have a principal typing, hence, for sake of simplicity, here we can restrict to system F without the `let` construct.

In this section we provide a practical and general schema to define $\preceq$ modularly on top of an entailment relation on type environments (which is expected to be at least sound, that is, if $\Gamma \preceq \Gamma'$ is valid, then whatever holds in Γ, holds in Γ' as well), and a subtyping relation (which is expected to be at least sound, that is, if $\Gamma \vdash \tau \preceq \tau'$ is valid, then under the assumptions in Γ, whatever has type τ, has type τ' as well).

To achieve that, a type system has to provide the following additional ingredients:

Environment Entailment A relation (not necessarily a pre-order) between type environments: $\Gamma_1 \preceq \Gamma_2$ means that Γ_1 entails Γ_2, hence Γ_1 contains at least as strong assumptions as those in Γ_2.

Subtyping relation A subtyping relation (not necessarily a pre-order) defined by a judgment of the form $\Gamma \vdash \tau_1 \preceq \tau_2$, meaning that τ_1 is a subtype of τ_2 in Γ.

Type variable substitution A standard notion of substitution σ which is a finite map from type variables to types[b], where $\sigma(\tau)$ and $\sigma(\Gamma)$ denote the usual capture avoiding substitution applied to a type and a type environment, respectively. We assume that terms do not contain free type variables, hence $\sigma(s) = s$ for all s. Furthermore, we assume that substitutions are well-behaved w.r.t. typings, that is, the following property is satisfied:

for all σ, Γ, s, τ $\Gamma \vdash s{:}\tau$ implies $\sigma(\Gamma) \vdash s{:}\sigma(\tau)$

With the ingredients above, the entailment relation $\preceq$ between typings can be defined by the following general rule:

$$(entail)\frac{\Gamma_2 \preceq \sigma(\Gamma_1) \qquad \Gamma_2 \vdash \sigma(\tau_1) \preceq \tau_2}{((\Gamma_1, \tau_1)) \preceq ((\Gamma_2, \tau_2))}$$

This rule captures the intuition that $\preceq$ is expected to be transitive, to be covariant w.r.t. subtyping and contravariant w.r.t. entailment between environments, and finally, to satisfy $(\Gamma, \tau) \preceq (\sigma(\Gamma), \sigma(\tau))$.

The following theorems express sufficient conditions on the entailment between type environments and on subtyping to ensure that the entailment defined by $(entail)$ is sound and complete.

Definition 5.1. An environment entailment $\preceq$ is sound iff for all Γ, Γ'
$\Gamma \preceq \Gamma' \Rightarrow$ for all s, τ $\Gamma' \vdash s{:}\tau \Rightarrow \Gamma \vdash s{:}\tau$;
it is sound and complete iff for all Γ, Γ'
$\Gamma \preceq \Gamma' \iff$ for all s, τ $\Gamma' \vdash s{:}\tau \Rightarrow \Gamma \vdash s{:}\tau$.

---

[b]In type systems with no type variables this notion collapses to the empty substitution.

Definition 5.2. A subtyping relation $\preceq$ is sound iff for all Γ, τ, τ'

$\Gamma \vdash \tau \preceq \tau' \Rightarrow$ for all s $\Gamma \vdash s{:}\tau \Rightarrow \Gamma \vdash s{:}\tau'$;

it is is sound and complete iff for all Γ, τ, τ'

$\Gamma \vdash \tau \preceq \tau' \iff$ for all s $\Gamma \vdash s{:}\tau \Rightarrow \Gamma \vdash s{:}\tau'$.

Theorem 5.1. *If the environment entailment and the subtyping relation are sound, then the typing entailment* $\preceq$ *defined by rule* (*entail*) *is sound as well.*

Theorem 5.2. *If the environment entailment and the subtyping relation are sound and complete, if all composable terms have a principal typing* (Γ_1, τ_1) *s.t. for all typings* (Γ_2, τ_2) *if* $(\Gamma_1, \tau_1) \leq (\Gamma_2, \tau_2)$, *then there exists a substitution* σ *s.t.*

(1) for all s, τ *if* $\sigma(\Gamma_1) \vdash s{:}\tau$, *then* $\Gamma_2 \vdash s{:}\tau$;
(2) for all s *if* $\Gamma_2 \vdash s{:}\sigma(\tau_1)$, *then* $\Gamma_2 \vdash s{:}\tau_2$.

Then each composable term has a $\preceq$*-principal typing, where* $\preceq$ *is the relation defined by rule* (*entail*).

In the hypothesis of Theorem 5.2, we have the following two corollaries:

(1) Linking $\vdash^{\preceq}$, with $\preceq$ defined by rule (*entail*), induces a sound compositional compilation for all typings (by Theorems 4.2 and 5.1);
(2) Compositional compilation $\vdash^{\preceq}_C$ with $\preceq$ defined by rule (*entail*) is sound and complete (by Theorems 3.1 and 5.2).

It is interesting to notice that in general properties 1. and 2. of Theorem 5.2 are not expected to hold for all pairs of typings t_1, t_2 s.t. $t_1 \leq t_2$; this is due to the fact that rule (*entail*) is sound but not complete w.r.t. $\leq$. However, recalling Remark 4.1 in Sect.4, this fact does not prevent the typable terms of the type system to have $\preceq$-principal typings for a sound relation $\preceq$ which does not coincide with $\leq$.

6. Conclusion

The contributions of the paper can be summarized as follows:

(1) A system-independent formal definition of compositional compilation (separate compilation and linking) and its expected properties. This work has been inspired by the seminal paper [5], where, however, definitions were given for a fixed language (a simple lambda-calculus) and issues of soundness and completeness were not considered.
(2) A sufficient condition for soundness and completeness of compositional compilation, that is, the existence of an entailment relation on typings s.t. for each

composable fragment there is a typing which entails all and only all the typings of the fragment. This condition is weaker than the principal typings [10] property, and coincides with it for relations which are sound w.r.t. typability of all terms.

(3) A modular way of defining an entailment relation between typings on top of an entailment relation between type environments and a subtyping relation which satisfy in turn appropriate soundness and completeness requirements.

Concerning the second point, we believe the result is significant since it shows that an independent characterization, designed starting from the intuition on what a linking procedure should guarantee, is then discovered to be equivalent to the principal typings property, thus confirming that this property is the right one when we want both sound and complete compositional compilation and soundness of the entailment relation. In this case, we have the additional benefit that linking is safe for all typings, and not only for those principal. However, it is interesting to note that, for only achieving sound and complete compositional compilation, one could in principle rely on the weaker property of $\preceq$-principal typings for some $\preceq$ entailment relation: in this case, if the type information carried by a fragment is $\preceq$-principal, then linking succeeds if and only if global recompilation does; however, linking of arbitrary typings might not be safe.

Our work demonstrates that many classical notions from type theory, where compilation is usually simplified to the hardest part, that is, type inference, can be reformulated in those contexts where binary code generation becomes an issue which cannot be neglected to guarantee compositionality. What happens is that, to achieve compositional compilation, one needs to define more abstract forms of binary code, as happens for types in compositional analysis. We refer to the full paper [4] for some examples illustrating this idea, which we believe can be applied to a variety of code transformations (as optimization) in different languages.

Acknowledgements

This work has been partially supported by MIUR EOS DUE - Extensible Object Systems for Dynamic and Unpredictable Environments.

Bibliography

1. R. Adams, W. Tichy, and A. Weinert. The cost of selective recompilation and environment processing. *ACM Transactions on Software Engineering and Methodology*, 3(1):3–28, 1994.

2. D. Ancona, F. Damiani, S. Drossopoulou, and E. Zucca. Polymorphic bytecode: Compositional compilation for Java-like languages. In *ACM Symp. on Principles of Programming Languages 2005*. ACM Press, January 2005.

3. D. Ancona and E. Zucca. Principal typings for Java-like languages. In *ACM Symp. on Principles of Programming Languages 2004*, pages 306–317. ACM Press, January 2004.

4. D. Ancona and E. Zucca. A formal framework for compositional compilation. Technical report, Dipartimento di Informatica e Scienze dell'Informazione, Università di Genova, April 2007.

5. L. Cardelli. Program fragments, linking, and modularization. In *ACM Symp. on Principles of Programming Languages 1997*, pages 266–277. ACM Press, 1997.

6. T. Jim. What are principal typings and what are they good for? In *ACM Symp. on Principles of Programming Languages 1996*, pages 42–53. ACM Press, 1996.

7. R. W. Schwanke and Gail E. Kaiser. Smarter recompilation. *ACM Transactions on Programming Languages and Systems*, 10(4):627–632, 1988.

8. Z. Shao and A.W. Appel. Smartest recompilation. In *ACM Symp. on Principles of Programming Languages 1993*, pages 439–450. ACM Press, 1993.

9. W. F. Tichy. Smart recompilation. *ACM Transactions on Programming Languages and Systems*, 8(3):273–291, 1986.

10. J. B. Wells. The essence of principal typings. In *ICALP'02 - 29th International Colloquium on Automata, Languages and Programming 2002*, number 2380 in Lecture Notes in Computer Science, pages 913–925. Springer, 2002.

TYPE INFERENCE FOR POLYMORPHIC METHODS
IN JAVA-LIKE LANGUAGES*

D. ANCONA, G. LAGORIO, and E. ZUCCA

DISI, Univ. of Genova, v. Dodecaneso 35, 16146 Genova, Italy
email: {davide,lagorio,zucca}@disi.unige.it

In languages like C++, Java and C#, typechecking algorithms require methods to be annotated with their parameter and result types, which are either fixed or constrained by a bound.

We show that, surprisingly enough, it is possible to infer the polymorphic type of a method where parameter and result types are left unspecified, as happens in most functional languages. These types intuitively capture the (less restrictive) requirements on arguments needed to safely apply the method.

We formalize our ideas on a minimal Java subset, for which we define a type system with polymorphic types and prove its soundness. We then describe an algorithm for type inference and prove its soundness and completeness. A prototype implementing inference of polymorphic types is available.

1. Introduction

Type inference is the process of automatically determining the types of expressions in a program. That is, when type inference is employed, programmers can avoid writing some (or all) type declarations in their programs.

At the source code level, the situation appears very similar to using untyped (or dynamically typed) languages, as in both cases programmers are not required to write type declarations. However, the similarities end there: when type inference is used, types are statically found and checked by the compiler so no "message not understood" errors can ever appear at runtime (as it may happen when using dynamically typed languages).

To most people the idea of type inference is so tightly tied to functional languages that hearing about one of them automatically springs to mind the other. While it is conceivable to have one without the other, it is a fact that all successful functional languages (like ML, CaML and Haskell) exploit type inference.

---
*This work has been partially supported by MIUR EOS DUE - Extensible Object Systems for Dynamic and Umpredictable Environments.

Type inference often goes hand in hand with another appealing concept: polymorphism. Indeed, even though type inference and polymorphism are independent concepts, in inferring a type for, say, a function f, it comes quite naturally trying to express "the best" type for f. Indeed, all above mentioned functional languages support both type inference and polymorphism. Outside the world of functional languages, most works on inferring type constraints for object-oriented languages [6,7,14–16] have dealt with structural types. However, in mainstream class-based object-oriented languages with nominal types, typechecking algorithms require methods to be annotated with their parameter types, which are either fixed or constrained by a (nominal) bound.

We show that, surprisingly enough, the approach of inferring the most general function types works smoothly for Java-like languages too. That is, we can define polymorphic types for methods and automatically infer these types when type annotations are omitted. These polymorphic types intuitively express the (minimal) requirements on arguments needed to safely apply the method.

The rest of the paper is organized as follows. In Section 2 we formally define a type system with polymorphic method types for Featherweight Java [8], in Section 3 we illustrate an algorithm for inferring polymorphic method types, and, finally, in Section 4 we discuss related and further work.

A preliminary version of the ideas exploited in this paper is in a previous work [10] by two of the authors (see Section 4 for a comparison). A small prototype that we have developed can be tried out using any Java-enabled web browser[†].

2. A type system with polymorphic method types

We formalize our approach on a minimal language, whose syntax is given in Figure 1. This language is basically Featherweight Java [8], a tiny Java subset which has become a standard example to illustrate extensions and new technologies for Java-like languages. However, to focus on the key technical issues and give a compact soundness proof, we do not even consider fields, constructors, and casts, since these features do not pose substantial new problems to our aim[‡]. The only new feature we introduce is the fact that type annotations for parameters can be, besides class names, *type variables* α (in the concrete syntax the user just omits these types and fresh variables are generated by the compiler). Correspondingly, the result type can be omitted, as indicated by the notation $[C]$.

We informally illustrate the approach on a simple example.

```
class A { A m(A anA) { return anA ; }}
```

[†] Available at http://www.disi.unige.it/person/LagorioG/justII/.
[‡] They can be easily handled by considering new kinds of constraints, see the following.

$$P ::= cd_1 \ldots cd_n$$
$$cd ::= \text{class } C \text{ extends } C' \, \{ \, mds \, \} \quad (C \neq \text{Object})$$
$$mds ::= md_1 \ldots md_n$$
$$md ::= mh \, \{ \text{return } e; \}$$
$$mh ::= [C] \, m(t_1 \, x_1, \ldots, t_n \, x_n)$$
$$t ::= C \mid \alpha$$
$$e ::= \text{new } C() \mid x \mid e_0.m(e_1, \ldots, e_n)$$

where class names declared in P, method names declared in mds, and parameter names declared in mh are required to be distinct

Figure 1.   Syntax

```
class B { B m(B    aB) { return   aB ; }}
class Example {
         polyM(x,y) { return x.m(y) ;                              }
   Object okA()      { return this.polyM(new A(), new A()) ; }
   Object okB()      { return this.polyM(new B(), new B()) ; }
   Object notOk()    { return this.polyM(new A(), new B()) ; }}
```

Polymorphic methods can be safely applied to arguments of different types; how-ever, their possible argument types are determined by a set of constraints, rather than by a single subtyping constraint as in Java generic methods. Intuitively, the polymorphic type of polyM should express that the method can be safely applied to arguments of any pair (α, β) s.t. α has a method m applicable to β, and the result type is that of m. Formally, polyM has the polymorphic type $\mu(\delta \, \alpha.m(\beta)) \Rightarrow \alpha \, \beta \rightarrow \delta$, which means that polyM has two parameters of type, respectively, α and β, and returns a value of type δ (right-hand side of $\Rightarrow$), pro-viding the constraint $\mu(\delta \, \alpha.m(\beta))$ is satisfied (left-hand side of $\Rightarrow$). This happens whenever class α provides a method m which can be safely applied to an argument of type β and returns a value of type δ.

According to the type of polyM, typechecking of methods Example.okA and Example.okB should succeed, while typechecking of Example.notOk should fail because it invokes polyM with arguments of types A and B, so, in turn, polyM requires a method m in A which can receive a B (and there is no such method in the example).

Type environments Δ are sequences of *class signatures* cs, which are triples consisting of a class name C, the name of the parent (that is, the direct super-class) C' and a sequence of *method signatures* mss. A method signature ms is a tuple consisting of a set of *constraints* Γ, a result type t, a method name m, and sequence of parameter types $t_1 \ldots t_n$.

In the simple language we consider, there are only two forms of constraints: the standard subtyping constraint $t \leq t'$, and $\mu(t\ t_0.m(t_1 \ldots t_n))$, meaning that type t_0 must have a method named $m^{\S}$ which is applicable to arguments of types $t_1 \ldots t_n$ and returns a result of type t. Fields, constructors and casts can be easily handled, as done in another work [2], by adding other form of constraints.

Clearly, a method type cannot be trivially extracted from the code as happens in standard Java, but a non-trivial inference process is required (see next section). Here we define the type system of the language (Figure 2) which checks that method types are consistent and that the program conforms to them, without specifying how method types can be inferred in practice.

$$(\mathrm{P})\frac{\Delta \vdash cd_i \diamond\ \forall i \in 1..n \qquad \vdash \Delta \diamond}{\Delta \vdash cd_1 \ldots cd_n \diamond}\ \Delta = cs_1 \ldots cs_n$$

$$(\mathrm{cd})\frac{\Delta; C \vdash md_i \diamond\ \forall i \in 1..n}{\Delta \vdash \texttt{class } C \texttt{ extends } C'\ \{md_1 \ldots md_n\}\diamond}\ (C, C', ms_1 \ldots ms_n) \in \Delta$$

$$(\mathrm{md})\frac{\begin{array}{c}\Delta; x_1 : t_1, \ldots, x_n : t_n, \texttt{this:}C; \Gamma \vdash e : t' \\ \Delta; \Gamma \vdash t' \leq t\end{array}}{\Delta; C \vdash [C_0]\ m(t_1\ x_1, \ldots, t_n\ x_n)\ \{\texttt{return } e;\}\diamond}\ \begin{array}{c}mtype(\Delta, C, m) = \\ \Gamma \Rightarrow t_1 \ldots t_n \rightarrow t \\ [t = C_0]\end{array}$$

$$(\mathrm{call})\frac{\Delta; \Pi; \Gamma \vdash e_i : t_i\ \forall i \in 0..n \qquad \Delta; \Gamma \vdash \mu(t\ t_0.m(t_1 \ldots t_n))}{\Delta; \Pi; \Gamma \vdash e_0.m(e_1, \ldots, e_n) : t}$$

$$(\mathrm{new})\frac{\Delta; \Gamma \vdash C \leq C}{\Delta; \Pi; \Gamma \vdash \texttt{new } C() : C} \qquad\qquad (\mathrm{x})\frac{}{\Delta; \Pi; \Gamma \vdash x : t}\ \Pi(x) = t$$

Figure 2. Rules for typechecking

By rule (P), a program is well-typed in the type environment Δ if Δ is well-formed (see the comments below), and every class declaration is well-typed in the type environment Δ.

A class declaration is well-formed in Δ (rule (cd)), if all its method declarations are well-formed in Δ and C (needed to correctly type this). The side condition ensures that the class extends the same class and declare the same num-

---

$\S$This method can be either directly declared or inherited.

ber of methods as asserted in Δ.

Rule (md) checks that a method declaration is well-typed in Δ and C. Actually, it is a schema that can be instantiated in two different ways: if the return type is not declared (that is, $[C_0]$ is empty), then the corresponding side conditions $t = C_0$ must be removed (that is, $[t = C_0]$ must be empty as well).

The notation $mtype(\Delta, C, m)$ denotes the type of method m of class C as specified in Δ. The body e must be well-typed in Δ and Π, the local environment assigning the proper types to the parameters and to this; furthermore, e is type-checked assuming that the type constraints in Γ hold. Finally, in Δ it should be derivable from Γ (see the comments below) that the type of e is a subtype of the return type declared for the method.

The last three rules define the typing judgment for expressions, which has form $\Delta; \Pi; \Gamma \vdash e : t$, and checks that expression e has type t in the class environment Δ, in the local environment Π, assuming that the constraints in Γ hold.

Rule (call) checks that the expressions denoting the receiver and the arguments are well-typed; furthermore, in Δ the constraint $\mu(t\ t_0.m(t_1 \ldots t_n))$ must be derivable from Γ, to ensure that the static type t_0 of the receiver has a method m compatible with the static types $t_1 \ldots t_n$ of the arguments.

Rule (new) is standard, except for the constraint $C \leq C$, which ensures that a definition for C is available.

For space limitations we have omitted the formal definition of the judgments $\vdash \Delta\diamond$ and $\Delta; \Gamma \vdash \gamma$ (where γ denotes a single constraint) which can be found in an extended version [3] of this paper.

A type environment is well-formed only if it satisfies a number of conditions, including those inherited from FJ: names of declared classes and methods are, respectively, unique in a program and a class declaration, all used class names are declared, and there are no cycles in the inheritance hierarchy. Furthermore, type variables appearing in a list of parameter types must be distinct, and constraints in method types must be *consistent*. Consistency of set of constraints is checked by a normalization procedure described in the next section. If the procedure succeeds, then the set of constraints is consistent and is transformed into an equivalent but simplified set where constraints are of the form $\alpha \leq t$ or $\mu(t\ \alpha.m(t_1 \ldots t_n))$. Finally, a type environment is well-formed if overriding of methods is *safe*. The following rule defines the overriding judgment.

$$
\text{(overriding)} \frac{\begin{array}{c} \Delta; \Gamma \vdash \sigma(\Gamma') \\ \{\Delta; \Gamma \vdash t_i \leq C_i \mid t_i' = C_i\} \\ \Delta; \Gamma \vdash \sigma(t') \leq t \end{array}}{\Delta \vdash mt \leftarrow mt'} \quad \begin{array}{l} mt = \Gamma \Rightarrow t_1 \ldots t_n \rightarrow t, \\ mt' = \Gamma' \Rightarrow t_1' \ldots t_n' \rightarrow t' \\ t_i' = \alpha_i \implies \sigma(\alpha_i) = t_i \end{array}
$$

This rule states that a method type safely overrides another if the constraints in the heir can be derived from those of its parent, modulo a substitution that maps type variables used as parameter types in the heir into the corresponding parameter types in the parent. This condition intuitively guarantees that the method body of the heir (which has been typechecked under the heir constraints) can be safely executed under its parent constraints. Moreover, parameter types in the heir which are classes must be more generic, and return type more specific. Note that on monomorphic methods the definition reduces to contravariance for parameter types and covariance for return type, hence to a more liberal condition than in standard FJ and Java.

The *entailment* judgment $\Delta; \Gamma \vdash \gamma$ is valid if in Δ the constraint γ is entailed by Γ. We will also write $\Delta \vdash \gamma$ for $\Delta; \emptyset \vdash \gamma$ (this means that γ hold in Δ).

The rules are available in the extended version [3] and are pretty straightforward, except that for constraints of the form $\mu(t\ C_0.m(t_1 \ldots t_n))$:

$$(\mu) \frac{\{\Delta; \Gamma \vdash t_i \leq C_i \mid t_i' = C_i\} \quad \Delta; \Gamma, \mu(t\ C_0.m(t_1 \ldots t_n)) \vdash \sigma(\Gamma')}{\Delta; \Gamma \vdash \mu(t\ C_0.m(t_1 \ldots t_n))} \quad \begin{array}{l} tvars(\sigma(\Gamma')) \subseteq \\ tvars(\mu(t\ C_0.m(t_1 \ldots t_n))) \\ mtype(\Delta, C_0, m) = \Gamma' \Rightarrow t_1' \ldots t_n' \to t' \\ t_i' = \alpha_i \implies \sigma(\alpha_i) = t_i \\ \sigma(t') = t \end{array}$$

Here the substitution σ ensures that the types of the arguments and of the returned value of the constraint matches the corresponding declaration of the method in Δ. The side condition $tvars(\sigma(\Gamma')) \subseteq tvars(\mu(t\ C_0.m(t_1 \ldots t_n)))$ ensures that the type variables of $\sigma(\Gamma')$ are included in those of $\mu(t\ C_0.m(t_1 \ldots t_n))$, in order to avoid unwanted clashes with the variables in Γ. This condition can be always satisfied either by a proper α-renaming of variables, or by substituting with ground terms the variables in Γ' which do not appear in $t_1' \ldots t_n' \to t'$.

Let us consider an instantiation of the rule above in the typechecking of the invocation `this.polyM(new A(), new A())` in method `Object okA()` in our initial code example; such an invocation typechecks since the judgment $\Delta \vdash \mu(A\ Example.polyM(A\ A))$ is valid, with Δ the type environment corresponding to the program. Indeed, $mtype(\Delta, Example, polyM) = \mu(\gamma\ \alpha.m(\beta)) \Rightarrow \alpha\ \beta \to \gamma$ and, by substituting α, β and γ with A we get $\mu(A\ A.m(A))$ which holds in Δ.

Note that in the premise of the rule we add $\mu(t\ C_0.m(t_1 \ldots t_n))$ to Γ. This is necessary to avoid infinite proof trees when typechecking recursive methods, as in the following example:

```
class C {
  m (x) { return x.m(x);}
  Object test () { return this.m(this); }
}
```

Here, polymorphic method m has type $\mu(\beta \, \alpha.\text{m}(\alpha)) \Rightarrow \alpha \rightarrow \beta$. The invocation this.m(this) in method test typechecks since the judgment $\Delta \vdash \mu(\text{C C.m(C)})$ holds, with Δ the type environment corresponding to the program. Indeed, $mtype(\Delta, \text{C}, \text{m}) = \mu(\beta \, \alpha.\text{m}(\alpha)) \Rightarrow \alpha \rightarrow \beta$ and, by substituting α and β with C we get the constraint $\mu(\text{C C.m(C)})$ which do not need to be proved again.

The type system with polymorphic method types we have defined is sound, that is, expressions which can be typed by using (the type information corresponding to) a well-formed program P can be safely executed w.r.t. this program, where reduction rules for $\rightarrow_P$ are standard. For lack of space we omit them here, but they can be found in the extended version [3] of this paper. This means in particular that these expressions are ground and do not require type constraints. The proof is given by the standard subject reduction and progress properties. The proof schema is similar to that given for Featherweight GJ [9]; roughly, in Featherweight GJ only a kind of constraints on type variables is considered, that is, that they satisfy their (recursive) upper bound. The details of these proofs can be found in the aforementioned technical report.

Theorem 2.1 (Progress). *If* $\Delta \vdash P\diamond$ *and* $\Delta; \emptyset; \emptyset \vdash \text{e} : t$, *then either* $\text{e} = \text{new } C()$ *or* $\text{e} \rightarrow_P \text{e}'$ *for some* e'.

Theorem 2.2 (Subject reduction). *If* $\Delta \vdash P\diamond$ *and* $\Delta; \Pi; \emptyset \vdash \text{e} : t$, $\text{e} \rightarrow_P \text{e}'$, *then* $\Delta; \Pi; \emptyset \vdash \text{e} : t'$, $\Delta \vdash t' \leq t$.

3. Inferring polymorphic method types

In this section we show how the typechecking defined in Section 2 can be made effective by defining an algorithm for generating method types and another for checking consistency, by normalization, of type constraints of method types.

The first algorithm can be derived in a straightforward way by a set of rules [3] which have been omitted here for space limitations. Rules are defined by following an approach similar to that adopted [2] for achieving principality in Java: each rule just records all constraints necessary to successfully typecheck a certain kind of expression, without performing any check; hence, generation of method types always succeeds.

For instance, the rule for generating constraints for a method invocation is as follows:

$$\text{(call)} \frac{\Pi \vdash \text{e}_i : \Gamma_i \Rightarrow t_i \; \forall i \in 0..n}{\Pi \vdash \text{e}_0.\text{m}(\text{e}_1, \ldots, \text{e}_n) : \Gamma_0, \ldots, \Gamma_n, \mu(\alpha \, t_0.\text{m}(t_1 \ldots t_n)) \Rightarrow \alpha} \; \alpha \text{ fresh}$$

The judgment for constraint generation has form $\Pi \vdash \text{e} : \Gamma \Rightarrow t$ where the local variable environment Π and the expression e are the input values, whereas the set of constraints Γ and the type t are the output values of the generation process. Note that the type t of the expression is only needed for generating type constraints and is not used for performing a real typechecking.

The algorithm that normalizes a set of constraints is described in pseudocode in Figure 3, together with its pre- and postcondition. If normalization fails, then the corresponding set of constraints is not consistent. The variable all contains the current set of constraints, and the variable done keeps track of those which have already been checked. Termination of the process is guaranteed by the use of done and by the fact that, given a certain program, the set of all possible constraints which can be generated from all is finite.

We write $\Delta \vdash \Gamma \sim \Gamma'$ to denote that $\Delta; \Gamma \vdash \Gamma'$ and $\Delta; \Gamma' \vdash \Gamma$ hold.

```
{all==Γ && done==∅ &&!failure}
while (∃γ ∈ (all \ done not in normal form)&&!failure) {
  done = done ∪ {γ};
  switch γ
    case C ≤ C':
      if (Δ⊬C ≤ C') failure = true;
    case μ(α C.m(t₁...tₙ)):
      mt = mtype(Δ,C,m);
      if (mt undefined) failure = true;
      else
        let mt = Γ'⇒t'₁...t'ₘ→t' in
        if (m!=n) failure = true;
        else
          substₗ = {αᵢ ↦ tᵢ | t'ᵢ = αᵢ};
          substₒ = {α ↦ substₗ(t')};
          all = substₒ(all) ∪ substₗ(Γ' ∪ {tᵢ ≤ Cᵢ | t'ᵢ = Cᵢ});
          done = subst(done);
    default:
      failure = true
  }
{!failure==(∃Γⁿᶠ in normal form and σ s.t. Δ⊢Γⁿᶠ ∼ σ(Γ))};
```

Figure 3. Simplification of constraints

Theorem 3.1 (Correctness of the algorithm). *The algorithm in Figure 3 is correct w.r.t. the given pre- and postcondition.*

Theorem 3.2 (Soundness of type inference). *If* $\vdash cd_1 \ldots cd_n : \Delta$, *then* $\Delta \vdash cd_1 \ldots cd_n \diamond$.

Theorem 3.3 (Completeness of type inference). *If* $P = cd_1 \ldots cd_n$, $\vdash cd_i : cs_i$ *for all* $i \in 1..n$ *and the simplification algorithm fails on* $cs_1 \ldots cs_n$, *then there exists no* Δ *s.t.* $\Delta \vdash cd_1 \ldots cd_n \diamond$.

More details on these results and their proofs can be found in the aforementioned extended technical report.

Extension to full FJ When considering full FJ, the other forms of constraints which come out can be easily accommodated in the schema. For instance, constraints of the form $\phi(t' \ t.f)$ (type t must have a field named f of type t') and $t \sim t'$ (t must be a subtype of t' or conversely) can be handled as the $t \leq t'$ constraints, in the sense that they must be just checked, whereas constraints of the form $\kappa(t(t_1 \ldots t_n))$, meaning that type t must have a constructor applicable to arguments of types $t_1 \ldots t_n$, are a simpler version of the $\mu(t' \ t.m(t_1 \ldots t_n))$ constraints, in the sense that they can generate new constraints when checked.

4. Related and further work

As mentioned, the idea of omitting type annotations in method parameters has been preliminarily investigated in a previous work [10]. However, the key problem of solving recursive constraint sets is avoided there by imposing a rather severe restriction on polymorphic methods.

The type inference algorithm presented here can be seen as a generalization of that for compositional compilation of Java-like languages [2]. Indeed, the idea leading to the work in this paper came out very nicely by realizing that the constraint inference algorithm adopted there for compiling classes in isolation extends smoothly to the case where parameter types are type variables as well.

However, there are two main differences: first, the compositional compilation algorithm [2] only eliminates constraints, whereas here new constraints can be added since other methods can be invoked in a method's body, thus making termination more an issue. Secondly, since we may also have type variables as method parameter types, substitutions are not necessarily ground.

Type inference in object oriented languages has been studied before; in particular, an algorithm for a basic language with inheritance, assignments and late-binding has been described [13,15]. An improved version of the algorithm is called CPA (Cartesian Product Algorithm) [1]. In these approaches types are set of classes, like in Strongtalk [4], a typechecker for Smalltalk. More recently, a modified CPA [16] has been designed which introduces *conditional constraints* and resolves the constraints by least fixed-point derivation rather than unification. Whereas the technical treatment based on constraints is similar to ours, their aim is analyzing standard Java programs (in order to statically verify some properties as downcasts correctness) rather than proposing a polymorphic extension of Java. As already pointed out, while in Java the only available constraint on type variables is subtyping, in our approach we can take advantage of a richer set of constraints, thus making method types more expressive; furthermore, while our system is based on type inference, in Java the type variables and the constraints associated with a generic method are not inferred, but have to be explicitly provided by the user.

Our type constraints are more reminiscent of *where-clauses* [5,12] used in the *PolyJ* language. In *PolyJ* programmers can write parameterized classes and interfaces where the parameter has to satisfy constraints (the where-clauses) which state the signatures of methods and constructors that objects of the actual parameter type must support. The fact that our type constraints are related to methods rather than classes poses the additional problem of handling recursion. Moreover, our constraints for a method may involve type variables which correspond not only to the parameters, but also to intermediate result types of method calls.

Type inference has been deeply investigated in the context of functional languages since the early 80s, where many systems proposed in literature are based on the Hindley/Milner system [11] with constraints; the relation between our approach and that system deserves further investigation.

We have shown how to infer the polymorphic type of a method where parameter and result types are left unspecified, as it happens in most functional languages. Polymorphic method types are expressed by a set of constraints which intuitively correspond to the minimal requirements on argument types needed to safely apply the method. In this way the type system proposed here turns out to be very flexible.

We have also developed a small prototype that implements the described type inference and simplification of constraints (though the implemented overriding rule is simpler, so less liberal, than the one described here). This prototype, written in Java, can be tried out using any web browser[¶].

We believe this is a nice result, which bridges the world of type inference for polymorphic functions and the one of object-oriented languages with nominal types, showing a relation which deserves further investigation.

On the more practical side, our work can serve as basis for developing extensions of Java-like languages which allow developers to forget about (some) type annotations as happens in scripting languages, gaining some flexibility without losing static typing. A different design alternative is to let programmers to specify

---

[¶]Available at http://www.disi.unige.it/person/LagorioG/justII/.

(some) requirements on arguments.

Finally, the system presented here is not complete w.r.t. the type system defined in Section 2, but we are planning to investigate whether completeness can be achieved.

Bibliography

1. O. Agesen. The cartesian product algorithm. In W. Olthoff, editor, *ECOOP'05 - Object-Oriented Programming*, volume 952 of *Lecture Notes in Computer Science*, pages 2–26. Springer, 1995.
2. D. Ancona, F. Damiani, S. Drossopoulou, and E. Zucca. Polymorphic bytecode: Compositional compilation for Java-like languages. In *ACM Symp. on Principles of Programming Languages 2005*. ACM Press, January 2005.
3. D. Ancona, G. Lagorio, and E. Zucca. Type inference for polymorphic methods in Java-like languages. Technical report, Dipartimento di Informatica e Scienze dell'Informazione, Università di Genova, 2007. Submitted for journal publication.
4. G. Bracha and D. Griswold. Strongtalk: Typechecking Smalltalk in a production environment. In *ACM Symp. on Object-Oriented Programming: Systems, Languages and Applications 1993*, pages 215–230, 1993.
5. M. Day, R. Gruber, B. Liskov, and A. C. Myers. Subtypes vs. where clauses: Constraining parametric polymorphism. In *ACM Symp. on Object-Oriented Programming: Systems, Languages and Applications 1995*, volume 30(10) of *SIGPLAN Notices*, pages 156–168, 1995.
6. J. Eifrig, S. F. Smith, and V. Trifonov. Sound polymorphic type inference for objects. In *ACM Symp. on Object-Oriented Programming: Systems, Languages and Applications 1995*, volume 30(10) of *SIGPLAN Notices*, pages 169–184, 1995.
7. J. Eifrig, S. F. Smith, and V. Trifonov. Type inference for recursively constrained types and its application to OOP. In *Mathematical Foundations of Programming Semantics*, volume 1 of *Electronic Notes in Theoretical Computer Science*. Elsevier Science, 1995.
8. A. Igarashi, B. C. Pierce, and P. Wadler. Featherweight Java: A minimal core calculus for Java and GJ. In *ACM Symp. on Object-Oriented Programming: Systems, Languages and Applications 1999*, pages 132–146, November 1999.
9. A. Igarashi, B. C. Pierce, and P. Wadler. Featherweight Java: a minimal core calculus for Java and GJ. *ACM Transactions on Programming Languages and Systems*, 23(3):396–450, 2001.
10. G. Lagorio and E. Zucca. Introducing safe unknown types in Java-like languages. In L.M. Liebrock, editor, *OOPS'06 - Object-Oriented Programming Languages and Systems, Special Track at SAC'06 - 21st ACM Symp. on Applied Computing*, pages 1429–1434. ACM Press, 2006.
11. R. Milner. A theory of type polymorphism in programming. *Journ. of Computer and System Sciences*, 17(3):348–375, 1978.
12. A. C. Myers, J. A. Bank, and B. Liskov. Parameterized types for Java. In *ACM Symp. on Principles of Programming Languages 1997*, pages 132–145. ACM Press, 1997.
13. J. Palsberg and M. I. Schwartzbach. *Object-Oriented Type Systems*. John Wiley & Sons, 1994.

14. J. Palsberg. Type inference for objects. *ACM Comput. Surv.*, 28(2):358–359, 1996.
15. J. Palsberg and M. I. Schwartzbach. Object-oriented type inference. In *ACM Symp. on Object-Oriented Programming: Systems, Languages and Applications 1991*, pages 146–161, 1991.
16. T. Wang and S. F. Smith. Precise constraint-based type inference for Java. In *ECOOP'01 - European Conference on Object-Oriented Programming*, volume 2072, pages 99–117. Springer, 2001.

SORTING STREAMED MULTISETS

T. GAGIE

Dipartimento di Informatica,
Università del Piemonte Orientale,
Alessandria, 15100 (AL), Italy
E-mail: travis@mfn.unipmn.it

Sorting is a classic problem and one to which many others reduce easily. In the streaming model, however, we are allowed only one pass over the input and sublinear memory, so in general we cannot sort. In this paper we show that, to determine the sorted order of a multiset s of size n containing σ distinct elements using one pass and $o(n \log \sigma)$ bits of memory, it is generally necessary and sufficient that its entropy $H = o(\log \sigma)$. Specifically, if $s = \{s_1, \ldots, s_n\}$ and $s_{i_1}, \ldots, s_{i_n}$ is the stable sort of s, then we can compute $i_1, \ldots, i_n$ in one pass using $O((H + 1)n)$ time, $O(\sigma)$ words plus $O((H + 1)n)$ bits of memory, and a simple combination of classic techniques. On the other hand, in the worst case it takes $\Omega(Hn)$ bits of memory to compute any sorted ordering of s in one pass.

Keywords: Sorting; Streaming algorithms; Compression.

1. Introduction

When in doubt, sort! Librarians, secretaries and computer scientists all know that when faced with lots of data, often the best thing is to organize them. For some applications, though, the data are becoming so overwhelming that we cannot sort. The streaming model was introduced for situations in which the flow of data cannot be paused or stored in its entirety; the model's assumptions are that we are allowed only one pass over the input and memory sublinear in its size (see, e.g., Babcock *et al.*'s [1] or Muthukrishnan's [6] surveys). Those assumptions mean we cannot sort in general, but in this paper we show we can when the data are very compressible.

Our inspiration comes from two older articles on sorting. In the first, "Sorting and seaching in multisets" from 1976, Munro and Spira [5] considered the problem of sorting a multiset s of size n containing σ distinct elements, in the comparison model. They showed sorting s takes $\Theta((H + 1)n)$ time, where $H = \sum_{i=1}^{\sigma} (n_i/n) \log(n/n_i)$ is the entropy of s, log means $\log_2$ and n_i is the frequency of the ith largest distinct element. This is a significant improvement over the $\Theta(n \log n)$ bound for sorting a set of size n.

In the second article, "Selection and sorting with limited storage" from 1980, Munro and Paterson [4] considered the problem of sorting a set s of size n using limited memory and few passes. They showed sorting s in p passes takes $\Theta(n/p)$ memory locations in the following model:[a]

> In our computational model the data is a sequence of n distinct elements stored on a one-way read-only tape. An element from the tape can be read into one of r locations of random-access storage. The elements are from some totally ordered set (for example the real numbers) and a binary comparison can be made at any time between any two elements within the random-access storage. Initially the storage is empty and the tape is placed with the reading head at the beginning. After each pass the tape is rewound to this position with no reading permitted. ... [I]n view of the limitations imposed by our model, [sorting] must be considered as the *determination* of the sorted order rather than any actual rearrangement.

An obvious question — but one that apparently has not been addressed decades later — is how much memory we need to sort a multiset in few passes; in this paper we consider the case when we are allowed only one pass. We assume our input is the same as Munro and Spira's, a multiset $s = \{s_1, \ldots, s_n\}$ with entropy H containing σ distinct elements. Our model is similar to Munro and Paterson's but, whereas they counted memory locations, we count words and bits; we assume words are $\Theta(\log n)$ bits long, an element fits in a constant number of words, and we can perform standard operations on words in unit time.

In Section 2 we consider the problem of determining the permutation π such that $s_{\pi(1)}, \ldots, s_{\pi(n)}$ is the stable sort of s (i.e., $s_{\pi(i)} \leq s_{\pi(i+1)}$ and, if $s_{\pi(i)} = s_{\pi(i+1)}$, then $\pi(i) < \pi(i+1)$). For example, if

$$s = a_1, b_1, r_1, a_2, c, a_3, d, a_4, b_2, r_2, a_5$$

(with subscripts serving only to distinguish copies of the same distinct element), then the stable sort of s is

$$a_1, a_2, a_3, a_4, a_5, b_1, b_2, c, d, r_1, r_2$$
$$= s_1, s_4, s_6, s_8, s_{11}, s_2, s_9, s_5, s_7, s_3, s_{10}$$

and

$$\pi = 1, 4, 6, 8, 11, 2, 9, 5, 7, 3, 10 \, .$$

---

[a]We have changed their variable names for consistency with our own.

We give a simple algorithm that computes π using one pass, $O((H+1)n)$ time, and $O(\sigma)$ words plus $O((H+1)n)$ bits of memory. A by-product of our algorithm is a data structure that stores a compressed representation of s, which may be of independent interest; it can be augmented to answer many standard queries efficiently or used as it is to efficiently find all the occurrences of any given element. In Section 3 we consider the simpler problem of determining a permutation ρ such that $s_{\rho(1)}, \ldots, s_{\rho(n)}$ is in sorted order (not necessarily stably-sorted). We prove that in the worst case it takes $\Omega(Hn)$ bits of memory to compute any such ρ in one pass.

It is not hard to show that if $H = o(\log \sigma)$, then our algorithm uses memory sublinear in the size of the input, i.e., $o(n \log \sigma)$ bits. Since entropy is minimized when the distribution is maximally skewed,

$$Hn \geq n \left(\frac{n - \sigma + 1}{n} \log \frac{n}{n - \sigma + 1} + \frac{\sigma - 1}{n} \log n \right) \geq (\sigma - 1) \log n \,.$$

Therefore, if $H = o(\log \sigma)$, then $O(\sigma \log n) \subseteq O(Hn) \subseteq o(n \log \sigma)$, so our algorithm uses $o(n \log \sigma)$ bits of memory. On the other hand, if $H = \Omega(\log \sigma)$, then our lower bound means no algorithm uses one pass and $o(n \log \sigma)$ bits of memory in the worst case.

2. Algorithm

The key to our algorithm is the fact $\pi = \ell_1 \cdots \ell_\sigma$, where ℓ_i is the sorted list of positions in which the ith smallest distinct element occurs. In our example from Section 1, $s = a, b, r, a, c, a, d, a, b, r, a$,

$$\ell_1 = 1, 4, 6, 8, 11$$
$$\ell_2 = 2, 9$$
$$\ell_3 = 5$$
$$\ell_4 = 7$$
$$\ell_5 = 3, 10 \,.$$

Since each ℓ_i is a strictly increasing sequence, we can store it compactly using Elias' gamma code [3]: we write the first number in ℓ_i, encoded in the gamma code; for $1 \leq j < n_i$, we write the difference between the $(j+1)$st and jth numbers, encoded in the gamma code. The gamma code is a prefix-free code for the positive integers; for $x \geq 1$, $\gamma(x)$ consists of $\lfloor \log x \rfloor$ zeroes followed by the $(\lfloor \log x \rfloor + 1)$-bit binary representation of x. In our example, we encode ℓ_1 as

$$\gamma(1) \, \gamma(3) \, \gamma(2) \, \gamma(2) \, \gamma(3)$$
$$= 1 \, 011 \, 010 \, 010 \, 011 \,.$$

Lemma 2.1. *We can store π in $O(H+1)n)$ bits of memory.*

Proof. Notice the numbers we write to encode ℓ_i sum to at most n. By Jensen's inequality, since $|\gamma(x)| \leq 2\log x + 1$ and log is concave, we store ℓ_i in at most $n_i(2\log(n/n_i) + 1)$ bits. Therefore, storing $\ell_1, \ldots, \ell_\sigma$ as described above takes

$$\sum_{i=1}^{\sigma} O\left(n_i(\log(n/n_i) + 1)\right) = O((H+1)n)$$

bits of memory. □

To compute $\ell_1, \ldots, \ell_\sigma$ in one pass, we keep track of which distinct elements have occurred and the positions of their most recent occurrences, which takes $O(\sigma)$ words of memory. For $1 \leq j \leq n$, if s_j is an occurrence of the ith smallest distinct element and that element has not occurred before, then we start the encoding of ℓ_i with $\gamma(j)$; if that element last occurred in position k, then we append $\gamma(j - k)$ to ℓ_i. Because we do not know in advance how many bits we will use to encode each ℓ_i, we keep the encoding in an expandable binary array [2]: we start with an array of size 1 bit; whenever the array overflows, we create a new array twice as big, copy the contents from the old array into the new one, and destroy the old array. We note appending a bit to the encoding takes amortized constant time.

Lemma 2.2. *We can compute $\ell_1, \ldots, \ell_\sigma$ in one pass using $O(\sigma)$ words plus $O((H+1)n)$ bits of memory.*

Proof. Since we are not yet concerned with time, for each element in s we can simply perform a linear search — which is slow but uses no extra memory — through the entire list of distinct elements to find the encoding we should extend. Since an array is never more than twice the size of the encoding it holds, the memory we use for the arrays is proportional to the total length of all encodings which, as shown in the proof of Lemma 2.1, is $O((H+1)n)$ bits. □

To make our algorithm time-efficient, we use search in a splay-tree [7] instead of linear search. At each node of the splay-tree, we store a distinct element as the key, the position of that element's most recent occurrence and a pointer to the array for that element. For $1 \leq j \leq n$, we search for s_j in the splay-tree; if we find it, then we extend the encoding of the corresponding list as described above, set the position of s_j's most recent occurrence to j and splay s_j's node to the root; if not, then we insert a new node storing s_j as its key, position j and a pointer to an expandable array storing $\gamma(j)$, and splay the node to the node to the root. Figure 1 shows the state of our splay-tree and arrays after we process the first 9 elements in our example; i.e., $a, b, r, a, c, a, d, a, b$. Figure 2 shows the changes when we process the next element, an r: we double the size of r's array from 4 to 8 bits in order to append $\gamma(10 - 3 = 7) = 00111$, set the position of r's most recent occurrence to 10 and splay r's node to the root. Figure 3 show the final state of our splay-tree and arrays after we process the last element, an a: we append $\gamma(11 - 8 = 3) = 011$ to a's array (but since only 10 of its 16 bits were already used, we do not expand it), set the position of a's most recent occurrence to 11 and splay a's node to the root.

Lemma 2.3. *We can compute* $\ell_1, \ldots, \ell_\sigma$ *in one pass using* $O((H + 1)n)$ *time, and* $O(\sigma)$ *words plus* $O((H + 1)n)$ *bits of memory.*

Proof. Our splay-tree takes $O(\sigma)$ words of memory and, so, does not change the bound on our memory usage. For $1 \leq i \leq \sigma$ we search for the ith largest distinct element once when it is not in the splay-tree, insert it once, and search for it $n_i - 1$ times when it is in the splay-tree. Therefore, by the Update Lemma [7] for splay-trees, the total time taken for all the operations on the splay-tree is

$$\sum_{i=1}^{\sigma} O \left(\log \frac{W}{\min(w_{i-1}, w_{i+1})} + n_i \log \frac{W}{w_i} + n_i \right) ,$$

where $w_1, \ldots, w_\sigma$ are any positive weights, W is their sum and $w_0 = w_{\sigma+1} = \infty$. Setting $w_i = n_i$ for $1 \leq i \leq \sigma$, this bound becomes

$$\sum_{i=1}^{\sigma} O \left((n_i + 2)(\log(n/n_i) + 1) \right) = O((H + 1)n) .$$

Because appending a bit to an array takes amortized constant time, the total time taken for operations on the arrays is proportional to the total length in bits of the encodings, i.e., $O((H + 1)n)$. □

After we process all of s, we can compute π from the state of the splay-tree and arrays: we perform an in-order traversal of the splay-tree; when we visit a node, we decode the numbers in its array and output their positive partial sums (this takes $O(1)$ words of memory and time proportional to the length in bits of the encoding, because the gamma code is prefix-free); this way, we output the concatenation of the decoded lists in increasing order by element, i.e., $\ell_1 \cdots \ell_\sigma = \pi$. In our example, we visit the nodes in the order a, b, c, d, r; when we visit a's node we

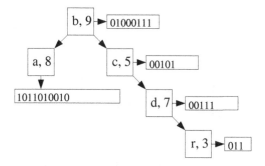

Fig. 1. Our splay-tree and arrays after we process $a, b, r, a, c, a, d, a, b$.

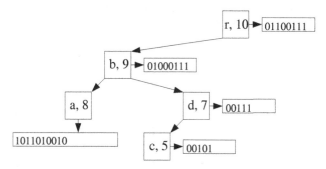

Fig. 2. Our splay-tree and arrays after we process $a, b, r, a, c, a, d, a, b, r$; notice we have doubled the size of the array for r, in order to append $\gamma(7) = 00111$.

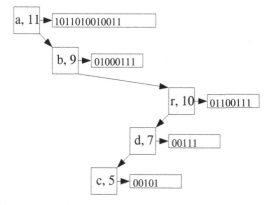

Fig. 3. Our splay-tree and arrays after we process $a, b, r, a, c, a, d, a, b, r, a$; notice we have not had to expand the array for a in order to append $\gamma(3) = 011$.

output

$$\gamma^{-1}(1) = 1$$
$$1 + \gamma^{-1}(011) = 1 + 3 = 4$$
$$4 + \gamma^{-1}(010) = 4 + 2 = 6$$
$$6 + \gamma^{-1}(010) = 6 + 2 = 8$$
$$8 + \gamma^{-1}(011) = 8 + 3 = 11 .$$

Our results in this section culminate in the following theorem:

Theorem 2.1. *We can compute π in one pass using $O((H+1)n)$ time, and $O(\sigma)$ words plus $O((H+1)n)$ bits of memory.*

As an aside, we note s can be recovered efficiently from our splay-tree and arrays: we start with an empty priority queue Q and insert a copy of each distinct element, with priority equal to the position of its first occurrence (i.e., the first encoded number in its array); for $1 \leq j \leq n$, we dequeue the element with minimum priority, output it, and reinsert it with priority equal to the position of its next occurrence (i.e., its previous priority plus the next encoded number in its array). This idea — that a sorted ordering of s partially encodes it — is central to our lower bound in the next section.

3. Lower Bound

Consider any algorithm A that, allowed one pass over s, outputs a permutation ρ such that $s_{\rho(1)}, \ldots, s_{\rho(n)}$ is in sorted order (not necessarily stably-sorted). Notice A generally cannot output anything until it has read all of s, in case s_n is the unique minimum; also, given the frequency of each distinct element, ρ tells us the arrangement of elements in s up to equivalence.

Theorem 3.1. *In the worst case, it takes $\Omega(Hn)$ bits of memory to compute any sorted ordering of s in one pass.*

Proof. Suppose $\sigma = 2^H$ and each $n_i = n/\sigma$, so the number of possible distinct arrangements of the elements in s is maximized,

$$\frac{n!}{\prod_{i=1}^{\sigma} n_i!} = \frac{n!}{((n/\sigma)!)^{\sigma}} .$$

It follows that in the worst case A uses at least

$$\log\left(n!/((n/\sigma)!)^\sigma\right)$$
$$= \log n! - \sigma \log(n/\sigma)!$$
$$\geq n\log n - n\log e - \sigma\left((n/\sigma)\log(n/\sigma) - (n/\sigma)\log e + O(\log(n/\sigma))\right)$$
$$= n\log n - n\log(n/\sigma) - O(\sigma\log(n/\sigma))$$
$$\geq n\log\sigma - O(n)$$
$$= \Omega(Hn)$$

bits of memory to store ρ. The first inequality holds by Stirling's formula — i.e., $x\log x - x\log e < \log x! \leq x\log x - x\log e + O(\log x)$ — and the last holds because $\sigma \leq n$ so $\sigma\log(n/\sigma) = O(n)$. $\square$

4. Future Work

Our lower bound does not hold outside the streaming model, when we are allowed more than one pass over the input; e.g., we can compute the stable sort of s using $O(1)$ words of memory if we are allowed n passes — on the ith pass we find and output the ith number in π. It is not hard to generalize our lower bound, though, especially if we restrict our attention to algorithms that produce no output during passes: if an algorithm uses b bits of memory, then in general it cannot output more than b bits after each pass and, so, must use $\Omega(Hn/b)$ passes in the worst case. We will prove a bound without restrictions in the full version of this paper.

It is also not hard to modify our algorithm to use less memory but more passes. Suppose we are allowed $O(\sigma)$ words plus b bits of memory. We proceed as usual until we reach an element s_j in s such that processing s_j would cause our arrays to use more than b bits in total. If s_j is at least as large as the largest element a in the splay-tree, then we ignore it; otherwise, we delete codewords from the end of a's array until we have enough space to process s_j. (We now use fully resizable arrays, which both expand and contract with the data they contain. If a's array becomes empty, we destroy it and delete a from the splay-tree.) At the end of the first pass, we have a prefix of π stored that, encoded, is approximately b bits long. We output this prefix decoded, use $O(1)$ words of memory to store the largest element a in the splay-tree and the last position k in the prefix, then destroy the splay-tree and arrays. Finally, we repeat this whole procedure, ignoring elements smaller than a and occurrences of a in positions less than or equal to k. This way, after $i \geq 1$ passes we have output a prefix of π that, if encoded, would be approximately ib bits long; it follows we output all of π in $O((H+1)n/b)$ passes.

A disadvantage of this modification is that we may waste time inserting elements into the splay-tree and storing the positions of their occurrences in s, then later delete them. Before each pass we can make a preliminary pass to find a pair a' and k' such that, by ignoring elements larger than a' and occurrences of a' in positions greater than k', we never have to delete codewords. Choosing a' and k' properly for each pass, we can compute π using $O((H + 1)n/b)$ passes, $O((H + 1)n)$ time, and $O(\sigma)$ words plus b bits of memory. We will give a complete description and analysis in the full version of this paper.

Acknowledgments

Many thanks to Giovanni Manzini for discussions, to the anonymous referees for comments, to my mother for proofreading and to Paola Innocenti for encouragement.

Bibliography

1. B. Babcock, S. Babu, M. Datar, R. Motwani, and J. Widom. Models and issues in data stream systems. In L. Popa, editor, *Proceedings of the 21st Symposium on the Principles of Database Systems (PODS '02)*, pages 1–16, 2002.
2. T. H. Cormen, C. E. Leiserson, R. L. Rivest, and C. Stein. *Introduction to Algorithms.* MIT Press, 2nd edition, 2001.
3. P. Elias. Universal codeword sets and representations of the integers. *IEEE Transactions on Information Theory*, 21(2):194–203, 1975.
4. J. I. Munro and M. S. Paterson. Selection and sorting with limited storage. *Theoretical Computer Science*, 12:315–323, 1980.
5. J. I. Munro and P. M. Spira. Sorting and searching in multisets. *SIAM Journal on Computing*, 5(1):1–8, 1976.
6. S. Muthukrishnan. *Data Streams: Algorithms and Applications.* Foundations and Trends in Theoretical Computer Science. Now Publishers, 2005.
7. D. D. Sleator and R. E. Tarjan. Self-adjusting binary search trees. *Journal of the ACM*, 32(3):652–686, 1985.

AN ANALYSIS OF A SIMPLE ALGORITHM
FOR RANDOM DERANGEMENTS

D. MERLINI, R. SPRUGNOLI, and M. C. VERRI

Dipartimento di Sistemi e Informatica
Viale Morgagni, 65 - Firenze (Italy)
E-mail: [merlini,sprugnoli]@dsi.unifi.it, mariacecilia.verri@unifi.it

We consider the uniform generation of random derangements, i.e., permutations without any fixed point. By using a rejection algorithm, we improve the straight-forward method of generating a random permutation until a derangement is obtained. This and our procedure are both linear with respect to the number of calls to the random generator, but we obtain an improvement of more than 36%. By using probability generating functions we perform an exact average analysis of the algorithm, showing that our approach is rather general and can be used to analyze random generation procedures based on the same rejection technique. Moreover, emphasis is given to combinatorial sums and a new interpretation of a known infinite lower triangular array is found.

Keywords: Derangements, rejection algorithms, probability generating functions.

1. Introduction

We consider the random, uniform generation of derangements, i.e., permutations without any fixed point. They were introduced during the XVIII century and Euler [3] describes the corresponding counting problem in this way: "Data serie quotcunque litterarum a, b, c, d, e etc., quorum numero sit n, invenire quot modis earum ordo immutari possit, ut nulla in eo loco reperiatur, quem initio occupaverat". Another famous formulation is as follows. Ten mathematicians arrive at the Faculty Club and leave their hats at the wardrobe. When they go out, everyone takes a hat at random; mathematicians are notoriously absent-minded. What is the probability that no one takes his own hat? If we mark the mathematicians and their hats with the numbers from 1 to 10, on exit the Club we obtain a permutation in the symmetric group S_{10}, and a mathematician who takes his own hat is a fixed point. Therefore, the required probability is $D_{10}/10!$, where $D_n = |\mathcal{D}_n|$ if $\mathcal{D}_n$ is the set of derangements over $[1..n]$. Another interesting application of the concept of derangements concerns the *stable marriage* or *ménage problem* (see, e.g., [4]).

The random, uniform generation of derangements is very simple. Since $D_n \approx$

$n!/e$, the obvious procedure of generating a random permutation and check if it is a derangement or not, and generating a new permutation in the negative case, is straight-forward and guarantees a linear time complexity, at least on the average; actually, as we will see, the average complexity is $\mu_1 \approx e(n-1)$. We measure complexity as the number of calls to random, the function that generates a random integer in a given interval; as we shall see in procedures generate1 and generate2, a fixed number of operations is related to each call; therefore, the procedures are also linear in time.

Other methods are also feasible. The general approach, proposed by Flajolet et al. [5], consists in giving a formal definition of the class $\mathcal{D}$ of derangements as the permutations only containing cycles of length greater than 1 (a fixed point is just a cycle of a single element): $\mathcal{D} := \text{SET}\{\text{CYCLE}_{>1}\{\mathcal{Z}\}\}$. Then the definition is transformed into a routine generating the random derangements in a uniform way. Ruskey [9] claims to use the recurrence $D_n = (n-1)D_{n-1} + (n-1)D_{n-2}$ for generating all the derangements in $\mathcal{D}_n$ in linear amortized time.

Our approach generates single derangements and is based on a rejection technique, as introduced in [1]. The method is rather general, as we observe at the end of Section 2, and the generation routine is very fast, with an average complexity $\mu_2 \approx (e-1)(n-1)$. Besides, it works without using any pre-compiled table and occupies minimum space, just the n elements of the permutation. Finally, in order to study its complexity, we use some triangular arrays which are known in the literature, but for which we give a different and more direct interpretation.

Actually, the random generation of derangements is not only important for its own, but it is the basis for other generations, very useful in the simulation of the behavior of several structures. For example: 1) permutations of n objects with exactly $k < n$ fixed points; 2) permutations of n objects having their first (last) fixed point at position k; 3) if we define a k-*disposition* of n objects as the first k objects in a permutation of the n objects (see [7]), problems analogous to 1) and 2) can be considered, and solved in a similar way.

In Section 2 we present our algorithms and the probability generating functions (p.g.f.) which will be used to perform their average case complexity analysis. In Section 3 we discuss the concept of the first fixed point in a permutation and develop the corresponding mathematical properties. Finally, in Section 4 we use these properties to compute the average number of calls to random and the corresponding variance of our main algorithm.

2. Derangements

By a classical application of the inclusion-exclusion principle, it is almost immediate to prove:

$$D_n = n! \left(1 - \frac{1}{1!} + \frac{1}{2!} - \cdots + \frac{(-1)^n}{n!} \right) = \left[\frac{n!}{e} \right], \tag{1}$$

where $[x]$ denotes the integer number closest to x. The sequence is A000166 in Sloane's encyclopedia [11] and the first values are (1, 0, 1, 2, 9, 44, 265, 1854, 14833, 133496) corresponding to the exponential generating function: $D(t) = e^{-t}/(1 - t)$. When dealing with approximate or asymptotic values, another expression for D_n, obtained from (1), can be more appropriate:

Theorem 2.1. *The derangement numbers satisfy the following formula:*

$$D_n = \frac{n!}{e} \left(1 - \frac{e(-1)^{n+1}}{(n + 1)!} + \cdots \right). \tag{2}$$

By (1), a simple procedure to generate a random derangement is:

proc generate1(n);
    repeat generate a random permutation $\pi \in \mathcal{S}_n$ **until** $\pi \in \mathcal{D}_n$;
end proc

The procedure to generate a random permutation will be called shuffle and is well-known (see, e.g., Knuth [8, Vol. 2]). It requires $n - 1$ calls to random(m), the function that generates a random integer in the interval $[1..m]$. In general, we define the complexity of a procedure as the number of calls to random, so that the complexity of shuffle is $n - 1$. It is intuitive from (1) that the complexity of the procedure generate1 is $e(n - 1)$ on the average, but we can obtain more precise results by using probability generating functions (see, e.g., [4,10]).

Theorem 2.2. *The average complexity and the variance of the procedure* generate1 *are* $\mu_1 = e(n - 1)$ *and* $\sigma_1^2 = e(e - 1)(n - 1)^2$.

Proof. Let $P_1(t) = \sum_{k=0}^{\infty} q_k t^k$ be the p.g.f. relative to the procedure generate1, where the term $q_k t^k$ denotes the fact that a derangement is generated with probability q_k after k calls to random. By (1) we have that a random permutation $\pi \in \mathcal{S}_n$ is a derangement with probability $1/e$ and is not with probability $(e - 1)/e$. The procedure performs a (possibly empty) sequence of non-derangements generations, followed by the generation of a derangement, each one with $n - 1$ calls to shuffle. Therefore:

$$P_1(t) = \sum_{k=0}^{\infty} \left(\frac{e-1}{e}t^{n-1}\right)^k \frac{1}{e}t^{n-1} = \frac{t^{n-1}}{e - (e-1)t^{n-1}}.$$

From this expression we have $\mu_1 = P'(1) = e(n-1)$ and by performing a differentiation again $\alpha_1 = P''(1) = e(n-1)(2en-n-2e)$; a simple computation finally yields $\sigma_1^2 = \alpha_1 + \mu_1 - \mu_1^2 = e(e-1)(n-1)^2$. □

The procedure generate1 is linear in time, but, since $e \approx 2.718$, we can hope to find a faster procedure, also if we cannot go under $n - 1$; in fact, all the elements in the permutation π (except possibly the last) must be generated, since they can be placed in any position. The method of *early refusal* (see, e.g., [1]) consists in stopping a generation as soon as it is clear that the generated object cannot be legal. In our case, when we generate the element k and it should be placed in position k, we obtain a fixed point and we are sure that the resulting permutation is not a derangement. This observation results in a new procedure, which has to be merged with the procedure shuffle.

```
proc generate2(n);
    found := false;
    while not found do
        for j:=1 to n do v[j] := j end for;
        j := n; fixed := false; over := false;
        while not over do p := random(j);
            if v[p] = j then fixed := true; over := true
                else a := v[j]; v[j] := v[p]; v[p] := a end if;
            j := j - 1; if j = 1 then over := true end if
        end while;
        if not fixed and v[1] <> 1 then found := true end if
    end while;
end proc
```

By this construction, we stop at the last fixed point; by symmetric reasons, we will analyze the procedure considering the first fixed point. In order to analyze the behavior of generate2 we need some new definitions. Given a permutation $\pi \in \mathcal{S}_n$, then π belongs to $\mathcal{D}_n$ or π has a *first fixed point* (f.f.p.), i.e., a fixed point at position k, while every position j, with $j < k$, is not fixed. For example, the permutation $(3\ 7\ 5\ 4\ 1\ 6\ 2)$ has two fixed points, 4 and 6, and 4 is its f.f.p.. Let $\mathcal{F}_{n,k}$ be the set of all $\pi \in \mathcal{S}_n$ such that π has its f.f.p. at position k; by abuse of language, we set $\mathcal{F}_{n,0} = \mathcal{D}_n$. Let us denote by p_k (understanding the index n) the probability that a permutation π has its f.f.p. at position k. Clearly $p_k = |\mathcal{F}_{n,k}|/n!$ for $k = 0, 1, \ldots, n$ so that p_0 is the probability that π is a derangement.

Theorem 2.3. *The p.g.f. corresponding to* generate2 *is:*

$$P_2(t) = \frac{p_0 t^{n-1}}{1 - (p_1 t + p_2 t^2 + \cdots + p_{n-1} t^{n-1} + p_n t^{n-1})}$$

Proof. To generate a derangement, we actually generate a sequence of false derangements, i.e., permutations with some fixed point. At the first fixed point we abandon the generation and start from scratch. Therefore, if this f.f.p. is at a position j, the cost of the generation is j calls to random with probability p_j, so that the contribution to the p.g.f. is $p_j t^j$. The only exception is for $j = n$, because the generation of the last element is obliged, and the contribution is $p_n t^{n-1}$. Finally, we generate the derangement, the cost of which is $n - 1$ with probability p_0. Therefore, the p.g.f. is:

$$P_2(t) = \sum_{j=0}^{\infty} (p_1 t + p_2 t^2 + \cdots + p_{n-1} t^{n-1} + p_n t^{n-1})^j p_0 t^{n-1}$$

from which the desired formula immediately follows. (This is indeed a p.g.f.; since $p_0 + p_1 + \cdots + p_n = 1$ we also have $P_2(1) = 1$). □

Once we have found the p.g.f., we are able to compute the average number of calls to random and the corresponding variance.

Theorem 2.4. *The average number of calls to* random *performed by the procedure* generate2 *is:*

$$\mu_2 = n - 1 - \frac{p_n}{p_0} + \frac{1}{p_0} \sum_{k=1}^{n} k p_k. \tag{3}$$

The corresponding variance is:

$$\sigma_2^2 = \left(\frac{1}{p_0} \sum_{k=1}^{n} k p_k \right)^2 + \frac{1}{p_0} \sum_{k=1}^{n} k^2 p_k - 2 \frac{p_n}{p_0^2} \sum_{k=1}^{n} k p_k + \left(\frac{p_n}{p_0} \right)^2 - (2n - 1) \frac{p_n}{p_0}.$$

Proof. By differentiating the p.g.f. $P_2(t)$ we get the following numerator:

$$(n - 1) p_0 t^{n-2} - (n - 1) p_0 t^{n-2} (p_1 t + p_2 t^2 + \cdots + p_{n-1} t^{n-1} + p_n t^{n-1}) +$$

$$+ p_0 t^{n-1} (p_1 + 2 p_2 t + \cdots + (n - 1) p_{n-1} t^{n-2} + (n - 1) p_n t^{n-2})$$

while the denominator is obviously $(1 - (p_1 t + \cdots + p_{n-1} t^{n-1} + p_n t^{n-1}))^2$. Now we set $t = 1$ and the denominator becomes p_0^2. In the numerator we add and subtract p_n in order to complete the last sum and get:

$$P_2'(1) = \frac{n-1}{p_0} - \frac{n-1}{p_0}(1-p_0) + \frac{1}{p_0}\sum_{k=1}^{n} kp_k - \frac{p_n}{p_0} = n - 1 - \frac{p_n}{p_0} + \frac{1}{p_0}\sum_{k=1}^{n} kp_k.$$

With the help of Maple, we differentiate $P_2'(t)$ and compute $\alpha_2 = P_2''(1)$; by applying formula $\sigma_2^2 = \alpha_2 + \mu_2 - \mu_2^2$ we obtain the assert. $\qquad\square$

Note: Let us consider the general problem of the random generation of a combinatorial object defined as the sequence of elementary items. If we use the method of early refusal, the previous theorem gives the expected complexity of the procedure, in the case that the last generated item is determined by the previous ones, as happens in our problem. Therefore, (3) is much more general than expected; it is sufficient that we interpret the probability p_k as the probability that the procedure is interrupted after the generation of the item in position k ($1 \le k \le n$).

3. The Triangle of First Fixed Points

The problem is now to determine the values $p_1, p_2, \ldots, p_n$ or, equivalently, the dimension of the sets $\mathcal{F}_{n,1}, \mathcal{F}_{n,2}, \ldots, \mathcal{F}_{n,n}$. We have:

Theorem 3.1. *The number of permutations in $\mathcal{S}_{n+1}$ having $k + 1$ as f.f.p. is:*

$$F_{n+1,k+1} = |\mathcal{F}_{n+1,k+1}| = \sum_{j=0}^{k}(-1)^j \binom{k}{j}(n-j)! \qquad k = 0, 1, 2, \ldots, n. \quad (4)$$

Proof. For $k = 0$ the formula gives $|\mathcal{F}_{n+1,1}| = n!$; in fact, we have $\pi(1) = 1$ as f.f.p., while the other elements can form any permutation, and so we actually have $n!$ permutations in $\mathcal{F}_{n+1,1}$. Let us now consider $k = 1$; we obviously have $n!$ permutations with position 2 as a fixed point. In this way, however, we also count the permutations having 1 as a fixed point, so we must subtract permutations having both 1 and 2 as fixed points. Therefore we find $F_{n+1,2} = n! - (n-1)!$ which agrees with (4). This reasoning suggests to apply the principle of inclusion and exclusion. In general, there are $n!$ permutations in $\mathcal{S}_{n+1}$ having $k + 1$ as a fixed point. In this way we include permutations having two fixed points: one at position $k + 1$ and the other at a position j, $1 \le j \le k$; therefore, we should eliminate $(n-1)!$ permutations for every value of j, that is $\binom{k}{1}$ times; so we have $n! - \binom{k}{1}(n-1)!$ permutations. Again, we have excluded permutations with three fixed points: one at position $k + 1$, one at position j and a third one at position r, with $1 \le j < r \le k$. Since there are $\binom{k}{2}$ possibilities of choosing j and r, we have obtained $n! - \binom{k}{1}(n-1)! + \binom{k}{2}(n-2)!$. By continuing, we obtain the desired expression. □

Table 1. Permutations in $\mathcal{S}_n$ having k as their f.f.p.

n/k	1	2	3	4	5	6	7
1	1						
2	1	0					
3	2	1	1				
4	6	4	3	2			
5	24	18	14	11	9		
6	120	96	78	64	53	44	
7	720	600	504	426	362	309	265

In Table 1 we give the upper part of the infinite triangle $(F_{n,k})_{n,k \in \mathbb{N}_0}$, where $\mathbb{N}_0 = \mathbb{N} \setminus \{0\}$. This triangle is already known in Combinatorics and corresponds to sequence A047920 in [11], where a paper by J. D. H. Dickson [2] is quoted, old as 1879. Formula (4) is ascribed to Philippe Deleham, while the property of Theorem 3.2 is due to Henry Bottomley. Our approach furnishes a more direct combinatorial interpretation of these numbers: $F_{n,k}$ is the number of permutations in $\mathcal{S}_n$ having their f.f.p. at position k.

Theorem 3.2. *The infinite triangle* $(F_{n,k})_{n,k \in \mathbb{N}_0}$ *is completely defined by the initial conditions* $F_{n,1} = (n-1)!$, $(n = 1, 2, \ldots)$ *and by the relation:*

$$F_{n+1,k+1} = F_{n+1,k} - F_{n,k} \qquad k = 1, 2, \ldots, n.$$

Proof. By simple properties of binomial coefficients, we have:

$$F_{n+1,k} - F_{n,k} = \sum_{j=0}^{k-1}(-1)^j \binom{k-1}{j}(n-j)! - \sum_{j=0}^{k-1}(-1)^j \binom{k-1}{j}(n-1-j)! =$$

$$= \sum_{j=0}^{k}(-1)^j \left(\binom{k-1}{j} + \binom{k-1}{j-1} \right)(n-j)! = \sum_{j=0}^{k}(-1)^j \binom{k}{j}(n-j)!$$

which corresponds to $F_{n+1,k+1}$, as desired. □

This theorem gives the link to the numerical interpretation of the triangle. It is just the array of the successive differences of factorial numbers (see column 1 in Table 1). This fact and the formula for derangements explain why derangement numbers appear on the main diagonal: $F_{n,n} = D_{n-1}$.

Now we give an asymptotic value and a good approximation of $F_{n+1,k+1}$:

Theorem 3.3. *For the numbers $F_{n+1,k+1}$ we have:*

$$F_{n+1,k+1} = n!e^{-k/n}\left(1 - \frac{k(n-k)}{2n^2(n-1)} + O\left(\frac{k^2(n-k)}{n^4}\right)\right).$$

Proof. Let us expand the formula for $F_{n+1,k+1}$:

$$F_{n+1,k+1} = n! - k(n-1)! + \binom{k}{2}(n-2)! - \binom{k}{3}(n-3)! + \cdots =$$

$$= n!\left(1 - \frac{k}{n} + \frac{k(k-1)}{2n(n-1)} - \frac{k(k-1)(k-2)}{6n(n-1)(n-2)} + \cdots\right).$$

Since $e^{-k/n} = 1 - \frac{k}{n} + \frac{k^2}{2n^2} - \frac{k^3}{6n^3} + \cdots$, we compute:

$$F_{n+1,k+1} - n!e^{-k/n} = n!\left(-\frac{k(n-k)}{2n^2(n-1)} + \frac{k(n-k)(3nk - 2n - 2k)}{6n^3(n-1)(n-2)} + \cdots\right)$$

and the result follows from this expression.   □

This is a good approximation and, because of $k(n-k)$, it is better for small and large k's and worse for $k \approx n/2$. As a consequence we have:

Corollary 3.1. *In every row of the infinite triangle $(F_{n,k})_{n,k\in N}$ the values are decreasing for increasing k.*

The row sums of the triangle are easily found:

Theorem 3.4. *For the row sums of the triangle $(F_{n,k})_{n,k\in N}$ we have* $\sum_{k=1}^{n} F_{n,k} = n! - D_n$.

Proof. A permutation is a derangement or has some fixed point; therefore $n! = D_n + \sum_{k=1}^{n} F_{n,k}$.   □

As we established in the previous section, we need the weighted row sums $S_n = \sum_{k=1}^{n} kF_{n,k}$. Table 2 illustrates the triangle $(kF_{n,k})_{n,k\in N}$.

Theorem 3.5. *If S_n are the row sums of the triangle of Table 2, we have:*

$$S_n = (n+1)!\sum_{j=2}^{n+1} \frac{(-1)^j(j-1)}{j!}.$$

Table 2. The weighted version of Table 1

n/k	1	2	3	4	5	6	7
1	1						
2	1	0					
3	2	2	3				
4	6	8	9	8			
5	24	36	42	44	45		
6	120	192	234	256	265	264	
7	720	1200	1512	1704	1810	1854	1855

Proof. Let $S_n = \sum_{k=1}^{n} k F_{n,k}$; by (4) and changing the order of summation:

$$S_{n+1} = \sum_{k=0}^{n}(k+1)\sum_{j=0}^{k}(-1)^j \binom{k}{j}(n-j)! = \sum_{j=0}^{n}(-1)^j(n-j)!\sum_{k=j}^{n}(k+1)\binom{k}{j}.$$

The internal sum is easy (see, e.g., [6, Formula (5.10)]):

$$\sum_{k=j}^{n}(k+1)\binom{k}{j} = (j+1)\sum_{k=j}^{n}\binom{k+1}{j+1} = (j+1)\binom{n+2}{j+2}.$$

Therefore we have:

$$S_{n+1} = \sum_{j=0}^{n}(-1)^j(n-j)!(j+1)\binom{n+2}{j+2} = (n+2)!\sum_{j=0}^{n}\frac{(-1)^j(j+1)}{(j+2)!}$$

and the statement of the theorem follows immediately. ☐

To find the average number of calls to `random`, by Theorem 2.4, we need the preceding row sums with a certain precision:

Theorem 3.6. *The asymptotic value of the row sums S_n is:*

$$S_n = \frac{e-2}{e}(n+1)! + (-1)^{n+1} - \frac{2(-1)^{n+1}}{n+2} + O\left(\frac{1}{n^2}\cdot\right) \qquad (5)$$

Proof. The development is rather standard:

$$S_n = (n+1)!\sum_{k=2}^{n+1}\frac{(-1)^k(k-1)}{k!} = (n+1)!\left(\sum_{k=1}^{n}\frac{(-1)^{k+1}}{k!} - \sum_{k=2}^{n+1}\frac{(-1)^k}{k!}\right).$$

Now we have:

$$\sum_{k=1}^{n}\frac{(-1)^{k+1}}{k!} = \left(1-\frac{1}{e}\right) + \frac{(-1)^{n+1}}{(n+1)!} + \frac{(-1)^{n+2}}{(n+2)!} + \cdots$$

$$\sum_{k=2}^{n+1}\frac{(-1)^k}{k!} = \left(1-1+\frac{1}{e}\right) + \frac{(-1)^{n+2}}{(n+2)!} + \cdots$$

$$S_n \approx (n+1)! \left(\frac{e-1}{e} + \frac{(-1)^{n+1}}{(n+1)!} + \frac{(-1)^{n+2}}{(n+2)!} + \cdots - \frac{1}{e} + \frac{(-1)^{n+2}}{(n+2)!} + \cdots \right)$$

and this is equivalent to the formula in the assert.   □

For the sake of completeness, we give a recurrence for $(S_n)_{n \in N}$:

Theorem 3.7. *The sequence $(S_n)_{n \in N}$ is defined by the initial condition $S_0 = 0$ and the recurrence relation $S_{n+1} = (n+2)S_n + (n+1)(-1)^n$, or, by the exponential generating function: $S(t) = (1 - e^{-t} - t^2 e^{-t})/(1-t)^2$.*

Proof. Let us consider Theorem 3.5 for S_{n+1}:

$$S_{n+1} = (n+2)\left((n+1)! \sum_{j=2}^{n+1} \frac{(-1)^j (j-1)}{j!} \right) + \frac{(n+2)!(-1)^n(n+1)}{(n+2)!}.$$

This is equivalent to the recurrence relation in the assert; by transforming it in terms of the exponential generating function $S(t) = \sum_{n \geq 0} S_n t^n / n!$ we obtain the differential equation: $S'(t) = tS'(t) + 2S(t) - te^{-t} + e^{-t}$, which corresponds to the function in the statement of the theorem.   □

4. Mean and Variance

We begin to compute the pieces appearing in the formula of Theorem 2.4:

Theorem 4.1. *The approximate value of p_n/p_0 is:*

$$\frac{p_n}{p_0} = \frac{D_{n-1}}{D_n} = \frac{1}{n} - \frac{(-1)^n}{n \cdot n!} + \cdots = \frac{1}{n}\left(1 - \frac{e(-1)^n}{n!} + \cdots \right).$$

Proof. We use the approximate value for D_n found in Theorem 2.1:

$$\frac{D_{n-1}}{D_n} = \frac{(n-1)!}{e}\left(1 - \frac{e(-1)^n}{n!} + \cdots \right) \cdot \frac{e}{n!}\left(1 + \frac{e(-1)^{n+1}}{(n+1)!} + \cdots \right) =$$

$$= \frac{1}{n}\left(1 - \frac{e(-1)^n}{n!} + \frac{e(-1)^{n+1}}{(n+1)!} + \cdots \right) = \frac{1}{n}\left(1 - \frac{e(-1)^n}{n!} + O\left(\frac{1}{(n+1)!} \right) \right)$$

as desired.   □

By using (2) and (5) we compute $(\sum_k kp_k)/p_0 = S_n/D_n$:

Theorem 4.2. *We have the following approximate value:*

$$\frac{\sum_k kp_k}{p_0} = (e-2)(n+1)\left(1 + \frac{e(e-1)}{e-2}\frac{(-1)^{n+1}}{(n+1)!} + \frac{e(e-1)}{e-2}\frac{(-1)^{n+2}}{(n+2)!} + \cdots \right).$$

Consequently, by taking the principal values, we find our main result:

Theorem 4.3. *The average number of calls to* random *performed by procedure* generate2 *is* $\mu_2 = (e - 1)(n - 1) + 2(e - 2) - \frac{1}{n} + O(n^{-n})$.

In order to compute the variance, since $(\sum_k k^2 p_k)/p_0$ is equal to $(\sum_k k^2 F_{n,k})/D_n$, we need the following result:

Theorem 4.4. *We have:*

$$\sum_{k=1}^{n} k^2 F_{n,k} = (n + 2)! \sum_{k=0}^{n-1} \frac{(-1)^k (k + 2)(k + 1)}{(k + 3)!} - (n + 1)! \sum_{k=0}^{n-1} \frac{(-1)^k (k + 1)}{(k + 2)!}$$

and, consequently, $\sum_{k=1}^{n} k^2 F_{n,k} \approx \frac{2e-5}{e}(n + 2)! - \frac{e-2}{e}(n + 1)!$.

Proof. By considering $n + 1$ and by changing the order of summation in $\sum_{k=0}^{n} (k + 1)^2 \sum_{j=0}^{k} (-1)^j \binom{k}{j} (n - j)!$ we obtain:

$$\sum_{j=0}^{n} \left(\frac{(-1)^j (n + 3)!(j + 2)(j + 1)}{(j + 3)!} - \frac{(-1)^j (n + 2)!(j + 1)}{(j + 2)!} \right);$$

at this point, it is sufficient to change $j \rightsquigarrow k$. By Theorems 3.5 and 4.2 the second sum is $\sum_k k F_{n,k} \approx (e - 2)(n + 1)!/e$, while for the first sum we have:

$$\sum_{k=0}^{n-1} \frac{(-1)^k (k + 2)(k + 1)}{(k + 3)!} = \sum_{k=0}^{n-1} (-1)^k \frac{(k + 3)(k + 2) - 2(k + 3) + 2}{(k + 3)!} =$$

$$= \sum_{k=0}^{n-1} \frac{(-1)^k}{(k + 1)!} - 2 \sum_{k=0}^{n-1} \frac{(-1)^k}{(k + 2)!} + 2 \sum_{k=0}^{n-1} \frac{(-1)^k}{(k + 3)!}.$$

In order to obtain the principal value, we extend these sums to infinity:

$$\sum_{k=0}^{n-1} \frac{(-1)^k}{(k + 1)!} \approx 1 - \frac{1}{e}, \quad \sum_{k=0}^{n-1} \frac{(-1)^k}{(k + 2)!} \approx \frac{1}{e}, \quad \sum_{k=0}^{n-1} \frac{(-1)^k}{(k + 3)!} \approx \frac{1}{2} - \frac{1}{e}.$$

By summing, we have $\left(1 - \frac{1}{e}\right) - 2 \cdot \frac{1}{e} + 2 \cdot \left(\frac{1}{2} - \frac{1}{e}\right) = 2 - \frac{5}{e} = \frac{2e-5}{e}$. $\qquad \square$

We are now in a position to compute the principal value of the variance:

Theorem 4.5. *For the variance relative to the procedure* generate2 *we have:*
$\sigma_2^2 \approx (e^2 - 2e - 1)(n - 1)^2 + (4e^2 - 7e - 7)(n - 1) + (4e^2 - 8e - 4)$.

Proof. Let us develop the various terms in the formula of Theorem 2.4:

$$\left(\frac{1}{p_0} \sum_k k p_k\right)^2 \approx (e-2)^2 (n+1)^2;$$

$$\frac{1}{p_0} \sum_k k^2 p_k \approx (2e-5)(n+2)(n+1) - (e-2)(n+1);$$

$$-2 \cdot \frac{p_n}{p_0^2} \sum_k k p_k \approx -2 \cdot \frac{(n-1)!}{e} \cdot \frac{e^2}{n!^2} \cdot \frac{e-2}{e} \cdot (n+1)! \approx -2(e-2);$$

$$\frac{p_n^2}{p_0^2} \approx \frac{1}{n^2}; \qquad (2n-1) \cdot \frac{p_n}{p_0} \approx \frac{2n-1}{n} \approx 2.$$

Putting all these contributions together we obtain the assert.   □

Acknowledgements

We wish to thank the referees for their helpful comments.

Bibliography

1. E. Barcucci, R. Pinzani, and R. Sprugnoli. The random generation of directed animals. *Theor. Comp. Sci*, 127(2):333–350, 1994.
2. J. D. H. Dickson. Discussion of two double series arising from the number of terms in determinants of certain forms. *Proc. London Math. Soc.*, 10:120–122, 1879.
3. L. Euler. Solutio quaestionis curiosae ex doctrina combinationum. *Opera Omnia*, 7(1):435–440, 1779.
4. P. Flajolet and R. Sedgewick. *Analytic combinatorics.* http://algo.inria.fr/ flajolet/Publications/books.html.
5. Ph. Flajolet, P. Zimmermann, and B. Van Cutsem. A calculus for the random generation of combinatorial structures. *Theor. Comp. Sci*, 132:1–35, 1994.
6. R. L. Graham, D. E. Knuth, and O. Patashnik. *Concrete Mathematics.* Addison-Wesley, New York, 1989.
7. D. Hanson, K. Seyffarth, and J. H. Weston. Matchings, derangements, rencontres. *Math. Magazine*, 56:224–229, 1983.
8. D. E. Knuth. *The art of computer programming.* Addison-Wesley, 1973.
9. F. Ruskey. The Combinatorial Object Server. http://www.theory.csc.uvic. ca/~cos/.
10. R. Sedgewick and P. Flajolet. *An Introduction to the Analysis of Algorithms.* Addison-Wesley, Reading, MA, 1996.
11. N. Sloane. On-line Encyclopedia of Integer Sequences. http://www.research. att.com/~njas/sequences.

THE MEASURE HYPOTHESIS AND EFFICIENCY OF POLYNOMIAL TIME APPROXIMATION SCHEMES

M. HAUPTMANN

Institute of Computer Science, University of Bonn,
53117 Bonn, Germany E-mail: hauptman@cs.uni-bonn.de

A polyomial time approximation scheme for an optimization problem X is an algorithm $\mathcal{A}$ such that for each instance x of X and each $\epsilon > 0$, $\mathcal{A}$ computes a $(1 + \epsilon)$-approximate solution to instance x of X in time is $O(|x|^{f(1/\epsilon)})$ for some function f. If the running time of $\mathcal{A}$ is instead bounded by $g(1/\epsilon) \cdot |x|^{O(1)}$ for some function g, $\mathcal{A}$ is called an efficient polynomial time approximation scheme. $PTAS$ denotes the class of all NP optimization problems for which a polytime approximation scheme exists, and $EPTAS$ is the class of all such problems for which an efficient polytime approximation scheme exists. It is an open question whether $P \neq NP$ implies the strictness of the inclusion $EPTAS \subseteq PTAS$. Bazgan [2] and independently Cesati and Trevisan [5] gave a separation under the stronger assumption $FPT \neq W[P]$. In this paper we prove $EPTAS \subsetneq PTAS$ under some different assumption, namely existence of NP search problems Π_R with a superpolynomial lower bound for the deterministic time complexity. This assumption is weaker than the NP Machine Hypothesis [13] and hence is implied by the Measure Hypothesis $\mu_p(NP) \neq 0$. Furthermore, using a sophisticated combinatorial counting argument we construct a recursive oracle under which our assumption holds but that of Cesati and Trevisan does not hold, implying that using relativizing proof techniques one cannot show that our assumption implies $FPT \neq W[P]$.

Keywords: Polynomial Time Approximation Schemes; PTAS versus EPTAS; Structural Complexity; Fixed Parameter Complexity.

1. Introduction

A polynomial time approximation scheme for an optimization problem X is an algorithm A such that for every instance x of X and every $\epsilon > 0$, A returns a $(1 + \epsilon)$-approximative solution $y = A(x, \epsilon)$ in time $O(|x|^{f(1/\epsilon)})$ for some function f. If instead the running time can be bounded by $O(g(1/\epsilon) \cdot |x|^c)$ for some constant c and some function g, algorithm A is called an *efficient polynomial time approximation scheme* (eptas).

NPO denotes the class of all NP optimization problems, $PTAS$ the class of all problems $X \in NPO$ that admit a polynomial time approximation scheme (ptas) and $EPTAS$ all problems in NPO that admit an efficient ptas. Obviously,

$EPTAS \subseteq PTAS$. It is an open problem whether the strictness of this inclusion follows from $P \neq NP$.

Cesati and Trevisan [5] and independently Bazgan [2] separate these two classes under the stronger assumption $W[P] \neq FPT$ from Fixed Parameter Complexity. Indeed, they showed the following chain of implications:

$$W[P] \neq FPT \implies EPTAS \neq PTAS \implies FPT \neq XP.$$

Here $FPT \subseteq W[P] \subseteq XP$ are classes of the W-hierarchy introduced by Downey and Fellows [7]. For further details we refer to [8] and to [10]. The assumption $FPT \neq W[P]$ was characterized in terms of bounded nondeterminism properties of NP search problems by Cai and Chen [4]. Cai and Chen [4] proved that $FPT \neq W[P]$ iff for each unbounded polynomial-time computable function $s: \mathbb{N} \to \mathbb{N}$, $NP[s(n)\log(n)] \not\subseteq P$, where $NP[f(n)]$ denotes the class of NP problems that can be solved in polynomial time with $O(f(n))$ nondeterministic steps.

We obtain the following results. We separate $PTAS$ from $EPTAS$ under some different assumption, namely existence of an NP search problem Π_R (where R denotes some polynomially balanced, polynomial-time decidable binary relation) and a superpolynomial function $t(n)$ such that Π_R is not solvable in time $O(t(n))$. Under this assumption which we simply call *Assumption (A)*, we construct for each strictly monotone recursive function f an NP optimization U_f such that U_f admits a polynomial time approximation scheme with running time $O(|x|^{f(1/\epsilon)})$ and such that $U_f \notin EPTAS$.

Let us point out some connections to the Quantitative Complexity Theory. *Assumption (A)* is a direct implication of the *NP Machine Hypothesis*, which states the existence of an NP machine accepting 0^* such that no 2^{n^ϵ}-time bounded machine can find infinitely many accepting computations. Jack Lutz defined polynomial measure μ_p [15] and p-dimension $\dim_p$ [16] as generalizations of the classical Lebesgue measure and the Hausdorff dimension. Scaled dimension was introduced by Hitchcock, Lutz and Mayordomo [12]. It was shown by Hitchcock and Pavan [13] that the Measure Hypothesis implies the NP Machine Hypothesis. On the other hand, results from Hitchcock ([11], Theorem 5.2) directly imply that *assumption (A)* already follows from the assumption that for some $i \in \mathbb{Z}$, $\dim_p^{(i)}(NP) = 1$. Here $\dim_p^{(i)}$ denotes the i-th order scaled dimension as introduced by Hitchcock, Lutz and Mayordomo [12].

Furthermore, we construct an oracle X relative to which *assumption (A)* holds but the assumption of Cai and Chen [4] fails. Hence there is no relativizing proof that our assumption implies $FPT \neq W[P]$. The oracle construction involves a sophisticated combinatorial counting argument which is based on ideas from

Beigel and Goldsmith [3].

The paper is organized as follows. Preliminaries are given in the next section. In section 3 we separate EPTAS from PTAS under *assumption (A)* stated above. In Section 4 we construct an oracle relative to which assumption (A) holds but $FPT \neq W[P]$ fails.

2. Preliminaries

Let $\Sigma = \{0,1\}$. A binary relation $R \subseteq \Sigma^* \times \Sigma^*$ is called $f(n)$-balanced if for each $(x,y) \in R$, $|y| \leq f(|x|)$. For such a relation R, let $L_R = \{x \in \Sigma^* \mid \exists\, y \in \Sigma^*\ (x,y) \in R\}$ be the projection of R to the first component. NP can be characterized as the set of all $L \subseteq \Sigma^*$ such that there exists a polynomially balanced polynomial-time decidable relation $R \subseteq \Sigma^* \times \Sigma^*$ with $L_R = L$.

Given such a relation R, Π_R denotes the associated *NP search problem*: Given some $x \in \Sigma^*$, either compute some string π such that $(x,\pi) \in R$ or return "NO" in case no such π exists. $NP[f(n)]$ denotes the class of all NP problems that are solvable in polynomial time with $O(f(n))$ nondeterministic steps - equivalently: the class of all problems L_R such that R is a polynomial-time decidable, $O(f(n))$-balanced binary relation. Especially, $\beta_k := NP[\log^k(n)] := GC(\log^k(n))$ ($k \in \mathbb{N}$) are the levels of the Kintala-Fischer hierarchy [14] which is also called the β-hierarchy. The possibility of downward separation within this hierarchy was invented by Beigel and Goldsmith [3], who proved that using relativizing proof techniques one cannot obtain any strictness result for this hierarchy.

NPO denotes the class of *NP optimization problems*. For the precise definition we refer to [1]. If $X \in NPO$, we call X an *NPO problem*.

3. Separating $PTAS$ from $EPTAS$

In this section we will prove $EPTAS \subsetneq PTAS$ under the following assumption.

Assumption (A): There is a language $L \in NP \setminus P$ and a polynomially bounded binary relation $R \subseteq \Sigma^* \times \Sigma^*$ with $L = L_R$ such that $\Pi_R \in DTIME(T(n)) \setminus DTIME(t(n))$ for two polynomial time computable superpolynomial functions $t(n), T(n)$ such that $t(n)^2 = O(T(n))$.

Here a function $f(n)$ is called *superpolynomial* if for each $c > 0$, $f(n) = \omega(n^c)$. Concerning polynomial-time approximation schemes, their running times are bounded by $O(|x|^{f(\epsilon)})$, where x denotes the instance and ϵ the accuracy parameter.

Our main result is stated in the following theorem.

Theorem 3.1. *Under assumption (A), for every strictly monotone recursive function* $f \colon \mathbb{N} \to \mathbb{N}$ *with* $f(1) = 1$ *there is an NPO problem* U_f *such that*

(1) U_f *has a ptas with running time* $O(|x|^{f(1/\epsilon)+1})$.

(2) *For every monotone increasing function* $g \colon \mathbb{N} \to \mathbb{N}$ *and every* $\alpha > 0$, U_f *does not have a ptas with running time* $g(1/\epsilon) \cdot |x|^{\alpha}$.

In particular, this implies $EPTAS \neq PTAS$.

In order to prove Theorem 3.1 we will first define a family of NPO problems $U_n, n \in \mathbb{N}$ and then construct U_f in stages in terms of problems U_n, such that in stage n we diagonalize against the first n Turing machines being efficient approximation schemes for problem U_f. The crucial point will be that although problems U_n will be approximable with better and better ratio (with n increasing), for every fixed $\epsilon > 0$ the time complexity of approximation within $1 + \epsilon$ will stay the same.

We will use the following convenntions. First, we only consider accuracy parameters $\epsilon = 1 + \frac{1}{n}, n \in \mathbb{N}$. In this sense, problem U_f will have a ptas with running time $O(|x|^{f(n)})$ for $\epsilon = 1/n$, but there exists no ptas with running time $g(n) \cdot |x|^{\alpha}$ for U_f. Second, we will consider binary relations $R \subseteq \Sigma^* \times \Sigma^*$ equivalently as functions $R \colon \Sigma^* \times \Sigma^* \to \{0, 1\}$ (where $R(x, y) = 1$ means $(x, y) \in R$).

Let $f \colon \mathbb{N} \to \mathbb{N}$ be some monotone increasing recursive function as above such that $f(1) = 1$. Let $A \subseteq \Sigma^*$ be some problem in NP, T_A some deterministic TM and p_A some polynomial such that

(1) For all $x \in \Sigma^*$, $x \in A$ iff there is some string π of length $|\pi| \leq p_A(|x|)$ such that $T_A(x, \pi)$ accepts in time $p_A(|x|)$.

(2) For $R = \{(x, \pi) \mid T_A(x, \pi)$ accepts$\}$, the associated NP search problem Π_R is solvable in time $T(n)$ but not in time $t(n)$.

We define a family $U_n, n \in \mathbb{N}$ of optimization problems as follows:

Definition of U_n**:**

Instances of U_n: $X = (x_1, \ldots, x_n, 0^k)$ such that $k \geq 1, x_1, \ldots, x_n \in \Sigma^*$ and

$$t(|x_j|) \leq |X|^{f(2^j)}, \quad j = 1, \ldots, n - 1. \tag{1}$$

Solutions: $\pi = (\pi_1, \ldots, \pi_n)$ with $\pi_j \in \Sigma^*$, $|\pi_j| \leq p_A(|x_j|), j = 1, \ldots, n$

Costs: $\quad c_n(X, \pi) = 2^n + \sum_{i=1}^{n} R(x_i, \pi_i) \cdot 2^{n-i} \in \left[2^n, 2^n + 2^{n+1} - 1\right].$

End of definition.

Here 0^k serves as a padding string, and $T_A(x_i, \pi_i) \in \{0, 1\}$ denotes the result of computation of machine T_A on input x_i, π_i (1 for accept, 0 for reject). The main properties of problems U_n are stated in the next two lemmas.

Lemma 3.1. *For all* $n \in \mathbb{N}$ U_n *is an NPO problem. There exists a two-variate polynomial* $q(x, y)$ *such that for all* $n \in \mathbb{N}$ U_n *is* $q(x, t_f(n))$- *time bounded, where* $t_f(n)$ *is a function such that* f *is computable in time* $t_f(n)$.

Lemma 3.2. *Under Assumption (A), problem* U_n *has the following properties.*

(1) For $j = 1, \ldots n-1$ *there is a* $\left(1 + 2^{-j}\right)$-*approximation algorithm for* U_n *with running time* $|x_1| + |x_2|^{f\left(2^2\right)} + \ldots + |x_j|^{f\left(2^j\right)} \leq n \cdot |X|^{f\left(2^j\right)} = O\left(|X|^{f\left(2^j\right)}\right)$ *(n being fixed).*

(2) For $j = 1, \ldots, n - 1$, *every approximation algorithm* $\mathcal{B}$ *for* U_n *with running time* $o\left(|X|^{f\left(2^j\right)}\right)$ *has approximation ratio at least* $1 + 2^{-(j+2)}$.

(3) There is no polynomial time approximation algorithm for U_n *with ratio better than* $1 + 2^{-(n+2)}$.

Proof. This follows from the construction of U_n, using the fact that the NP search problem Π_R cannot be solved deterministically in time $t(n)$. □

Proof of Theorem 3.1:. We will construct an NPO problem U_f in stages, using a monotone increasing sequence of strings $x_0, x_1, \ldots, x_n, \ldots$. U_f restricted to the n-th interval $I_n := [x_{n-1}, x_n)$ will be equal to U_n. Let $(T_i, c_i, \alpha_i), i \in \mathbb{N}$ be some effective enumeration of triples (T_i, c_i, α_i) where T_i is a Turing machine, $c_i > 0$ some constant and $\alpha_i \in \mathbb{N}$ such that every such triple (T, c, α) occurs infinitely often. We will construct $x_1, \ldots, x_n, \ldots$ such that for every $n \in \mathbb{N}$ the following requirement (C_n) is satisfied:

(C_n) For $j = 1, \ldots, n$ both (a) and (b) hold.

   (a) For $m = 1, \ldots, n - 1$: If $f(2^m) \geq \alpha_j + 1/n$ then there exists some $y_{j,m} \in I_n$ such that $T_j(y_{j,m}, 2^{m+3})$ is not a $(1 + 2^{-(m+3)})$-approximate solution to instance $y_{j,m}$ of U_f in time bounded by $c_j \cdot |y_{j,m}|^{\alpha_j}$.

   (b) There is some $z_j \in I_n$ such that $T_j(z_j, 2^{n+3})$ is not a $(1 + 2^{-(n+3)})$-approximate solution to instance z_j of U_f in time $c_j \cdot |z_j|^{\alpha_j}$.

Construction of U_f:
Stage 0: $x_0 := 0$.

Stage $n > 0$: Compute $f(2^1), \ldots, f(2^n), f(2^{n+1})$. By Brute Force find the lexicographically first strings $y_{j,m}, j = 1, \ldots, n, m \in \{1, \ldots, n-1\}$ with $f(2^m) \geq \alpha_j + 1$ and z_j with $y_{j,m}, z_j \geq x_{n-1}$ such that (C_n) becomes true. Such pairs exist because of properties 2 and 3 from Lemma 3.2. Let t_n be the time needed to compute $f(j), 1 \leq j \leq n$ and to find strings $y_{j,m}$ and z_j. Let $x_n := 0^{t_n+1}$ and $U_f | I_n := U_n$.
End of construction.

U_f *is an NPO problem:* There is a linear time algorithm to compute for given $x \in \Sigma^*$ the number $n \in \mathbb{N}$ such that $x \in I_n$, by computing the number $n - 1$ in at most $|x|$ steps. Since in stage $n - 1$ we compute $f(n), |x| \geq t_f(n)$, and therefore using Lemma 3.1 we conclude that U_f is bounded by some polynomial $p(|x|)$ and hence an NPO problem.

U_f *admits a polynomial time approximation scheme:* For given x and n, in order to compute a $(1 + 1/n)$-approximate solution to instance x of U_f we first compute the number $m \in \mathbb{N}$ with $x \in I_m$. If $2^{m-1} \geq n$ we compute a $(1 + 2^{-j})$-approximate solution for $j = \lceil \log(n) \rceil$ in time $|x|^{f(2^j)} \cdot m \leq |x|^{f(2^j)+1}$. Otherwise we compute an optimum solution y^* to instance x by brute force. Since $2^{m-1} < n$ for only finite many m (and therefore finite many x) and $2^{\lceil \log(n) \rceil} < 2n$, the running time is bounded by $O\left(|x|^{f(2n)+1}\right)$ and hence by $O\left(|x|^{f(2n)+1}\right)$.

$U_f \notin EPTAS$: Assume U_f admits a ptas T with running time $g(n) \cdot |x|^\alpha$ for some function g and some constant α. Then for every $n \in \mathbb{N}$ there exists some $i \in \mathbb{N}$ such that $T_i = T, \alpha_i = \alpha$ and $c_i = g(n)$. But for $m \geq n + 3$, in I_m there exist $y \in I_m$ such that either $T_i(y, 2^m)$ is not a $(1 + 2^{-m})$-approximate solution for instance y of U_f or $T_i(y, 2^m)$ does not stop after at most $c_i \cdot |y|^{\alpha_i}$ steps, a contradiction ! This proves the claim and hence Theorem 3.1. □

4. Oracle Constructions

We will now construct an oracle X relative to which Assumption (A) holds but $FPT \neq W[P]$ doesn't. Recall that in [4] $FPT \neq W[P]$ was shown being equivalent to

Assumption (B) For every unbounded polynomial-time computable function $s: \mathbb{N} \to \mathbb{N}$, $NP[s(n) \log(n)] \not\subseteq P$.

We start by defining the appropriate relativized classes.

Definition 4.1. For $X \subseteq \Sigma^*$ and $f: \mathbb{N} \to \mathbb{N}$,

$$NP^X[f(n)] := \{L \subseteq \Sigma^* | \text{there exists an } O(f(n))\text{-balanced binary relation}$$
$$R \subseteq \Sigma^* \times \Sigma^* \text{ such that } L = L_R \text{ and } R \in P^X\}$$

It is easy to construct an oracle making assumption (B) false, namely by taking a sufficiently powerful oracle.

Theorem 4.1. *For every polynomial-time computable unbounded function $s(n)$ there exists a recursive set $X \subseteq \Sigma^*$ such that $NP^X[s(n)\log(n)] \subseteq P^X$.*

Proof. Let X be some $DTIME\left(n^{O(s(n))}\right)$-complete set, then the inclusion obviously holds. For a precise argument (yielding a slightly more general result) see the proof of Lemma 4.1 below. □

In order to construct an *oracle relative to which assumption (B) becomes true*, one needs to diagonalize against polynomially bounded oracle machines accepting inputs (x, y) with $|y|$ bounded by $s(|x|)\log(|x|)$ for some nonconstant polytime computable function $s(n)$. We can enumerate polynomially bounded TMs M_i computing functions $s_i(n)$, but by no means we know in advance which of these functions is bounded. Hence we will guess $s_i(n)$ being bounded by some constant C, and if this guess was incorrect, then we will observe the incorrectness after finite amount of time, namely find some n such that $s_i(n) > C$. We perform such a guessing process, and each time a violation occurs, we increase the constant C and perform one diagonalization step against $NP^X[s_i(n)\log(n)]$ being equal to P^X. We obtain:

Theorem 4.2. *(An Oracle relative to which Assumption (B) holds)*
There existst some recursive set $X \subseteq \Sigma^*$ such that for every unbounded polynomial-time computable function $s(n)$, $NP^X[s(n)\log(n)] \not\subseteq P^X$.

We will now separate assumptions (A) and (B) by an oracle construction.

Theorem 4.3. *(An Oracle relative to which (A) is true but (B) is false)* *There exists a recursive set $X \subseteq \Sigma^*$ such that (1) and (2) hold.*

(1) $NP^X[\log^2(x)] \subseteq P^X$
(2) For the relation $R_X := \{(x, y)|x = 0^n, n \in \mathbb{N}, |y| = 2n, y \in X\}$,

$$\Pi_{R_X} \in DTIME^X\left(2^{n^3}\right) \setminus DTIME^X\left(2^n\right).$$

Proof Idea: Let $\tilde{X}$ be some $DTIME\left(n^{O(\log n)}\right)$-complete problem with respect to polynomial-time Karp reductions. Then $X' := \{1xx|x \in \tilde{X}\}$ is $DTIME\left(n^{O(\log n)}\right)$-complete as well. We let $X = X' \cup X''$ where X'' consists of strings of even length only. We use X'' for a diagonalization process in order to assure (2).

The following two lemmas indicate how powerful the set may be in order to make (1) become true.

Lemma 4.1.
For every $DTIME\left(n^{O(\log n)}\right)$-complete problem Y, $NP^Y[\log^2(n)] \subseteq P^Y$.

Proof. Let R be $c \cdot \log^2(n)$ - balanced for some $c > 0$ with $R \in P^Y$. Let $R = L(M, Y)$ for some polytime bounded oracle machine M. We have to show that $\Pi_R \in FTIME^Y\left(n^{O(1)}\right)$. For input x of length n there are less than $n \cdot 2^{c \cdot \log^2(n)} = n \cdot n^{c \cdot \log(n)} = n^{O(\log(n))}$ strings of length bounded by $c \cdot \log^2(n)$, hence a straight forward algorithm will enumerate all such strings and for each of them ask the question to oracle machine M with oracle Y. The running time of this oracle algorithm is bounded by

$$\underbrace{p(n + c \cdot \log^2(n))}_{\text{running time of } M} \cdot \underbrace{n^{O(\log(n))}}_{\sharp\text{strings of that length}} = n^{O(\log(n))},$$

If we replace the oracle questions by calls of a $n^{O(\log(n))}$-time bounded algorithm M_Y for Y, the total running time can be bounded by

$$n^{O(\log(n))} \cdot \underbrace{q(n)^{O(\log(q(n)))}}_{\text{time for one call of } M_Y} = n^{O(\log(n))}$$

where $q(n) := p(n + c \cdot \log^2(n))$ is polynomially bounded. Hence we can reduce this problem to Y (Y is $DTIME(n^{O(\log(n))})$- complete) and obtain $L \in P^Y$. $\square$

Lemma 4.2. For every $DTIME\left(n^{O(\log n)}\right)$-hard problem Y which is complete for a class $\mathcal{C}$ of languages such that $DTIME(t(n)) \subseteq \mathcal{C}$ implies $DTIME\left(n^{O(\log(n))} \cdot t\left(n^{O(1)}\right)\right) \subseteq \mathcal{C}$, $NP^Y[\log^2(n)] \subseteq P^Y$.

Proof. Let $L \in NP^Y[\log^2(n)]$ and $Y \in DTIME(t(n))$. We perform the complete-enumeration oracle algorithm as in the previous proof and obtain a running time bounded by

$$\underbrace{n^{O(\log(n))}}_{\sharp \text{ strings to be enum.}} \cdot \underbrace{p(n + c \cdot \log^2(n))}_{\text{single call of the Oracle TM for } L} \cdot \underbrace{t(p(n + c \cdot \log^2(n)))}_{\text{solving one instance of } Y}$$

which is bounded by $n^{O(\log(n))} \cdot t(n^{O(1)})$. Hence $L \in \mathcal{C}$, and L is polynomial-time reducible to Y, therefore $L \in P^Y$. $\square$

Now if we take an arbitrary set $X'' \subseteq \bigcup_{n \in \mathbb{N}} \Sigma^{2n}$ which is complete for such a class $\mathcal{C}$, the disjoint union $X := X' \cup X''$ still satisfies the conditions in Lemma 4.2, hence condition (1) from Theorem 4.3 will still hold.

Proof of Theorem 4.3. Let $X = X' \cup X''$ where X' consists of odd-length strings only and X'' consists of even-length strings only. We choose

$$C^X := \{(i, x, 0^s) | M_i \text{ on input } x \text{ with oracle } X \text{ accepts within } s \text{ steps}$$
$$\text{and } O(\log^2(n)) \text{ nondeterministic steps} \}.$$

Then C^X is $\leq_m^p$-complete for $NP^X[\log^2(n)]$. Let $p(n)$ be a polynomial such that $C^X \in NTIME[\log^2(n)](p(n))$ (i.e. solvable in time $p(n)$ with $O(\log^2(n))$ nondeterministic steps). We will encode C^X into X' in a polynomial manner and use X'' for diagonalisation in order to assure (2). The encoding will be as follows: For all strings $x \in \Sigma^*$,

$$x \in C^X \iff 1^{p(|x|)^2} 0 \, x \in X.$$

We are now ready to construct X. Let $M_1, \ldots, M_n, \ldots$ denote an enumeration of $O(2^n)$-time bounded Oracle machines such that without loss of generality M_i is $i \cdot 2^n$ - time bounded.

Construction of X in stages

```
/* At the end of stage s X is defined up to        */
/* strings of length n_s. During stage s diagonalization */
/* against L(M_i) = L_X is performed by choosing    */
/* n > n_{s-1} and assuring 0^n ∈ L(M - i)ΔL_X      */
```

Stage 0: $n_0 := 0, \quad X := \emptyset$

Stage $s > 0$:
/* X is defined up to length n_{s-1} */
Choose $n > n_s$ to be a power of 2 and sufficiently large.
Define X up to length $l := n^3 - 1$.
Define C^X up to strings y with $p(|y|)^2 + 1 + |y| \leq n^3 - 1$.

/* $L_X(1^n)$ depends on strings of length n^3. */

Compute $M_s(1^n, X)$.

If $M_s(1^n, X)$ accepts then
    Let y be a **legal** string of length n^3.
    $X := X \cup \{y\}$.

$n_s := \max\{l, s \cdot 2^n\}$

Freeze X up to length n_s.

Freeze C^X up to strings of length m with $p(m)^2 + 1 + m \leq n_s$.

End of Stage s.

It remains to define which strings y of length n^3 are **legal** and what it means to choose n **sufficiently large**. The initial idea is simply to pick a string y which was not asked by the computation $M_s(x, X)$. Such string of length n^3 exists since M_i has running time bounded by $s \cdot 2^n$ and there are 2^{n^3} strings of length n^3 available (we choose n such that $s \cdot 2^n < 2^{n^3}$). The problem is that the encoding of C^X into X may depend on this choice, and the result of $M_s(x, X)$ may in turn depend on this coding and so on.

We accomplish this difficulty by using an approach from Beigel and Goldberg: We show that due to the way the coding of C^X into X is arranged, there are more strings of length n^3 available than are influencing the coding of C^X into X in the range up to length $s \cdot 2^n$:

$M_s(x, X)$ has running time bounded by $s \cdot 2^n$ and therefore may ask at most $s \cdot 2^n$ oracle questions about strings of length bounded by $s \cdot 2^n$.

Due to the encoding, these strings may encode strings from C^X of length bounded by $\sqrt{s \cdot 2^n} = \sqrt{s} \cdot 2^{n/2}$. Each of these encoding strings w in turn may depend on at most

$$p(|w|) \cdot 2^{\log^2(|w|)} = p\left(s^{2^{-1}} \cdot 2^{n/2^1}\right) \cdot 2^{\log^2\left(s^{2^{-1}} \cdot 2^{n/2^1}\right)}$$

strings of this smaller length and so on.

Since X is already fixed up to length $l - 1$, the recursion can be cut off at strings of length $\leq l - 1$. Therefore the number of such terms is bounded by

$$\log \log(s \cdot 2^n) - \log \log(l-1) \leq \log(\log s + n) - \log \log(n) \leq c \cdot \log(n) = \Theta(\log(n))$$

for some constant $c > 0$. Hence the total number of strings being influenced by the choice of y is bounded by

$$s \cdot 2^n \cdot \prod_{i \leq c \cdot \log(n)} p\left(s^{2^{-i}} \cdot 2^{n/2^i}\right) \cdot 2^{\log^2\left(s^{2^{-i}} \cdot 2^{n/2^i}\right)}$$

$$= s \cdot 2^n \cdot \prod_{i \leq c \cdot \log(n)} \left(s^{2^{-i}} \cdot 2^{n/2^i}\right)^{O(1)} \cdot 2^{\log^2\left(s^{2^{-i}} \cdot 2^{n/2^i}\right)}.$$

Since $\log^2\left(s^{2^{-i}} \cdot 2^{n/2^i}\right) = \left(2^{-i} \cdot \log(s) + \frac{n}{2^i}\right)^2 = O(n^2)$, the total number of strings is bounded by $s \cdot 2^n \cdot O(\log(n)) \cdot 2^{O(n)} \cdot 2^{O(n^2)} = 2^{O(n^2)}$, supposed we choose s sufficiently small compared to n, i.e. choose n large, namely $s = 2^{\log s}$, $\log(s) = O(n^2)$.

Hence we find a string y of length n^3 such that adding y to X does not change the result of computation $M_s(x, X)$, therefore the diagonalization step is well-defined. This completes the proof of Theorem 4.3. □

5. Conclusion

We have proved a separation of the classes $PTAS$ and $EPTAS$ under the assumption that there are NP search problems with a superpolynomial lower bound on the deterministic time complexity. We have shown that there exists no relativizing proof that our assumption implies $FPT \neq W[P]$, hence in this sense our result can be seen as independent from the separation result given by Cesati and Trevisan. It remains as an open problem to prove the strictness of the inclusion $EPTAS \subseteq PTAS$ under assumption $P \neq NP$.

Acknowledgement. We would like to thank Marek Karpinski and Claus Viehmann for valuable discussions.

Bibliography

1. G. Ausiello, P. Crescenzi, G. Gambosi, V. Kann, A. Marchetti-Spaccamela, M. Protasi. Complexity and Approximation. Springer, 1999
2. C. Bazgan. Schemas d'approximation et complexite' parametree. *Thesis, INRIA, Orsay, France*, 1995.
3. R. Beigel and J. Goldsmith. Downward separation fails catastrophically for limited nondeterminism classes. In *Structure in Complexity Theory Conference*, pages 134–138, 1994.
4. L. Cai and J. Chen. On fixed-parameter tractability and approximability of np optimization problems. *Journal of Computer and System Sciences*, 54(3):465–474, 1997.
5. M. Cesati and L. Trevisan. On the efficiency of polynomial time approximation schemes. *Information Processing Letters*, 64(47):165–171, 1997.
6. Y. Chen and M. Grohe. An Isomorphism Between Subexponential and Parameterized Complexity Theory. *Proceedings of the 21st IEEE Conference on Computational Complexity (CCC'06)*, PP.314-328, 2006.
7. R. G. Downey and M. R. Fellows. Fixed-parameter tractability and completeness. In *Congr. Num. 87*, pages 161–187, 1992.
8. R. G. Downey and M. R. Fellows. Parameterized Complexity. Springer, 1997
9. J. Flum, M. Grohe and M. Weyer. Bounded fixed-parameter tractability and log2n nondeterministic bits , *Journal of Computer and System Sciences* 72:34-71, 2006.
10. J. Flum and M. Grohe. Parameterized Complexity Theory. Springer, 2006
11. J. M. Hitchcock. Small spans in scaled dimension. *SIAM Journal on Computing*, 34(1):170–194, 2004.
12. J. M. Hitchcock, J. H. Lutz, and E. Mayordomo. Scaled dimension and nonuniform complexity. *Journal of Computer and System Sciences*, 69:97–122, 2004.

13. J. M. Hitchcock and A. Pavan. Hardness hypotheses, derandomization, and circuit complexity. In *Proceedings of the 24th Conference on Foundations of Software Technology and Theoretical Computer Science*, pages 336–347, 2004.

14. C.M.R. Kintala and P. Fischer. Refining nondeterminism in relativized complexity classes. *SIAM Journal on Computing*, 13:329–337, 1984.

15. J. H. Lutz. Category and measure in complexity classes. *SIAM Journal on Computing*, 19:1100–1131, 1990.

16. J. H. Lutz. Dimension in complexity classes. In *IEEE Conference on Computational Complexity*, pages 158–169, 2000.

DICHOTOMY RESULTS FOR FIXED POINT COUNTING IN BOOLEAN DYNAMICAL SYSTEMS

SVEN KOSUB

Fakultät für Informatik, Technische Universität München,
D-85748 Garching, Germany
`kosub@in.tum.de`

CHRISTOPHER M. HOMAN

Department of Computer Science, Rochester Institute of Technology,
Rochester, NY 14623, USA
`cmh@cs.rit.edu`

We present dichotomy theorems regarding the computational complexity of counting fixed points in boolean (discrete) dynamical systems, i.e., finite discrete dynamical systems over the domain $\{0, 1\}$. For a class $\mathcal{F}$ of boolean functions and a class $\mathcal{G}$ of graphs, an $(\mathcal{F}, \mathcal{G})$-system is a boolean dynamical system with local transitions functions lying in $\mathcal{F}$ and graph in $\mathcal{G}$. We show that, if local transition functions are given by lookup tables, then the following complexity classification holds: Let $\mathcal{F}$ be a class of boolean functions closed under superposition and let $\mathcal{G}$ be a graph class closed under taking minors. If $\mathcal{F}$ contains all min-functions, all max-functions, or all self-dual and monotone functions, and $\mathcal{G}$ contains all planar graphs, then it is #P-complete to compute the number of fixed points in an $(\mathcal{F}, \mathcal{G})$-system; otherwise it is computable in polynomial time. The theorem relies on an evident conjecture for an open case. In contrast, we prove a dichotomy theorem for the case that local transition functions are given by formulas (over logical bases). A corresponding theorem for boolean circuits coincides with the theorem for formulas.

1. Introduction

Efforts to understand the behavior of complex systems have led to various models for finite discrete dynamical systems, including (finite) cellular automata, discrete recurrent Hopfield networks, and concurrent and communicating finite state machines. A fairly general class of systems was introduced in [4]. There, a finite discrete dynamical system (over a finite domain $\mathcal{D}$) is defined as: (a) a finite undirected graph, where vertices correspond to variables and edges correspond to an interdependence between the two connected variables, (b) for each vertex v, a local transition function that maps tuples of values (belonging to $\mathcal{D}$) of v and v's neighbors to values of v, and (c) an update schedule that governs which variables are allowed to update their values in which time steps. Formal definitions can be found in Sec. 2.

A central goal in the study of dynamical systems is to classify them according to how easy it is to predict their behavior. In a finite, discrete setting, a certain behavioral pattern is considered predictable if it can be decided in polynomial time whether a given system will show the pattern [6]. Although the pattern reachability problem is, in general, an intractable problem, i.e., at least NP-hard (see, e.g., [2,11,20]), many tractable classes of patterns and systems have been identified. However, there is still a serious demand for exhaustive characterizations of *islands of predictability*.

A fundamental behavioral pattern is the *fixed point* (a.k.a., homogeneous state, or equilibrium). A value assignment to the variables of a system is a fixed point if the values assigned to the variables are left unchanged after the system updates them. Note that fixed points are invariant under changes of the update regime. In this sense, they can be seen as a particularly robust behavior. A series of recent papers has been devoted to the identification of finite systems with tractable/intractable fixed-point analyses [3,13,21–23]. Precise boundaries are known for which systems finding fixed points can be done in polynomial time. For the fixed-point counting problem this is far less so.

Contributions of the paper. We prove dichotomy theorems on the computational complexity of counting fixed points in boolean (discrete) dynamical systems, i.e., finite discrete dynamical systems over the domain $\{0, 1\}$. For a class $\mathcal{F}$ of boolean functions and a class $\mathcal{G}$ of graphs, an $(\mathcal{F}, \mathcal{G})$-system is a boolean dynamical system with local transition functions lying in $\mathcal{F}$ and a graph lying in $\mathcal{G}$. Following [13], Post classes (a.k.a., clones) and forbidden-minor classes are used to classify $(\mathcal{F}, \mathcal{G})$-systems. In Sect. 4 we state the following theorem (Theorem 4.1): Let $\mathcal{F}$ be a class of boolean function closed under superposition and let $\mathcal{G}$ be a minor-closed graph class. If $\mathcal{F}$ contains all min-functions, all max-functions, or all self-dual and monotone functions, and $\mathcal{G}$ contains all planar graphs, then it is #P-complete to compute the number of the fixed points in an $(\mathcal{F}, \mathcal{G})$-system; otherwise it is computable in polynomial time. Here, the local transition functions are supposed to be given by lookup tables. In , we prove a conditional version of the theorem requiring an evident conjecture for the only open case. In addition, we prove a dichotomy theorem (Theorem 4.2) for the case that local transition functions are given by formulas (over logical bases). Moreover, the corresponding theorem for boolean circuits coincides with the theorem for formulas. The theorem has a significantly more complicated structure than the one for lookup tables.

Related work. There is a series of work regarding the complexity of certain computational problems for finite discrete dynamical systems (see, e.g., [1–3,11,20–23] and the references therein). The problem of counting fixed points of boolean dynamical systems has been studied in [21–23]. To summarize: counting the number of fixed points is in general #P-complete. So is counting the number of fixed points for boolean dynamical systems with monotone local transition functions over planar bipartite graphs or over uniformly sparse graphs. We note that all system classes considered here are based on formula or circuit representations. That is, if they fit into our scheme at all, then the intractability results fall into the scope of Theorem 4.2 (and are covered there). Detailed studies of computational problems related to fixed-point existence have been reported in [3,13]. In [13], a complete classification of the fixed-point existence problem with respect to the analysis framework we use in this paper was shown.

2. The Dynamical Systems Framework

In this section we present a formal framework for dynamical systems. A fairly general approach is motivated by the theoretical study of simulations. The following is based on [4,13].

The underlying network structure of a dynamical system is given by an undirected graph $G = (V, E)$ without multi-edges and loops. We suppose that the set V of vertices is ordered. So, without loss of generality, we assume $V = \{1, 2, \ldots, n\}$. For any vertex set $U \subseteq V$, let $N_G(U)$ denote the neighbors of U in G, i.e.,

$$N_G(U) =_{\text{def}} \{ j \mid j \notin U \text{ and there is an } i \in U \text{ such that } \{i, j\} \in E \}.$$

If $U = \{i\}$ for some vertex i, then we use $N_G(i)$ as a shorthand for $N_G(\{i\})$. The degree d_i of a vertex i is the number of its neighbors, i.e., $d_i =_{\text{def}} \|N_G(i)\|$.

A *dynamical system* S *over a domain* $\mathcal{D}$ is a pair (G, F) where $G = (V, E)$ is an undirected graph (the *network*) and $F = \{f_i \mid i \in V\}$ is a set of *local transition functions* $f_i : \mathcal{D}^{d_i+1} \to \mathcal{D}$. The intuition of the definition is that each vertex i corresponds to an active element (entity, agent, actor etc.) which is always in some state x_i and which is capable to change its state, if necessary. The domain of S formalizes the set of possible states of all vertices of the network, i.e., for all $i \in V$, it always holds that $x_i \in \mathcal{D}$. A vector $\vec{x} = (x_i)_{i \in V}$ such that $x_i \in \mathcal{D}$ for all $i \in V$ is called a *configuration of* S. The local transition function f_i for some vertex i describes how i changes its state depending on the states of its neighbors $N_G(i)$ in the network and its own state.

We are particularly interested in dynamical system operating on a discrete time-scale. A *discrete dynamical system* $\mathcal{S} = (S, \alpha)$ consists of a dynamical system S and a mapping $\alpha : \{1, \ldots, T\} \to \mathcal{P}(V)$, where V is a set of vertices of the network of S and $T \in \mathbb{N}$. The mapping α is called the *update schedule* and specifies which states updates are realized at certain time-steps: for $t \in \{1, \dots, T\}$, $\alpha(t)$ specifies those vertices that simultaneously update their states in step t.

A discrete dynamical system $\mathcal{S} = (S, \alpha)$ over domain $\mathcal{D}$ induces a global map $\mathbf{F}_{\mathcal{S}} : \mathcal{D}^n \to \mathcal{D}^n$ where n is the number of vertices of S. For each vertex $i \in V$, define an *activity function* φ_i for a set $U \subseteq V$ and $\vec{x} = (x_1, \dots, x_n) \in \mathcal{D}^n$ by

$$\varphi_i[U](\vec{x}) =_{\text{def}} \begin{cases} f_i(x_{i_1}, \dots, x_{i_{d_i+1}}) & \text{if } i \in U \\ x_i & \text{if } i \notin U \end{cases}$$

where $\{i_1, i_2, \dots, i_{d_i+1}\} = \{i\} \cup N_G(i)$. For a set $U \subseteq V$, define the *global transition function* $\mathbf{F}_S[U] : \mathcal{D}^n \to \mathcal{D}^n$ for all $\vec{x} \in \mathcal{D}^n$ by

$$\mathbf{F}_S[U](\vec{x}) =_{\text{def}} (\varphi_1[U](\vec{x}), \dots, \varphi_n[U](\vec{x})).$$

Note that the global transition function does not refer to the update schedule, i.e., it only depends on the dynamical system S and not on $\mathcal{S}$. The function $\mathbf{F}_{\mathcal{S}} : \mathcal{D}^n \to \mathcal{D}^n$ computed by the discrete dynamical system $\mathcal{S}$, the *global map* of $\mathcal{S}$, is defined by

$$\mathbf{F}_{\mathcal{S}} =_{\text{def}} \prod_{k=1}^{T} \mathbf{F}_S[\alpha(k)].$$

The central notion for our study of dynamical systems is the concept of a fixed point, i.e., a configuration which does not change under any global behavior of the system. Let $S = (G, \{f_i \mid i \in V\})$ be a dynamical system over domain $\mathcal{D}$. A configuration $\vec{x} \in \mathcal{D}^n$ is said to be a *local fixed point of S for* $U \subseteq V$ if and only if $\mathbf{F}_S[U](\vec{x}) = \vec{x}$. A configuration $\vec{x} \in \mathcal{D}^n$ is said to be a *fixed point of S* if and only if $\vec{x}$ is a local fixed point of S for V. Note that a fixed point does not depend on a concrete update schedule: a configuration $\vec{x} \in \mathcal{D}^n$ is a fixed point of S if and only if for all update schedules $\alpha : \{1, \dots, T\} \to \mathcal{P}(V)$, it holds that $\mathbf{F}_{(S,\alpha)}(\vec{x}) = \vec{x}$.

3. The Analysis Framework

In this section we specify our analysis framework for $(\mathcal{F}, \mathcal{G})$-systems. Following [13], local transition functions are classified by Post classes, i.e., superpositionally closed classes of boolean functions, and graphs are classified using the theory of graph minors as a tool. In the following we gather relevant notation.

3.1. Transition Classes

We adopt notation from [5]. An n-ary boolean function f is a mapping $f : \{0, 1\}^n \to \{0, 1\}$. Let BF denote the class of all boolean functions. There are two

0-ary boolean functions: $c_0 =_{\text{def}} 0$ and $c_1 =_{\text{def}} 1$ (which are denoted in formulas by the symbols 0 and 1). There are two 1-ary boolean functions: $\text{id}(x) =_{\text{def}} x$ and $\text{not}(x) =_{\text{def}} 1 - x$ (denoted in formulas by x for $\text{id}(x)$ and $\bar{x}$ for $\text{not}(x)$). We say that a class $\mathcal{F}$ is *Post* if and only if $\mathcal{F}$ contains the function id and $\mathcal{F}$ is closed under the introduction of fictive variables, permutations of variables, identification of variables, and substitution (see, e.g., [5] for definitions). It is a famous theorem by Post [16] that the family of all Post classes is a countable lattice with respect to set inclusion. In particular, each Post class is the intersection of a finite set of meet-irreducible classes, which are the following.

The classes R_0 *and* R_1. For $b \in \{0, 1\}$, a boolean function f is said to be *b-reproducing* if and only if $f(b, \ldots, b) = b$. Let R_b denote the class of all b-reproducing functions.

The class M. For binary n-tuples $\vec{a} = (a_1, \ldots, a_n)$ and $\vec{b} = (b_1, \ldots, b_n)$, we say that $(a_1, \ldots, a_n) \leq (b_1, \ldots, b_n)$ if and only if for all $i \in \{1, \ldots, n\}$, it holds that $a_i \leq b_i$. An n-ary boolean function f is said to be *monotone* if and only if for all $\vec{x}, \vec{y} \in \{0, 1\}^n$, $\vec{x} \leq \vec{y}$ implies $f(\vec{x}) \leq f(\vec{y})$. Let M denote the class of all monotone boolean functions.

The class D. An n-ary boolean function f is said to be *self-dual* if and only if for all $(x_1, \ldots, x_n) \in \{0, 1\}^n$, it holds that $f(x_1, \ldots, x_n) = \text{not}(f(\text{not}(x_1), \ldots, \text{not}(x_n)))$. Let D denote the class of all self-dual functions.

The class L. A boolean function f is linear if and only if there exists constants $a_1, \ldots, a_n \in \{0, 1\}$ such that $f(x_1, \ldots, x_n) = a_0 \oplus a_1 x_1 \oplus \cdots \oplus a_n x_n$. Note that $\oplus$ is understood as addition modulo 2 and xy is understood as multiplication modulo 2. Let L denote the class of all linear functions. The logical basis of L is $\{\oplus, 0, 1\}$.

The classes S_b *and* S_b^k. For $b \in \{0, 1\}$, a tuple set $T \subseteq \{0, 1\}^n$ is said to be *b-separating* if and only if there is an $i \in \{1, \ldots, n\}$ such that for $(t_1, \ldots, t_n) \in T$ holds $t_i = b$. A boolean function f is *b-separating* if and only if $f^{-1}(b)$ is b-separating. A function f is called *b-separating of level k* if and only if every $T \subseteq f^{-1}(b)$ such that $\|T\| = k$ is b-separating. Let S_b denote the class of b-separating functions and let S_b^k denote the class of all functions which are b-separating of level k.

The classes E *and* V. We denote by E the class of all AND functions, i.e., the class of all functions f, the arity of which is n, such that for some set $J \subseteq \{1, \ldots, n\}$, the equality $f(x_1, \ldots, x_n) = \min_{i \in J} x_i$ is satisfied for all $x_1, \ldots, x_n \in \{0, 1\}$. The logical basis over E is $\{\wedge, 0, 1\}$. Dually, we denote by V the class of all OR functions, i.e., the class of all functions f, the arity of which is n, such that for some set $J \subseteq \{1, \ldots, n\}$, the equality $f(x_1, \ldots, x_n) = \max_{i \in J} x_i$ is satisfied for all $x_1, \ldots, x_n \in \{0, 1\}$. The logical basis of V is

$\{\vee, 0, 1\}$.

The class N. An n-ary boolean function f is a projection if and only if there is an $i \in \{1, \ldots, n\}$ such that for all $x_1, \ldots, x_n \in \{0, 1\}$, it holds that $f(x_1, \ldots, x_n) = x_i$. A boolean function f is the negation of a projection if and only if there is an $i \in \{1, \ldots, n\}$ such that for all $x_1, \ldots, x_n \in \{0, 1\}$, it holds that $f(x_1, \ldots, x_n) = \mathrm{not}(x_i)$. A boolean function f is constant if and only if there exists a $b \in \{0, 1\}$ such that for all $x_1, \ldots, x_n \in \{0, 1\}$, it holds that $f(x_1, \ldots, x_n) = b$. Let N denote the class of boolean functions which are projections, negations of projections, or constant functions.

Note that the classes possess the following inclusion structure (see, e.g., [5]):

- $S_0 \subseteq \cdots \subseteq S_0^k \subseteq S_0^{k-1} \subseteq \cdots \subseteq S_0^2 \subseteq R_1$
- $S_1 \subseteq \cdots \subseteq S_1^k \subseteq S_1^{k-1} \subseteq \cdots \subseteq S_1^2 \subseteq R_0$
- $E \subseteq M$ and $V \subseteq M$
- $N \subseteq L$

No other inclusions hold among these classes. Moreover, all Post classes have a finite logical basis. Particular relevance for our studies have the following classes:

$D_2 =_{\mathrm{def}} D \cap M$	with logical basis $\{(x \wedge y) \vee (x \wedge z) \vee (y \wedge z)\}$
$D_1 =_{\mathrm{def}} D \cap R_0 \cap R_1$	with logical basis $\{(x \wedge y) \vee (x \wedge \bar{z}) \vee (y \wedge \bar{z})\}$
$S_{00} =_{\mathrm{def}} S_0 \cap M \cap R_0$	with logical basis $\{x \vee (y \wedge z)\}$
$S_{10} =_{\mathrm{def}} S_1 \cap M \cap R_1$	with logical basis $\{x \wedge (y \vee z)\}$
$E_2 =_{\mathrm{def}} E \cap S_{10}$	with logical basis $\{\wedge\}$
$V_2 =_{\mathrm{def}} V \cap S_{00}$	with logical basis $\{\vee\}$

3.2. Network Classes

We adopt notation from [9]. Let X and Y be two undirected graphs. We say that X is minor of Y if and only if there is a subgraph Y' of Y such that X can be obtained by contracting edges of Y'. Let $\preceq$ be the relation on graphs defined by $X \preceq Y$ if and only if X is a minor of Y. A class $\mathcal{G}$ of graphs is said to be *closed under taking minors* if and only if for all graphs G and G', if $G \in \mathcal{G}$ and $G' \preceq G$, then $G' \in \mathcal{G}$. Let $\mathcal{X}$ be any set of graphs. $\mathrm{Forb}_{\preceq}(\mathcal{X})$ denotes the class of all graphs without a minor in $\mathcal{X}$ (and which is closed under isomorphisms). More specifically, $\mathrm{Forb}_{\preceq}(\mathcal{X}) =_{\mathrm{def}} \{G \mid G \not\preceq X \text{ for all } X \in \mathcal{X}\}$. The set $\mathcal{X}$ is called the set of *forbidden minors*. Note that $\mathrm{Forb}_{\preceq}(\emptyset)$ is the class of all graphs. As usual, we write $\mathrm{Forb}_{\preceq}(X_1, \ldots, X_n)$ instead of $\mathrm{Forb}_{\preceq}(\{X_1, \ldots, X_n\})$. Forbidden-minor classes are monotone with respect to $\preceq$, i.e., $X \preceq Y$ implies $\mathrm{Forb}_{\preceq}(X) \subseteq \mathrm{Forb}_{\preceq}(Y)$. The celebrated Graph Minor Theorem, due to Robertson and Seymour [19], shows that there are only countably many network classes closed under taking minors: A class $\mathcal{G}$ of graphs is closed under taking minors if and only if there is a finite set $\mathcal{X}$ such that $\mathcal{G} = \mathrm{Forb}_{\preceq}(\mathcal{X})$.

Two graph classes are particularly relevant to our study: planar graphs and graphs having a vertex cover of size one. Let K^n denote the complete graphs on n vertices and let $K_{n,m}$ denote the complete bipartite graph having n vertices in one component and m vertices in the other component. The well-known Kuratowski-Wagner theorem (see, e.g., [9]) states that a graph G is planar if and only if G belongs to $\mathrm{Forb}_{\preceq}(K_{3,3}, K^5)$. Moreover, a graph X is planar if and only if $\mathrm{Forb}_{\preceq}(X)$ has bounded treewidth [18]. As we use the treewidth of a graph only in a black-box fashion, we refer to, e.g., [9] for a definition. A class $\mathcal{G}$ of graphs is said to have *bounded treewidth* if and only if there is a $k \in \mathbb{N}$ such that all graphs in the class have treewidth at most k. Let $G = (V, E)$ be a graph. We say that a subset $U \subseteq V$ is a *vertex cover* of G if and only if for all edges $\{u, v\} \in E$, it holds that $\{u, v\} \cap U \neq \emptyset$. It is known that the class of graphs having a vertex cover of size at most k is closed under taking minors [7]. Moreover, G has a vertex cover of size one if and only if G belongs to $\mathrm{Forb}_{\preceq}(K^3 \oplus K^2)$ [7], where for graphs G and G', $G \oplus G'$ denotes the graph obtained by the disjoint union of G and G'. A class of graphs is said to have *bounded degree* if and only if there is a $k \in \mathbb{N}$ such that all graphs in the class have a maximum vertex-degree of at most k. It is known that a graph X has a vertex cover of size one if and only if $\mathrm{Forb}_{\preceq}(X)$ has bounded degree [13].

4. Islands of Tractability for Fixed Point Counting

In this section we are interested in the computational complexity of the following counting problem. Let $\mathcal{F}$ be a class of boolean functions and let $\mathcal{G}$ be a class of graphs.

Problem:	#FIXED POINTS$(\mathcal{F}, \mathcal{G})$
Input:	An $(\mathcal{F}, \mathcal{G})$-system S, i.e., a boolean dynamical system $S = (G, \{f_1, \ldots, f_n\})$ such that $G \in \mathcal{G}$ and for all $i \in \{1, \ldots, n\}$, $f_i \in \mathcal{F}$
Output:	The number of fixed points of S

The complexity of the problem depends on how transition functions are represented. We consider the cases of lookup table, formula, and circuit representations. The corresponding problems are denoted by #FIXED POINTS$_T$, #FIXED POINTS$_F$, and #FIXED POINTS$_C$. It is obvious that all problem versions belong to #P. We say that a problem is intractable if it is #P-hard (with respect to Turing reductions, as described in, e.g., [12]), and it is tractable if it is solvable in polynomial time.

Due to space limitations, many of the proofs are omitted from this extended abstract. They can be found in the full paper [14].

4.1. The Case of Local Transition Functions Given By Lookup Tables

We start by identifying tractable counting problems.

Lemma 4.1. $\#\text{FIXED POINTS}_T(L, \text{Forb}_{\preceq}(\emptyset))$ *is solvable in polynomial time.*

Proof. Notice that for a linear function $f(x_1, \ldots, x_n) = a_0 \oplus a_1 x_2 \oplus a_2 x_2 \oplus \cdots \oplus a_n x_n$, the proposition $x_i \leftrightarrow [a_0 \oplus a_1 x_2 \oplus a_2 x_2 \oplus \cdots \oplus a_n x_n]$ is true if and only if $a_0 \oplus a_1 x_2 \oplus a_2 x_2 \oplus \cdots \oplus a_n x_n \oplus x_i \oplus 1$ is satisfiable. So, each dynamical system with linear, boolean local transition functions constitutes a system of linear equations over Z_2, for which the number of solutions can be computed in polynomial time using Gaussian elimination (cf. [8]). $\quad\square$

In [13], it has been shown that the decision version of $\#\text{FIXED POINTS}_T(\text{BF}, \text{Forb}_{\preceq}(X))$ for planar graphs X can be solved in polynomial time [13]. This result is obtained by a reduction to a certain type of constraint satision problems. Actually, the reduction establishes injections between the fixed points of a dynamical system and the satisfying assignments of the corresponding constraint satision problem. Consequently, the numbers of fixed points and the numbers of satisfying assignments are equal.

Lemma 4.2. *Let X be a planar graph. Then,* $\#\text{FIXED POINTS}(\text{BF}, \text{Forb}_{\preceq}(X))$ *is solvable in polynomial time.*

We turn to the intractable fixed-point counting problems. Let H be a 2CNF such that each clause consists of exactly one positive and one negative literal. H is called a Horn-2CNF formula. Moreover, suppose H possesses a planar graph representation, i.e., the graph $\Gamma(H) = (V, E)$ with vertex set $V = \{x_1, \ldots, x_n, C_1, \ldots, C_m\}$, where the x_i's are the variables and the C_i's are the clauses of H, and edge set $E = \{\{x_i, C_j\} \mid x_i$ is a variable in $C_j\}$ is planar. Then, H is called a planar Horn 2-CNF formula. $\#\text{PLANAR HORN-2SAT}$ is the problem of counting all satisfying assignments of a given planar Horn-2CNF formula. The proof of the following proposition uses techniques from [15,17,24].

Proposition 4.1. $\#\text{PLANAR HORN-2SAT}$ *is $\#$P-complete even if each variable is allowed to occur in four clauses only.*

The following results all rely on the hardness of $\#\text{PLANAR HORN-2SAT}$.

Lemma 4.3. $\#\text{FIXED POINTS}_T(E_2, \text{Forb}_{\preceq}(K_{3,3}, K^5))$ *is $\#$P-complete.*

Proof. We reduce from #PLANAR HORN-2SAT assuming that each variable occurs only four times in the formula. Let $H = C_1 \wedge \cdots \wedge C_m$ be a planar Horn-2CNF formula. Define a dynamical system $S = (G, F)$ as follows. $G = (V, E)$ is given by $V =_{\text{def}} \{1, \ldots, n\}$ and $E =_{\text{def}} \{\{i, j\} \mid (\overline{x_i} \vee x_j) = C_r \text{ for some } r \in \{1, \ldots, m\}\}$. Since H has a planar graph representation, G is planar, i.e., $G \in \text{Forb}_{\preceq}(K_{3,3}, K^5)$. The local transition functions are specified in the following way. For a vertex $i_0 \in V$ let $\{i_1, \ldots, i_r\}$ be the set of all vertices such that $(\overline{x_{i_j}} \vee x_{i_0})$ is a clause in H. Then, f_{i_0} is the function given by the formula $H_{i_0} = x_{i_0} \wedge x_{i_1} \wedge \cdots \wedge x_{i_r}$. Notice that all local transition functions belong to E_2 and also notice that the maximum degree of a vertex in G is four. Thus, we can compute the lookup tables in polynomial time depending on the size of H. Moreover, it is easily seen that $(x_{i_0} \leftrightarrow \bigwedge_{j=1}^r x_{i_j}) \equiv \bigwedge_{j=1}^r (\overline{x_{i_j}} \vee x_{i_0})$. Hence, the number of satisfying assignments of H is equal to the number of fixed-point configurations of S_H. This shows that #PLANAR HORN-2SAT reduces to #FIXED POINTS$_T(E_2, \text{Forb}_{\preceq}(K_{3,3}, K^5))$. $\qquad \square$

Lemma 4.4. *#FIXED POINTS$_T(V_2, \text{Forb}_{\preceq}(K_{3,3}, K^5))$ is #P-complete.*

Proposition 4.2. *#FIXED POINTS$_T(D_1, \text{Forb}_{\preceq}(K_{3,3}, K^5))$ is #P-complete.*

The remaining case of D_2 functions is special. We conjecture that the fixed-point counting problem for dynamical systems with local transition functions in D_2 and planar networks is intractable. This is based on the following weaker proposition.

Proposition 4.3. *#FIXED POINTS$_T(D_2, \text{Forb}_{\preceq}(\emptyset))$ is #P-complete.*

Finally, we combine the results to obtain the following conditional dichotomy theorem.

Theorem 4.1. *Let $\mathcal{F}$ be a Post class of boolean functions and let $\mathcal{G}$ be a graph class closed under taking minors. Under the assumption that #FIXED POINTS$_T(D_2, \text{Forb}_{\preceq}(K_{3,3}, K^5))$ is an intractable problem, the following holds: If $(\mathcal{F} \supseteq V_2$ or $\mathcal{F} \supseteq E_2$ or $\mathcal{F} \supseteq D_2)$ and $\mathcal{G} \supseteq \text{Forb}_{\preceq}(K_{3,3}, K^5)$, then #FIXED POINTS$_T(\mathcal{F}, \mathcal{G})$ is intractable, otherwise #FIXED POINTS$_T(\mathcal{F}, \mathcal{G})$ is tractable.*

Proof. If $(\mathcal{F} \supseteq V_2$ or $\mathcal{F} \supseteq E_2$ or $\mathcal{F} \supseteq D_2)$ and $\mathcal{G} \supseteq \text{Forb}_{\preceq}(K_{3,3}, K^5)$, then #FIXED POINTS$_T(\mathcal{F}, \mathcal{G})$ is #P-complete by Lemma 4.3, Lemma 4.4, and by the assumption made for D_2. Suppose the premise is not satisfied. First, assume that $\mathcal{F} \not\supseteq V_2$, $\mathcal{F} \not\supseteq E_2$, and $\mathcal{F} \not\supseteq D_2$. The maximal Post class having this property is L. By Lemma 4.1, #FIXED POINTS$_T(L, \text{Forb}_{\preceq}(\emptyset))$ is tractable. It remains to consider the case $\mathcal{G} \not\supseteq \mathrm{Forb}_{\preceq}(K_{3,3}, K^5)$. Then, $\mathcal{G} \subseteq \mathrm{Forb}_{\preceq}(X)$ for some planar graph X. By Lemma 4.2, #FIXED POINTS$_T(\mathrm{BF}, \mathcal{G})$ is solvable in polynomial time.   □

4.2. Succinctly Represented Local Transition Functions

In this section we state a dichotomy theorem for the fixed-point counting problem when transition are given by formulas or circuits. As usual, the size of formula is the number of symbols from the basis used to encode the formula, the size of a circuit is the number of gates (from the basis) it consists of (including the input gates). Both succinct representations of functions lead to the same result.

Theorem 4.2. Let $\mathcal{F}$ be a Post class of boolean functions and let $\mathcal{G}$ be a graph class closed under taking minors. Then, #FIXED POINTS$_F(\mathcal{F}, \mathcal{G})$ is intractable if one of the following conditions is satisfied.

(1) $\left(\mathcal{F} \supseteq \mathrm{S}_{00} \text{ or } \mathcal{F} \supseteq \mathrm{S}_{10} \text{ or } \mathcal{F} \supseteq \mathrm{D}_2\right)$ and $\mathcal{G} \supseteq \mathrm{Forb}_{\preceq}(K^3 \oplus K^2)$.
(2) $\left(\mathcal{F} \supseteq \mathrm{V}_2 \text{ or } \mathcal{F} \supseteq \mathrm{E}_2\right)$ and $\mathcal{G} \supseteq \mathrm{Forb}_{\preceq}(K_{3,3}, K^5)$.

Otherwise, #FIXED POINTS$_F(\mathcal{F}, \mathcal{G})$ is tractable. Moreover, the same classification is true for #FIXED POINTS$_C(\mathcal{F}, \mathcal{G})$.

5. Conclusion

Fixed points are an important and robust (in the sense that they exist independently of any update schedule) feature of discrete dynamical systems. We presented two dichotomy theorems on the complexity of counting the number of fixed points in such a system. Both results demonstrate that the linear boolean functions are the only function class such that fixed point counting is tractable independent of representations and of degrees of variable dependency.

The main open issue of this paper is resolving the intractability conjecture for fixed point counting in systems with local transition functions from D_2 over planar graphs. More generally, it is tempting to apply our analysis framework (Post classes and forbidden minors) to a precise identification of islands of predictability for more schedule-based behavioral patterns, e.g., gardens of Eden, predecessors, or fixed-point reachability.

Bibliography

1. C. Barrett, H. Hunt III, M. Marathe, S. Ravi, D. Rosenkrantz, R. Stearns. Predecessor and permutation existence problems for sequential dynamical systems. In *Proc. Conference on Discrete Models for Complex Systems (DMCS'03)*, DMTCS Proceedings #AB, pp. 69–80, 2003.

2. C. Barrett, H. Hunt III, M. Marathe, S. Ravi, D. Rosenkrantz, R. Stearns. Complexity of reachabillity problems for finite discrete dynamical systems. *J. Comput. Syst. Sci.*, 72(7):1317–1345, 2006.

3. C. Barrett, H. Hunt III, M. Marathe, S. Ravi, D. Rosenkrantz, R. Stearns, P. Tošić. Gardens of Eden and fixed points in sequential dynamical systems. In *Proc. 1st International Conference on Discrete Models: Combinatorics, Computation and Geometry (DM-CCG'01)*, DMTCS Proceedings #AA, pp. 241–259, 2001.

4. C. Barrett, H. Mortveit, C. Reidys. Elements of a theory of computer simulation II: Sequential dynamical systems. *Appl. Math. Comput.*, 107(2–3):121–136, 2000.

5. E. Böhler, N. Creignou, S. Reith, H. Vollmer. Playing with Boolean blocks, part I: Post's lattice with applications to complexity theory. *ACM SIGACT News*, 34(4):38–52, 2003.

6. S. Buss, C. Papadimitriou, J. Tsitsiklis. On the predictability of coupled automata: An allegory about chaos. *Complex Syst.*, 5:525–539, 1991.

7. K. Cattell, M. Dinneen. A characterization of graphs with vertex cover up to five. In *Proc. International Workshop on Orders, Algorithms, and Applications (ORDAL'94)*, LNCS #831, pp. 86–99. Springer, 1994.

8. N. Creignou, M. Hermann. Complexity of generalized satisfiability counting problems. *Inf. Comput.*, 125(1):1–12, 1996.

9. R. Diestel. *Graph Theory*. Graduate Texts in Mathematics. Springer, 2003.

10. J. Flum, M. Grohe. The parameterized complexity of counting problems. *SIAM J. Comput.*, 33(4):892–922, 2004.

11. F. Green. NP-complete problems in cellular automata. *Complex Syst.*, 1(3):453–474, 1987.

12. L. Hemaspaandra, M. Ogihara. *The Complexity Theory Companion*. Texts in Theoretical Computer Science. An EATCS Series. Springer, 2002.

13. S. Kosub. Dichotomy results for fixed-point existence problems for boolean dynamical systems. Technical Report TUM-I0701, Fakultät für Informatik, Technische Universität München, January 2007.

14. S. Kosub, C. Homan. Dichotomy results for fixed point counting in boolean dynamical systems. Technical Report TUM-I0706, Fakultät für Informatik, Technische Universität München, January 2007.

15. N. Linial. Hard enumeration problems in geometry and combinatorics. *SIAM J. Algebraic Discrete Methods*, 7(2):331–335, 1986.

16. E. Post. The two-valued iterative systems of mathematical logic. *Annals of Mathematical Studies* #5, Princeton University Press, 1941.

17. S. Provan, M. Ball. The complexity of counting cuts and of computing the probability that a graph is connected. *SIAM J. Comput.*, 12(4):777–788, 1983.

18. N. Robertson, P. Seymour. Graph minors. V. Excluding a planar graph. *J. Comb. Theory, Ser. B*, 41(1):92–114, 1986.

19. N. Robertson, P. Seymour. Graph minors. XX. Wagner's conjecture. *J. Comb. Theory, Ser. B*, 92(2):325–357, 2004.

20. K. Sutner. On the computational complexity of finite cellular automata. *J. Comput. Syst. Sci.*, 50(1):87–97, 1995.

21. P. Tošić. On complexity of counting fixed point configurations in certain classes of graph automata. ECCC #05-51, 2005.

22. P. Tošić. On the complexity of counting fixed points and gardens of Eden in sequential dynamical systems on planar bipartite graphs. *Int. J. Found. Comput. Sci.*, 17(5):1179–1203, 2006.
23. P. Tošić, G. Agha. On computational complexity of counting fixed points in symmetric boolean graph automata. In *Proc. 4th International Conference on Unconventional Computation (UC'05)*, LNCS #3699, pp. 191–205. Springer, 2005.
24. S. Vadhan. The complexity of counting in sparse, regular, and planar graphs. *SIAM J. Comput.*, 31(2):398–427, 2002.

DEFINABLE SETS IN WEAK PRESBURGER ARITHMETIC

CHRISTIAN CHOFFRUT

LIAFA, Université Paris 7 & CNRS,
2, pl. Jussieu – 75251 Paris Cedex – 05, France
E-mail: cc@liafa.jussieu.fr
http://www.liafa.jussieu.fr/~cc

ACHILLE FRIGERI*

Dipartimento di Matematica, Politecnico di Milano & LIAFA, Université Paris 7
via Bonardi, 9 – 20133 Milano, Italia
E-mail: achille.frigeri@polimi.it

We show that it is recursively decidable whether or not a given relation defined by a first-order formula in the structure $\langle \mathbb{Z}; +, < \rangle$ is first-order definable in $\langle \mathbb{Z}; + \rangle$.

Keywords: Presburger arithmetic, arithmetical definability.

Introduction

Presburger arithmetic is the fragment of arithmetic concerning integers with addition and order. Presburger's supervisor considered the decidability of this fragment too modest a result to deserve a Ph.D. degree and he accepted it only as a Master's Thesis in 1928. Looking at the number of citations, we may say that history revised this depreciative judgment long ago. There still remains, at least as far as we can see, some confusion concerning the definition itself of the structure: is the domain $\mathbb{Z}$ or $\mathbb{N}$? Must we take the order relation or not? (The main popular mathematical websites disagree on this respect). The original paper deals with the additive group of positive and negative integers with no binary relation, but in a final remark of the communication, the author asserts that the same result, to wit quantifier elimination, holds on the structure of the "whole" integers, i.e., the natural numbers with the binary relation $<$. In 7, which is the main reference on the subject, Presburger arithmetic is defined as the elementary theory of integers with equality, addition, having 0 and 1 as constant symbols and $<$ as binary pred-

---

*Supported by Vinci program, AutoMathA ESF project and GNSAGA.

icate, see also 13. On the other hand, the majority of "modern" papers referring to Presburger arithmetic is concerned with natural numbers where order relation is unnecessary as it is first-order expressible.

The origin of the present work is the simple remark that considering the set of integers $\mathbb{Z}$, the binary relation matters. Here, we study the decidability of the definability in the structure $\langle \mathbb{Z}; + \rangle$ for a given relation defined in $\langle \mathbb{Z}; +, < \rangle$. We show that it is indeed recursively decidable and we prove this result by revisiting the notion of linear set introduced by Ginsburg and Spanier [6] in the sixties.

Despite its simplicity, this arithmetic is central in many areas of theoretical and applied computer science. From a theoretical point of view, it has many surprising properties: 1) it admits quantifier elimination [7,11,13] and therefore it is decidable, 2) given a formula on the expansion of the structure obtained by adding the function which to each integer assigns the maximal power of 2 which divides it, it is decidable whether or not it is definable by a Presburger formula over $\mathbb{N}$ (Cobham-Semënov theorem [12], improved in 9 with a polynomial-time algorithm), and 3) Presburger arithmetic is self-definable (i.e., there is a Presburger definable criterion for definability [10]). Moreover, there is a strong and old connection between language theory, Presburger definable sets and rational relations on $\mathbb{Z}$ and $\mathbb{N}$ dating back to the sixties [1,3,6]. The concept is also widely used in many application areas, such as program analysis and model-checking and more specifically timed automata: roughly speaking, the main idea is that we can describe an infinite system with unbounded integer variables using Presburger formulas as guards [5] (see also the introduction of 14 for some historical remarks on the role of Presburger arithmetic in the development of theoretical and applied computer science).

1. Preliminaries

1.1. *Variants of Presburger arithmetic*

As observed above, a source of confusion is the lack of agreement in the definition of Presburger arithmetic itself. We make the convention of calling *weak Presburger arithmetic* the structure $z^W = \langle \mathbb{Z}; =; +; 0, 1 \rangle$ originally studied in 11, while by z we mean the *(standard) Presburger arithmetic* $\langle \mathbb{Z}; =, <; +; 0, 1 \rangle$. The *positive Presburger arithmetic* is the structure $\mathcal{X} = \langle \mathbb{N}; =; +; 0, 1 \rangle$ and we observe that in this case the $<$ predicate (as restriction of the order on $\mathbb{Z}$ to $\mathbb{N}$) is already definable in $\mathcal{X}$. All these three structures are decidable in the sense that given a closed formula, it is recursively decidable whether or not it holds. In particular z^W and z admit quantifier elimination in the augmented languages with the additional unary functional symbol "$-$" and the (recursive) set of binary functional symbols $(\equiv_m)_{m\in\mathbb{N}\backslash\{0,1\}}$, having the usual meaning of opposite and modulo respectively, while for $\mathcal{N}$ it suffices to add the binary functional symbols $(<_m)_{m\in\mathbb{N}\backslash\{0\}}$, where $x <_m y$ if, and only if, $x < y \wedge x \equiv_m y$ [1,4].

1.2. Logical definability

Here we are concerned with the *definability* issue. We recall that given a logical structure $\mathcal{D}$ with domain D and a first-order formula on this structure, say $\phi(x_1,\ldots,x_n)$, where $x_1,\ldots,x_n$ is the set of free variables, the n-ary relation R *defined* by ϕ is the set of n-tuples $(a_1,\ldots,a_n)$ such that ϕ holds true when the variable x_i is assigned the value a_i, i.e., $R = \{(a_1,\ldots,a_n) \in D^n \mid \mathcal{D} \models \phi(a_1,\ldots,a_n)\}$.

Example 1.1. E.g., the formula $(x_1 = x_2 = 1) \vee (x_1 + x_2 = 0)$ defines, in the structure z, the union of a point and of a line in the discrete plane. □

2. $\mathbb{N}$-linear and $\mathbb{Z}$-linear sets

2.1. Some notations

The free abelian monoid and the free abelian group on k generators are respectively identified with $\mathbb{N}^k$ and $\mathbb{Z}^k$ with the usual additive structure. The addition is extended from elements to subsets: if $X, Y \subseteq \mathbb{N}^k$ (resp. $X, Y \subseteq \mathbb{Z}^k$), $X + Y \subseteq \mathbb{N}^k$ (resp. $X + Y \subseteq \mathbb{Z}^k$) is the set of all sums $x + y$, where $x \in X$ and $y \in Y$. It might be convenient to consider the elements of $\mathbb{N}^k$ and $\mathbb{Z}^k$ as vectors of the $\mathbb{Q}$-vector space $\mathbb{Q}^k$. Given v in $\mathbb{N}^k$ or in $\mathbb{Z}^k$, the expression $\mathbb{N}v$ represents the subset of all vectors nv where n ranges over $\mathbb{N}$. This expression can be similarly extended to $\mathbb{Z}v$ whenever v is in $\mathbb{Z}^k$. Thus if $v_1,\ldots,v_n \in \mathbb{Z}^k$, $\mathbb{Z}v_1 + \cdots + \mathbb{Z}v_n$ represents the subgroup generated by $v_1,\ldots,v_n$ in $\mathbb{Z}^k$ and sometimes it will be denoted by $\langle v_1,\ldots,v_n\rangle$.

2.2. Linear sets

The following discussion requires (the adaptation of) few definitions. The symbol $\mathbb{K}$ stands either for $\mathbb{N}$ or for $\mathbb{Z}$ when concerning the free abelian group $\mathbb{Z}^k$ or for $\mathbb{N}$ when concerning the free abelian monoid $\mathbb{N}^k$.

Definition 2.1. A subset of $\mathbb{Z}^k$ (resp. $\mathbb{N}^k$) is $\mathbb{K}$-*linear* if it is of the form

$$a + \sum_{i=1}^{n} \mathbb{K}b_i, \qquad a, b_i \in \mathbb{Z}^k \text{ (resp. } \mathbb{N}^k), \; i = 1,\ldots,n. \tag{1}$$

It is $\mathbb{K}$-*simple* if the vectors b_i are linearly independent in $\mathbb{Q}^k$. It is $\mathbb{K}$-*semilinear* if it is a finite union of $\mathbb{K}$-linear sets, and $\mathbb{K}$-*semisimple* if it is a finite disjoint union of $\mathbb{K}$-simple sets. A subset of $\mathbb{Z}^k$ is $\mathbb{Z}$-*quasisimple* if it is of the form $A+\sum_{i=1}^{n} \mathbb{Z}b_i$, where $\sum_{i=1}^{n} \mathbb{Z}b_i$ is $\mathbb{Z}$-simple and $A \subseteq \mathbb{Z}^k$ is finite and for all $a, a' \in A$, the vector $(a - a')$ belongs to $\sum_{i=1}^{n} \mathbb{Q}b_i$.

Example 2.1. The set $\mathbb{Z}(1, 0) \cup \mathbb{Z}(0, 1)$ is $\mathbb{Z}$-semilinear. It is also $\mathbb{N}$-semilinear and $\mathbb{N}$-semisimple (it is equal to the union of $\mathbb{N}(1, 0)$, $(-1, 0) + \mathbb{N}(-1, 0)$, $\mathbb{N}(0, 1)$ and $(0, -1) + \mathbb{N}(0, -1)$). The set $\{(1, 0), (0, 1)\} + \mathbb{Z}(2, 0) + \mathbb{Z}(0, 2)$ is $\mathbb{Z}$-quasisimple. The set $\{(0, 1, 0), (1, 1, 1)\} + \mathbb{Z}(2, 0, 0) + \mathbb{Z}(0, 2, 0)$ is $\mathbb{Z}$-semilinear but not $\mathbb{Z}$-quasisimple. $\qquad\square$

Ginsburg and Spanier proved [6] the following result for $\mathbb{N}^k$, but it can readily be seen to hold for $\mathbb{Z}^k$.

Theorem 2.1. *Given a subset X of $\mathbb{N}^k$ (resp. $\mathbb{Z}^k$) the following assertions are equivalent:*

(1) X is first-order definable in $\mathcal{N}$ (resp. z);
(2) X is $\mathbb{N}$-semilinear in $\mathbb{N}^k$ (resp. $\mathbb{Z}^k$);
(3) X is $\mathbb{N}$-semisimple in $\mathbb{N}^k$ (resp. $\mathbb{Z}^k$).

Example 2.2. The formula in Example 1.1 defines the union of the two $\mathbb{Z}$-linear sets $\{(1, 1)\}$ and $\mathbb{Z}(1, -1)$. $\qquad\square$

Clearly, a finite union of $\mathbb{Z}$-linear sets is also a finite union of $\mathbb{N}$-linear sets but the converse does not hold, e.g., a moment's reflection will convince the reader that the set $\mathbb{N}$ is not expressible as a finite union of $\mathbb{Z}$-linear sets. Still every $\mathbb{Z}$-linear set is z^W-definable. Indeed, given $X = a + \sum_{i=1}^{n} \mathbb{Z}b_i$, then $x = (x_1, \ldots, x_k) \in X$ if, and only if, the following formula holds (where $b_j^{(i)}$ represents the i-th component of the vector b_j):

$$\mathcal{P}(x) = \exists z_1 \cdots \exists z_n \left(\bigwedge_{i=1}^{k} (x_i = a^{(i)} + \sum_{j=1}^{n} z_j b_j^{(i)}) \right). \tag{2}$$

Would the family of finite unions of $\mathbb{Z}$-linear sets by chance capture the notion of set definable in the structure z^W? This is not the case, since this family is not closed under taking the complement. Actually we will see that the Boolean closure of the family of $\mathbb{Z}$-linear sets is precisely the class of z^W-definable sets, see Theorem 4.1.

3. Properties of $\mathbb{Z}$-linear sets

Our decidability result is based on the equivalence between definable sets in the structure z^W and the Boolean closure of the $\mathbb{Z}$-linear sets. This characterization is obtained, in particular, by proving that the class of $\mathbb{Z}$-linear sets enjoys many properties such as closure under finite sum, projection, direct product and, more interestingly, intersection.

3.1. *Closure properties*

We start with an elementary technical result.

Lemma 3.1. *Let S be a $\mathbb{Z}$-simple set in $\mathbb{Z}^k$. Then, for every $v \in \mathbb{Z}^k$, $S + \mathbb{Z}v$ is $\mathbb{Z}$-simple.*

Proof. We argue by induction and assume that $S = \sum_{i=1}^n \mathbb{Z}b_i$, for some $b_i \in \mathbb{Z}^k$ such that $\{b_1, \ldots, b_n\}$ is a linearly independent set of vectors in $\mathbb{Z}^k$. We may further assume that $\{b_1, \ldots, b_n, v\}$ is linearly dependent since otherwise we are done. We have $hv \in \sum_{i=1}^n \mathbb{Z}b_i$ for some $h \in \mathbb{N}$ which implies $v \in R = \langle b_1/h, \ldots, b_n/h \rangle$ as a lattice in $(\mathbb{Z}/h)^k$. In particular R is a free abelian group on n generators and $S + \mathbb{Z}v$ is a free subgroup of R. There exist $c_1, \ldots, c_n \in (\mathbb{Z}/h)^k$ such that $S + \mathbb{Z}v = \langle c_1, \ldots, c_n \rangle = \sum_{i=1}^n \mathbb{Z}c_i$ (see [8, Theorem 4, (I,§10)]). But $S + \mathbb{Z}v \subseteq \mathbb{Z}^k$, so that $c_i \in \mathbb{Z}^k$, for every $1 \leq i \leq k$. Finally, if the vectors $c_i \in \mathbb{Z}^k$ are independent in $(\mathbb{Z}/h)^k$, they are certainly free in $\mathbb{Z}^k$ and so $S + \mathbb{Z}v$ is a $\mathbb{Z}$-simple set. □

As a consequence we have the following two corollaries which show a first important departure from the $\mathbb{N}$-linear and $\mathbb{Z}$-linear sets.

Corollary 3.1. *Every $\mathbb{Z}$-linear set is $\mathbb{Z}$-simple.*

Corollary 3.2. *The family of $\mathbb{Z}$-simple sets is closed under projection, direct product and finite sum.*

The *dimension* of a simple set $A = a + \sum_{i=1}^n \mathbb{Z}b_i$ is the integer $\dim A = n$, while for a union of simple sets is the maximum dimension of these sets. E.g., the dimension of the set in Example 2.2 and of the first in Example 2.1 is equal to 1, while for the others of Example 2.1 is equal to 2.

In order to prove the closure under intersection, we recall a classical and useful theorem of linear algebra (for each integer n, $GL_n(\mathbb{Z})$ represents the group of all $n \times n$ invertible matrices with entries in $\mathbb{Z}$).

Theorem 3.1 (Smith normal form, [2, p. 74]). *Let* $A \in \mathbb{Z}^{m \times n}$ *be a matrix of rank s. Then there exist two matrices* $U \in GL_m(\mathbb{Z})$ *and* $V \in GL_n(\mathbb{Z})$, *such that*

$$A' = UAV = \begin{pmatrix} D & 0 \\ 0 & 0 \end{pmatrix},$$

where $D = (d_{ij}) \in \mathbb{Z}^{s \times s}$ *is an integer diagonal matrix such that* d_{ii} *divides* d_{jj}, *for* $1 \leq i \leq j \leq s$.

Proposition 3.1. *Let* $A \in \mathbb{Z}^{m \times n}$ *and* $b \in \mathbb{Z}^m$. *The set* S *of solutions in* $\mathbb{Z}^n$ *of the linear system* $Ax = b$ *is an effective* $\mathbb{Z}$-*simple set of dimension equal to* $n - s$, *where* s *is the rank of* A.

Proof. If $A' = UAV$ is the Smith normal form of A, then the given system is equivalent to $UAVV^{-1}x = Ub$. Let $V^{-1}x = y$ and $Ub = b'$. The set of solutions of $A'y = b'$ is the $\mathbb{Z}$-simple set $S' = c + \sum_{i=s+1}^{m} \mathbb{Z}e_i$, where $c^{(j)} = b'^{(j)}/a_{jj}$ for $1 \leq j \leq s$ and $c^{(j)} = 0$ for $s < j \leq n$, and e_i stands for the i-th vector of the canonical basis. Indeed, since the matrix V^{-1} has integer entries, thus y is a vector with integer entries and therefore the system admits solutions in $\mathbb{Z}^n$ if, and only if, a_{jj} divides $b'^{(j)}$ for $1 \leq j \leq s$. The vectors $\hat{c} = Vc$ and $\hat{e}_i = Ve_i$ have integer entries and $\hat{e}_{s+1}, \ldots, \hat{e}_m$ are linearly independent because V is unimodular (i.e., $|V| = \pm 1$). Since equality $S = VS'$ holds, we have $S = \hat{c} + \sum_{i=s+1}^{m} \mathbb{Z}\hat{e}_i$. The effectiveness should be clear, knowing that obtaining the Smith normal form is effective [15]. □

This leads us to the main result of this section.

Theorem 3.2. *The intersection of two simple sets of dimension* n *and* m *is a simple subset of dimension less than or equal to* $\min\{n, m\}$. *In particular the family of* $\mathbb{Z}$-*simple sets is closed under finite intersection.*

Proof. Let $P = a + \sum_{i=1}^{n} \mathbb{Z}b_i$ and $Q = c + \sum_{j=1}^{m} \mathbb{Z}d_j$ be two $\mathbb{Z}$-simple sets in $\mathbb{Z}^k$ and assume without loss of generality that $n \leq m$. Consider the linear system $\sum_{i=1}^{n} b_i x_i - \sum_{i=n+1}^{n+m} d_{i-n} x_i = c - a$ and let S be the set of solutions in $\mathbb{Z}^{m+n}$ obtained by applying Theorem 3.1, with $A = [b_1, \ldots, b_n, -d_1, \ldots, -d_m]$. Observe that its rank is greater than or equal to m so that S is $\mathbb{Z}$-simple with dimension $\ell \leq n$. Its projection on the first n coordinates $S' = \pi_n(S)$ is $\mathbb{Z}$-linear: $S' = u + \sum_{i=1}^{\ell} \mathbb{Z}v_i$, for some $u \in \mathbb{Z}^n$ and $v_i \in \mathbb{Z}^n$, $i = 1, \ldots, \ell$. Clearly $P \cap Q$ can be written as $\{a + \sum_{i=1}^{n} x_i b_i \mid (x_1, \ldots x_n) \in S'\}$, so let B be the $k \times n$ matrix whose column vectors are $b_1, \ldots, b_n$ and V the $n \times \ell$ matrix whose column vectors are $v_1, \ldots, v_\ell$. Then the intersection can be obtained as a composition of two affine transformations $\phi : \mathbb{Z}^n \to \mathbb{Z}^k$, defined by $\alpha \mapsto a + \alpha B$, and $\psi : \mathbb{Z}^\ell \to \mathbb{Z}^n$, defined by $\beta \mapsto u + \beta V$ (the matrices operate to the left on row vectors):

$$P \cap Q = \phi(\psi(\mathbb{Z}^\ell)) = a + (u + \mathbb{Z}^\ell V)B = (a + uB) + \mathbb{Z}^\ell(VB).$$

This proves that $P \cap Q$ is $\mathbb{Z}$-linear and, via Corollary 3.1, that it is actually $\mathbb{Z}$-simple. □

3.2. Quasisimple sets

The following two propositions deal with quasisimple sets which are slight generalizations of simple sets, see Definition 2.1. For lack of space, we omit the proofs, which use only elementary algebra results.

Proposition 3.2. *Let S and T be $\mathbb{Z}$-simple sets in $\mathbb{Z}^k$. Suppose $\dim S = \dim T$ and $T \subset S$. Then $X = S \setminus T$ is a $\mathbb{Z}$-quasisimple set.*

Proposition 3.3. *Let S be a finite union of $\mathbb{Z}$-simple sets of dimension k in $\mathbb{Z}^k$. Then S is $\mathbb{Z}$-quasisimple.*

The last result of this paragraph concerns a weak condition of equality of two quasisimple sets of maximum dimension. Intuitively, it means that it suffices for two quasisimple sets to be equal almost everywhere (in some precise sense) in order to be equal.

Proposition 3.4. *Two quasisimple sets of maximum dimension k are equal if, and only if, for all integers n there exists an hypercube $[\alpha_1, \alpha_1 + n] \times \cdots \times [\alpha_k, \alpha_k + n] \subseteq \mathbb{Z}^k$ on which they agree.*

Proof. The condition is clearly necessary. In order to prove that it is sufficient, consider an homomorphism $\phi : \mathbb{Z}^k \to G$ onto some finite group recognizing two $\mathbb{Z}$-semilinear subsets X and Y, i.e., $\phi^{-1}\phi(X) = X$ and $\phi^{-1}\phi(Y) = Y$. Let n be a common multiple of degrees of the k elements $\phi(1, 0, \ldots, 0)$, $\phi(0, 1, \ldots, 0)$, $\ldots, \phi(0, \ldots, 0, 1)$. Then a vector $(v_1, \ldots, v_k)$ belongs to X (resp. Y) if, and only if, so does the vector $([v_1], \ldots, [v_k])$, where $[v_i]$ is the remainder of the division of v_i by n, so if X and Y agree in $[0, n]^k$, they are equal. □

Corollary 3.3. *Let $X, Y \subseteq \mathbb{Z}^k$ be two quasilinear subsets of maximum dimension k and let $Z \subseteq \mathbb{Z}^k$ be a finite union of linear subsets of dimension less than k. Then $X = Y$ if, and only if, $X \setminus Z = Y \setminus Z$.*

4. Definable sets in weak Presburger arithmetic

4.1. An algebraic characterization of definable sets

The Boolean closure of the linear sets enjoys some properties which we will take advantage of when characterizing z^W-definable sets. In particular, condition (iii) of the following lemma is useful for our decision procedure. From now on, "linear" and "simple" mean $\mathbb{Z}$-linear and $\mathbb{Z}$-simple.

Lemma 4.1. *The following families of subsets of $\mathbb{Z}^k$ are equal:*

(i) *the Boolean closure of linear sets;*

(ii) *the family of all finite unions of the form $S \cap \bigcap_{j=1}^{J} \overline{T}_j$, where the sets S and T_j are $\mathbb{Z}$-simple;*

(iii) *the family of all finite unions of the form $S \setminus (\bigcup_{j=1}^{J} T_j)$, where the sets S and T_j are $\mathbb{Z}$-simple, $T_j \subset S$ and $\dim T_j < \dim S$.*

Proof. Clearly the families (ii) and (iii) are included in the Boolean closure of the linear sets. The family (ii) contains all linear sets (take $J = 0$) and all their complements (take $S = \mathbb{Z}^k$ and $J = 1$). Furthermore the complement of a set of the form $S \cap \bigcap_{j=1}^{J} \overline{T}_j$ is a finite union of linear sets and their complements, thus the complement of a finite union of such sets is a finite union of intersections of linear sets and their complements. Since the intersection of linear sets is again linear, this shows that the family (ii) is closed under complement, and thus coincides with the Boolean closure. We now show that each set of the form (ii) is equivalent to a union of sets of the form (iii). Indeed, because of equality $S \setminus (\bigcup_i T_i) = S \setminus (\bigcup_{1 \le i \le r}(S \cap T_i))$, without loss of generality we may assume that all the sets T_i are $\mathbb{Z}$-simple subsets of S. Assume further that the first $p \le r$ of them have the same dimension as S, with $p = 0$ if no sets T_i has the same dimension as S. Then by repeatedly applying Proposition 3.2 to $S \setminus (\bigcup_i T_i) = (\cdots((S \setminus T_1) \setminus T_2) \cdots \setminus T_p) \setminus (\bigcup_{i > p} T_i)$ we may transform $S \setminus (\bigcup_i T_i)$ into a finite union of sets of the required form. $\square$

Theorem 4.1. *The family of z^W-definable sets is the Boolean closure of the family of $\mathbb{Z}$-linear sets.*

Proof. Clearly, all linear sets are z^W-definable, see expression (2). Let us verify the converse. Using the quantifier elimination result, all z^W-definable sets belong to the Boolean closure of the relations which are solutions of a system of linear equations or of modular equations of the type $\sum_{i=1}^{n} a_i x_i \equiv_m b$. In the former case, this is a consequence of Proposition 3.1. As for the latter case, let us proceed by induction on n. Let $n = 1$, then we must solve the equation $ax \equiv_m b$. If b is not a multiple of the greatest common divisor d of a and m, there is no solution. Otherwise a/d has an inverse modulo m/d and the set of solutions is defined by $(a/d)^{-1}(b/d) + \mathbb{Z}(m/d)$. Now, if $n > 1$, let $t = \sum_{i=1}^{n-1} a_i x_i$. The congruence $\sum_{i=1}^{n} a_i x_i \equiv_m b$ is equivalent to $\bigvee_{j=0}^{m-1} \left(t \equiv_m j \wedge a_n x_n \equiv_m (b - j) \right)$, and so by the induction hypothesis, we may conclude. □

4.2. A special case

The case studied here can be considered as the top level case in the recursive procedure of the next paragraph. The following notation is useful: given a $\mathbb{N}$-simple set $S = a + \sum_{i=1}^{m} \mathbb{N}b_i$, we denote by $S^{\mathbb{Z}}$ the $\mathbb{Z}$-simple set $a + \sum_{i=1}^{m} \mathbb{Z}b_i$.

Theorem 4.2. *Let $X \subseteq \mathbb{Z}^k$ be a z-definable set of the form*

$$X = T \cup \bigcup_{i=1}^{m} Y_i,$$

where $Y_i = a^i + \sum_{j=1}^{k} \mathbb{N}b_j^i$ for some linearly independent vectors b_j^i (i.e. it is a $\mathbb{N}$-simple set of dimension k) and T is a finite union of $\mathbb{N}$-simple sets of dimension less than k. Then X is z^W-definable if, and only if, it can be decomposed as $S \cup (P \setminus R)$, where:

(1) $P = \bigcup_{1 \leq i \leq m}(a^i + \sum_{j=1}^{k} \mathbb{Z}b_j^i) = \bigcup_{1 \leq i \leq m} Y_i^{\mathbb{Z}};$
(2) R and S are z^W-definable sets which are included in a finite union of $\mathbb{Z}$-simple sets of dimension less than k;
(3) $R \subseteq P$ and $S \cap P = \varnothing$.

Proof. Clearly the condition is sufficient. Suppose X is z^W-definable and express it as in (ii) of Lemma 4.1. Isolate all the simple sets of dimension k. By the set-theoretic equality $\bigcup_i (E_i \setminus F_i) = (\bigcup_i E_i) \setminus (\bigcup_i F_i \setminus (\bigcup_{j \neq i}(E_j \setminus F_j)))$, if every set E_i is a simple set of maximal dimension, by Proposition 3.3 their union is a quasisimple set and we may write

$$X = S \cup \left((A + \sum_{j=1}^{k} \mathbb{Z}d_j) \setminus R \right),$$

where $A \subseteq \mathbb{Z}^k$ is finite, the vectors d_j are linearly independent, S and R are z^W-definable sets included in a finite union of $\mathbb{Z}$-simple sets of dimension less than k. Now we prove that the symmetric difference of $\bigcup_{i=1}^{m}(a^i + \sum_{j=1}^{k} \mathbb{Z}b_j^i)$ and $(A + \sum_{j=1}^{k} \mathbb{Z}d_j)$ is included in a finite union of linear subsets of dimension less than k. Indeed, if we take a vector in $A + \sum_{j=1}^{k} \mathbb{Z}d_j$ not belonging to $R \cup T$ (which is contained in $R \cup T^{\mathbb{Z}}$, that is, in a finite union of $\mathbb{Z}$-simple sets of dimension less

than k), it must belong to one of the sets Y_i, and thus to $\bigcup_{i=1}^{m} \left(a^i + \sum_{j=1}^{k} \mathbb{Z}b_j^i\right)$.
Conversely, consider a set Y_i, namely $Y = a + \sum_{j=1}^{k} \mathbb{N}b_j$ (we drop the upper
indices to simplify the notation). Then we show $Y^\mathbb{Z} \subseteq A + \sum_{j=1}^{k} \mathbb{Z}d_j$, except
for a union of $\mathbb{Z}$-simple sets of dimension less than k. We observe that S is in
particular z-definable, so $S = \bigcup_{1 \le i \le m} S_i$, where every S_i is an $\mathbb{N}$-simple set
of dimension less than k. For each S_i, let $J_i \subseteq I = \{1, \ldots, k\}$ be the maximal
ordered set of indices $1 \le j_1 < \cdots < j_p \le k$, such that S_i is not parallel to
the vectors b_j, $j \in J_i$, and let $\pi_i : \mathbb{Z}^k \to \mathbb{Z}^{|J_i|}$ be the projection defined by
$\pi_i((x_j)_{j \in I}) = ((x_j)_{j \in J_i})$. So, we can define $\widehat{S}_i = \pi_i^{-1}(S_i)$, if $J_i \ne I$, and
$\widehat{S}_i = \varnothing$ otherwise. E.g., if S consists of the unique simple subset $(1, 0, 1) +$
$\mathbb{N}(0, 2, 2) + \mathbb{N}(3, 0, 0) = \{(1 + 3p, 2n, 2n + 1) \mid n, p \in \mathbb{N}\}$, it is parallel to the
vector $(1, 0, 0)$ and we have $\widehat{S} = \{(p, 2n, 2n + 1) \mid p \in \mathbb{Z}, n \in \mathbb{N}\}$. We want now
to show by induction on i that the subset

$$W_i = (a + \mathbb{Z}b_1 + \cdots + \mathbb{Z}b_{i-1} + \mathbb{N}b_i + \cdots + \mathbb{N}b_k) \setminus \left(\bigcup_{1 \le j \le m} \widehat{S}_j \right)$$

is included in $A + \sum_{j=1}^{k} \mathbb{Z}d_j$. This is clear for $i = 1$. Now assume $1 < i \le k$
and consider a vector $v \in W_i$. Since it does not belong to any subset S_j parallel
to b_i, the subset $v + \mathbb{N}b_i$ is included in $A + \mathbb{Z}d_1 + \cdots + \mathbb{Z}d_k$, except maybe for
finitely many elements which are the possible intersections of this linear set with
the subsets S_j parallel to none of the vectors $b_1, \ldots, b_k$. This implies for every
sufficiently large n, $v + nb_i = a_n + \lambda_n^1 d_1 + \cdots + \lambda_n^k d_k$, for some $\lambda_n^1, \ldots, \lambda_n^k \in \mathbb{Z}$
and $a_n \in A$. Since the set A is finite, the elements $a_n \in A$ start to repeat, so there
exist $n_1, r \in \mathbb{N}$ such that $a_{n_1} = a_{n_1+r}$. Moreover we have $a_{n_1+i} = a_{n_1+r+i}$ for
$i \ge 0$, since by computing $v + (n_1 + r)b_i - (v + n_1 b_i)$, we obtain $rb_i = \sum_{j=1}^{k} \mu_r^j d_j$,
where $\mu_r^j = \lambda_{n+r}^j - \lambda_n^j$. Now for all integers n let $m \in \mathbb{Z}$ and $0 \le r' \le r$ be such
that $n = n_1 + mr + r'$, then

$$v + nb_i = (v + (n_1 + r')b_i) + mrb_i = a_{n_1+r'} + \sum_{j=1}^{k} (\lambda_{n_1+r'}^j + m\mu_r^j)d_j,$$

which shows that $v + \mathbb{Z}b_i \subseteq A + \mathbb{Z}d_1 + \cdots + \mathbb{Z}d_k$. Because of Corollary 3.3, X
can be written as $S \cup (P \setminus R)$, where S and R are z^W-definable sets which are
included in simple sets of dimension less than k and which are computable from
T and from the sets Y_i. To end the proof we must verify the last item. Indeed, we
have $S \cup (P \setminus (R \setminus S)) = S \cup (P \cap (\overline{R} \cup S)) = S \cup (P \cap S) \cup (P \setminus R) = S \cup (P \setminus R)$, and
observe that since R is included in P so is $R \setminus S$ which shows that we may assume
$S \cap R = \varnothing$. Furthermore, we have $S \cup (P \setminus R) = (S \cap P) \cup (S \setminus P) \cup (P \cap \overline{R}) =$
$(S \setminus P) \cup (P \cap (S \cup \overline{R}))$. Since $S \cap R = \varnothing$ holds, we have $S \cup \overline{R} = \overline{R}$ which

shows that without loss of generality we may suppose $S \cap P = \varnothing$. This implies

$$X \setminus P = S, \quad P \setminus X = R. \qquad \square$$

4.3. The procedure

We recall our problem. Given a subset $X \subseteq \mathbb{Z}^k$ which is z-definable, i.e., specified as a finite disjoint union of $\mathbb{N}$-simple sets, decide whether or not it is actually z^W-definable and, in the affirmative case, give a representation as Boolean combination of $\mathbb{Z}$-simple sets. We cannot directly use Theorem 4.2, because it requires that one of the simple sets in the specification have dimension k. So we proceed as follows.

(1) Let $X \subseteq \mathbb{Z}^k$ be the union of the sets

$$X_i = a^{(i)} + \sum_{j=1}^{J_i} \mathbb{N} b_j^{(i)}, \quad 1 \le i \le m.$$

Consider the affine subspaces of $\mathbb{Q}^k$, $\mathcal{H}_i = \left(a^{(i)} + \sum_{j=1}^{J_i} \mathbb{Q} b_j^{(i)} \right)$ and suppose (possibly changing some indices) $\mathcal{H}_1, \ldots, \mathcal{H}_r$, $r \le m$, are the maximal (for the inclusion) elements of the collection $\{ \mathcal{H}_i \mid 1 \le i \le m \}$.

(2) Compute all the sets $\mathcal{H}_i' = \mathcal{H}_i \cap \mathbb{Z}^k$ and observe that they are z^W-definable. Indeed for a subset of the form $H = \left(a + \sum_{j=1}^{J} \mathbb{Q} b_j \right) \cap \mathbb{Z}^k$, where $a, b_j \in \mathbb{Z}^k$, there exist $k - J$ linear equations $F_1(y) = 0, \ldots, F_{k-J}(y) = 0$ whose set of solutions is exactly the subspace generated by the vectors b_j. Then H is defined by the Presburger formula

$$\exists y \big((x = y + a) \wedge (F_1(y) = 0) \wedge \ldots \wedge (F_{k-J}(y) = 0) \big).$$

Clearly, X is z^W-definable if, and only if, all the intersections $Y_i = X \cap \mathcal{H}_i'$ are z^W-definable and moreover $X = \bigcup_{i=1}^r Y_i$.

(3) For all $1 \le i \le r$, consider an isomorphism $\mu_i : (\mathcal{H}_i - a^{(i)}) \to \mathbb{Q}^{J_i}$ such that $\tau_i(\mathcal{H}_i' - a^{(i)}) = \mathbb{Z}^{J_i}$. Such isomorphism clearly exists and it can be expressed, relatively to $\mathcal{H}_i'$, in z^W, as like as $\tau_i = \mu_i \circ (-a^{(i)})$. Then $\tau_i(Y_i)$ is z^W-definable if, and only if, Y_i is z^W-definable.

(4) Finally we can apply Theorem 4.2 to $\tau_i(Y_i) \subseteq \mathbb{Z}^{J_i}$, since it has at least one component of maximal dimension J_i, obtaining the sets P_i, S_i, and R_i that satisfy all conditions of 4.2. Now $Y_i = \tau_i^{-1}(S_i) \cup \left(\tau_i^{-1}(P_i) \cap \tau_i^{-1}(R_i) \right)$, and observe that the inverse images of P_i, S_i, and R_i by τ again satisfy the three conditions, in particular $\tau_i^{-1}(P_i)$ is $\mathbb{Z}$-simple.

(5) Now apply the procedure recursively to the sets $\tau_i^{-1}(S_i)$ and $\tau_i^{-1}(R_i)$.

(6) It only remains to observe that if we fail in applying Theorem 4.2, the set X actually was not z^W-definable.

Bibliography

1. A. Bès. A Survey of Arithmetical Definability. *Bull. Belg. Math. Soc. Simon Stevin*, suppl.:1–54, 2001.
2. H. Cohen. *A Course in Computational Algebraic Number Theory*, volume 138 of *Graduate Texts in Mathematics*. Springer-Verlag, 1993.
3. S. Eilenberg and M.-P. Schützenberger. Rational Sets in Commutative Monoids. *J. Algebra*, 13:173–191, 1969.
4. H. Enderton. *A Mathematical Introduction to Logic*. Academic Press, 1972.
5. FAST homepage. http://www.lsv.ens-cachan.fr/fast/.
6. S. Ginsburg and E. H. Spanier. Semigroups, Presburger formulas, and languages. *Pacific J. Math.*, 16:285–296, 1966.
7. D. Hilbert and P. Bernays. *Grundlagen der Mathematik I*, chapter 7, pages 368–377. Springer-Verlag, 2nd edition, 1968.
8. S. Lang. *Algebra*. Addinson Wesley, 1965.
9. J. Leroux. A Polynomial Time Presburger Criterion and Synthesis for Number Decision Diagrams. In *LICS '05*, pages 147–156, 2005.
10. A. A. Muchnik. The definable criterion for definability in Presburger arithmetic and its applications. *Theoret. Comput. Sci.*, 290:1433–1444, 2003.
11. M. Presburger. Über die Vollständigkeit eines gewissen Systems der Arithmetik ganzer Zahlen, in welchem die Addition als einzige Operation hervortritt. In *Comptes-rendus du I Congrès des Mathématiciens des Pays Slaves, Varsovie 1929*, pages 92–101, 395, Warsaw, 1930.
12. A. L. Semënov. Presburgerness of predicates regular in two number systems. *Siberian Math. J.*, 18(2):289–299, 1977.
13. C. Smoryński. *Logical Number Theory I*, chapter III, pages 307–329. Springer-Verlag, 1991.
14. R. Stansifer. Presburger's Article on Integer Arithmetic: Remarks and Translation. Technical Report TR84–639, Cornell University, Computer Science Department, http://techreports.library.cornell.edu:8081/Dienst/UI/1.0/Display/cul.cs/TR84-639, 1984.
15. A. Storjohann. Near Optimal Algorithms for Computing Smith Normal Forms of Integer Matrices. In *ISSAC '96*, pages 1–8, 1996.

ON DEFINING PROOFS OF KNOWLEDGE
IN THE BARE PUBLIC-KEY MODEL

GIOVANNI DI CRESCENZO

Telcordia Technologies, Piscataway,
NJ, USA. E-mail: `giovanni@research.telcordia.com`

IVAN VISCONTI*

Dipartimento di Informatica ed Applicazioni, Università di Salerno,
84084 Fisciano (SA), Italy. E-mail: `visconti@dia.unisa.it`

One contribution provided by the groundbreaking concept of interactive proofs is the notion of proofs of knowledge, where a prover can convince a verifier that she knows a secret related to a public statement. This notion was formalized in the conventional complexity-theoretic model of interactive protocols and showed to be very useful for cryptographic applications, such as entity authentication schemes.

Motivated by these applicability considerations, in this paper, we consider proofs of knowledge in a cryptographic model, called the bare public-key model (BPK model in short), where round-efficient interactive proofs with strong variants of security against provers (i.e., soundness) and security against verifiers (i.e., zero-knowledge) have been presented. We formally define notions of proofs of knowledge in the BPK model, and show that there are 4 distinct such notions for each of the previously studied four known notions of soundness. Finally, under the existence of any homomorphic one-way function family, (a generalization of) a 4-round argument system for all $\mathcal{NP}$ languages from the literature is a proof of knowledge that is secure against concurrent attacks from provers or verifiers.

Keywords: Zero-Knowledge, Proofs of Knowledge, Bare Public-Key Model

1. Introduction

Zero-knowledge proofs, introduced in a seminal paper [14] by Goldwasser, Micali and Rackoff, are methods for a prover to convince a verifier of the validity of a statement without revealing any additional information. They are often applied to cryptographic protocols as they are secure both against malicious provers trying to prove false statements (this is called the soundness property) and against

---

*Part of this work done in 2004 while Ivan Visconti was a post-doctoral fellow at the Département d'Informatique of the Ecole Normale Supérieure in Paris, France.

malicious verifiers trying to obtain additional information (this is called the zero-knowledge property). These proofs are also called *proofs of membership* as the statements proved are of the form $x \in L$, for some instance x and language L. Since their introduction, a large amount of research has been devoted to zero-knowledge proofs, including concrete protocols for different classes of languages and relations, and improvements on both efficiency aspects (such as the communication and round complexity) as well as their security notions (such as stronger notions of soundness and zero-knowledge). In particular, the original notion [14] was augmented into a notion [13] that is closed under sequential composition, thus remaining zero-knowledge even if a malicious verifier sequentially runs polynomially many protocols. Later, motivated by the use of such protocols in networks like the Internet several researchers realized the need of extending the zero-knowledge notion so that it holds against malicious verifiers that can concurrently run polynomially many protocols (thus resulting in the *concurrent zero-knowledge* notion [9]); furthermore, an even stronger notion of *resettable zero-knowledge* protocols was introduced [5]; these are protocols that remain zero-knowledge even against verifiers that can additionally reset provers to previous states. However, for the notion of concurrent zero-knowledge, super-constant lower bounds on the round complexity have been given [6]. As these bounds severely limit applicability, this notion is being studied in other models, where it is possible to achieve, in particular, constant-round concurrent zero-knowledge. Among the several studied models, the model that currently seems to have the minimal set-up or network assumptions is the bare public-key (BPK) model [5], where verifiers register their public key in a public file during a set-up stage, and there is no interactive preprocessing stage, no trusted third party, no common random or trusted reference string, and no assumption on the asynchronicity of the network.

While the BPK model simplifies the work for achieving the zero-knowledge property, the work for achieving soundness becomes instead more complex. Indeed, in this model separations were showed [15] between different notions of soundness that instead coincide in the standard model. This separation is a consequence of the use of the verifier's private key (corresponding to the public key that is in the public file) during the protocol. A malicious prover could somehow exploit such an use of the private key in order to convince the verifier of a false theorem. Under standard intractability assumptions, it was showed [15] that there are four distinct meaningful notions of soundness, i.e., one-time, sequential, concurrent and resettable soundness. Moreover, it was showed that previous constant-round resettable zero-knowledge arguments in the BPK model [5] and their improvement [15] enjoy sequential soundness and it was conjecture that both protocols do not satisfy concurrent soundness.

An enhanced notion for proof systems first discussed by Goldwasser, Micali and Rackoff [14] and formally investigated by Feige, Fiat and Shamir [10], is that of *proofs of knowledge*, where a prover convinces a verifier that she knows a string y such that $R(x, y) = 1$, where x is a common instance and R is a relation. Zero-knowledge proofs of knowledge found several applications in cryptographic protocols, such as identification (or entity authentication) schemes. This notion was later revisited [3], and and a revised formal definition was presented which has been used very often in the literature (also, a slight variant of this definition has appeared [12], and assumptions have been presented [3] under which these two definitions are equivalent.) The proof of knowledge property requires the existence of an efficient witness extraction procedure that outputs a legal witness for the statement proved by the adversarial prover. These authors also discussed distinctions between soundness and witness extractability in proof systems. We will see that such distinctions are both conceptual and formal and happen to be even more relevant in the BPK model.

Considering both concurrent/resettable zero-knowledge and proofs of knowledge, we stress that black-box (i.e., the adversary as an oracle, without looking at its code) resettable zero-knowledge arguments of knowledge exist only for trivial languages [5]. Non-black-box techniques were used [2] to obtain a resettable zero-knowledge argument of knowledge although this protocol is only proved to be sequentially sound. A constant-round concurrently-sound resettable zero-knowledge argument in the BPK model has been presented [7] with hardness assumptions with respect to super-polynomial-time adversaries. Recently [8], a constant-round concurrently-sound concurrent zero-knowledge argument of knowledge in the BPK model has been constructed under standard complexity-theoretic and number-theoretic assumptions.

Our results. Motivated by the fact [10] that identification schemes are often been considered one major application of zero-knowledge proofs of knowledge, and that the latter have yet to be defined in the BPK model, in this paper we study notions of witness extraction in the BPK model. Specifically, we study arguments of knowledge in the BPK model and we formalize this concept using the notion of witness extraction [3,10,11,14].

Analogously to what has been previously noted [15] for the soundness notion, the verifier's use of a public key can be used by malicious provers to affect the extractability of the argument system. We introduce four notions of witness extraction: one-time, sequential, concurrent and resettable and, similarly to the soundness case [15], we show that these notions are meaningful and depend on the power of the adversarial prover. In particular when many arguments of knowledge are executed, we consider the strong witness extraction property that concerns the extraction of a witness from each proof, i.e., when the prover succeeds in many proofs, he has to prove knowledge of a witness in each proof. Therefore we confirm that even in the BPK model the notions of soundness and witness extraction are distinct, and in fact we show that for each of the four notions of soundness previously identified [15] the four notions of witness extraction are distinct. The proofs of these statements, although building on previous proofs for the soundness case [15], require new ideas.

Naturally, we then consider the problem of designing arguments of knowledge for any language in $\mathcal{NP}$ that satisfy any among the defined witness extraction notions. In Section 4 we generalize a previous protocol [8] to show that assuming the existence of homomorphic one-way function families, this generalization of a previous 4-round argument system [8] satisfies concurrent soundness, concurrent witness extraction and concurrent zero-knowledge. Our contribution with respect to the previous protocol [8] is two-fold: we prove that a generalized version of it additionally satisfies concurrent witness-extraction (as the previous protocol was only proved to satisfy concurrent soundness and concurrent zero-knowledge), and we weaken the assumption to the existence of homomorphic one-way function families (while the previous protocol assumed the intractability of a specific number-theoretic problem; i.e., computing discrete logarithms).

2. Defining Proofs of Knowledge in the BPK Model

We now give new notions of one-time, sequential, concurrent and resettable soundness and witness extraction attacks in the BPK model. For the definition of the BPK model, of notions of one-time, sequential, concurrent and resettable soundness, and the definition of concurrent zero-knowledge in this model the reader is referred to previous work [8,15,16].

Malicious provers and attacks in the BPK model. Let s be a positive polynomial and P^* be a probabilistic polynomial-time algorithm that takes as first input 1^n.

P^* is an *s-sequential malicious* prover if it runs in at most $s(n)$ stages in the following way: in stage 1, P^* receives a public key pk and outputs an n-bit string x_1. In every even stage, P^* starts from the final configuration of the previous stage, sends and receives messages of a single interactive protocol on input pk and can decide to abort the stage in any moment and to start the next one. In every odd stage $i > 1$, P^* starts from the final configuration of the previous stage and outputs an n-bit string x_i. An *s-one-time malicious* prover is defined as an s-sequential malicious prover that is restricted to generate a different x_i in each odd stage.

P^* is an *s-concurrent malicious* prover if on input a public key pk of V, can perform the following $s(n)$ interactive protocols with V: 1) if P^* is already running i protocols $0 \leq i < s(n)$ he can start a new protocol with V choosing the new statement to be proved; 2) he can output a message for any running protocol, receive immediately the response from V and continue.

P^* is an *s-resetting malicious* prover, if on input the public key pk of a verifier, he gets access to $s(n)$ oracles for the verifier.

Given an *s-sequential malicious* prover P^* and an honest verifier V, a *sequential soundness attack* is performed in the following way: 1) the first stage of V is run on input 1^n and a random string so that a pair (pk, sk) is obtained; 2) the first stage of P^* is run on input 1^n and pk and x_1 is obtained; 3) for $1 \leq i \leq s(n)/2$ the $2i$-th stage of P^* is run letting it interact with V that receives as input sk, x_i and a random string r_i, while the $(2i + 1)$-th stage of P^* is run to obtain x_{i+1}. A *one-time soundness attack* is defined as a sequential attack, with the only difference that all x_i are distinct.

Given an *s-concurrent malicious* prover P^* and an honest verifier V, a *concurrent soundness attack* is performed in the following way: 1) the first stage of V is run on input 1^n and a random string so that a pair (pk, sk) is obtained; 2) P^* is run on input 1^n and pk; 3) whenever P^* starts a new protocol choosing a statement x_i, V is run on inputs x_i, a new random string r_i and sk.

Given an *s-resetting malicious* prover P^* and an honest verifier V, a *resetting soundness attack* is performed in the following way: 1) the first stage of V is run on input 1^n and a random string so that a pair (pk, sk) is obtained; 2) P^* is run on input 1^n and pk; 3) random string r_i, for $i = 1, \ldots, s(n)$, is independently generated; 4) P^* is allowed to interact with oracles for the second stage of V on input sk and one of the $s(n)$ random strings r_i.

These definitions directly imply the notion of *i-th session* between P^* and V as the interaction where V uses random string r_i as her random tape.

Witness extraction in the BPK model. We present a definition of witness extraction (and thus of arguments of knowledge) in the BPK model. Our starting point would naturally be the current definition of (black-box) witness extraction [3] in the standard model, under the name of 'validity'. Accordingly, we would like to present a natural extension of this definition in the BPK model. Before presenting our definition, we need to settle on two convention issues arising from the previous definitions [3,4,12].

We note that originally [3] cheating provers were modeled as probabilistic algorithms; in a next work [12] they are modeled as deterministic algorithms; in a more recent work [4] three conditions are showed which, when satisfied, make the two notions equivalent if we restrict to proofs of knowledge for polynomial-time relations. These three conditions do not appear to cause any loss of generality. Accordingly, in our notion in the BPK model, we model provers as probabilistic algorithms.

We also note that in the original work [3] the authors define two notions: first, a *validity* notion where, briefly speaking, an extractor is required to exist for any prover that makes the verifier accept with sufficiently high probability, on input any instance x that belongs to the relation domain dom R_L; second, a *strong validity* notion where the same condition is required on input any instance x that does *not* belong to dom R_L. Finally, in the recent work [4], the validity notion presented there, which we rename *witness extraction*, incorporates both validity and strong validity from the original work [3] by requiring that the same condition holds for all x.

The conjunction of validity and soundness implies strong validity for $\mathcal{NP}$ relations [3]. By definition, witness extraction is equivalent to the conjunction of validity and strong validity. As briefly sketched in the more recent work [4], it also holds that witness extraction (with negligible knowledge error) implies soundness for $\mathcal{NP}$ relations.

In our notion in the BPK model, it suffices to use the witness extraction notion of this recent work [4] as a starting point.

Even after settling these two conventions, in order to define an analogue notion in the BPK model, we need to address a few non-trivial technical points, which we first discuss in detail.

Witness extraction vs soundness. In light of the previously mentioned relationships between soundness, validity, strong validity, and witness extraction, it is of interest and technically meaningful to define, orthogonally to the four soundness notions, four analogous notions for witness extraction in the BPK model: one-time, sequential, concurrent and resettable witness extraction. (We note in particular that one-time witness extraction has a natural meaning if we think of one-time password authentication.) Not surprisingly, it will still hold in the BPK model that witness extraction (with negligible knowledge error) implies soundness. Our results in Section 3 will show that the 4 witness extraction notions are all distinct and thus meaningful, even for each notion of soundness, and that in some cases even the strongest soundness notion is not sufficient to guarantee the weakest witness extraction notion for a given protocol.

The formalization of proofs of knowledge [3] intends to capture the knowledge communicated by the prover to the verifier during a single execution of the protocol (as opposed to, say, the knowledge that the prover has on its private memory, which in general may not be used during the protocol). More formally, this is defined by requiring that there exists a polynomial-time function ρ, and an extractor algorithm E that is given oracle access to the prover, such that for any adversarial prover P^*, for any n-bit input string x, the following holds: if the acceptance probability $p(n)$ of P^* is larger than some knowledge error $k(n)$, then, denoting as tr the transcript of the interaction between P^* and E, and as r_E the random coins used by E, it holds that $\rho(r_E, x, tr)$ returns a witness w for x and E runs in expected time bounded by $poly(n)/(p(n) - k(n))$. Note that this is an inherently black-box formulation, in that E is given oracle access to P^*. This formalization refers to a single-session and single-statement setting.

In extending this formalization to a multi-session and multi-statement model (such as the BPK model), we require a protocol to satisfy witness extraction in this model if on *each* protocol session using as input a certain statement, some appropriate knowledge (e.g., a witness for that statement) is communicated by the prover to the verifier and such a knowledge has to be communicated *during that specific session* (as opposed to, say, being derived from other sessions). This is especially important in the BPK model, where some session transcripts could reveal information, for instance, about the verifier's secret key, to a cheating prover that might later be able to convince the verifier in a new session without knowing the witness. (Indeed some of our separations in Section 3 use this idea.) In applications such as identification schemes, this would be quite dangerous as a new prover could use the transcript of previous identifying sessions to be positively identified as a different user.

More formally, this is defined by requiring that there exists a polynomial-time function ρ, and an extractor algorithm E that is given oracle access to the prover, such that for any adversarial prover P^*, for any polynomially-long sequence of n-bit input strings $x_1, \ldots, x_s$ possibly chosen by P^*, the following holds: for any $i \in \{1 \ldots, s\}$ such that the acceptance probability $p_i(n)$ in the i-th session of P^* is larger than some knowledge error $k(n)$, then, denoting as tr_i the transcript of the interaction between P^* and E in the i-th session, it holds that $\rho(r_E, x_i, tr_i)$ returns a witness w_i for x_i and E runs in expected time bounded by $\max_{i=1}^{n} poly(n)/(p_i(n) - k(n))$, where $tr_1, \ldots, tr_s$ are the s transcripts, one for each session between P^* and E.

The extractor's input in the BPK model. As already pointed out by Bellare and Goldreich [3], the notion of proofs of knowledge aims at capturing the knowledge communicated by the prover to the verifier during the proof, where, by 'knowledge' we mean the computational advantage over the verifier that the prover shows to possess while running the protocol. We stress that the BPK model requires protocols to happen in two phases: a key generation phase, where all verifiers deposit one public key on the common public file and keep their private key secret; and a proof phase, where a prover and a verifier use the public file as an additional input during a proof for some statement, and the verifier uses the private key as another additional input during the proof. Accordingly, the computational advantage over the verifier that the prover is supposed to show during the protocol needs to take into account the verifier's secret key.

A first observation we make is that there are two definitional options here: either we allow the extractor to take as input the verifier's secret key, or we don't. We opt for giving the extractor the verifier's secret key[a], the reason being that otherwise even protocols that very naturally seem to be proofs of knowledge may not be so according to a definition where the extractor does not have access to the verifier's secret key. To see this, consider, for instance an interactive proof of knowledge π modified as follows: before starting the execution of π as a subprotocol, the verifier gives a 3-round witness-indistinguishable proof of knowledge of the secret key associated with the public key; later, the prover only starts π if the verifier's proof was accepting. While the modified protocol appears to maintain its property of being a proof of knowledge, it is not hard to check that if there exists a black-box extractor running in expected polynomial time for this protocol that is not given the verifier's secret key and is successful in returning a valid witness, then a trivialization result is obtained; specifically, either it is easy to compute witnesses (i.e., the protocol is not run at all and a witness computed in stand-alone by the extractor), or it is easy to compute secret keys when given public keys as input (i.e., the extractor computes the secret key and runs the protocol).

We now present a formal definition of the four variants of witness extraction in the BPK model. We will use the notion of one-time, sequential, concurrent and resettable provers, as previously defined, and we define the notions of *one-time, sequential, concurrent and resettable witness extraction attacks* from provers, similarly to the analogous notions of soundness attacks, the only difference being that in each attack, during the key-generation phase, the pair (pk, sk) is generated by one extractor algorithm (rather than by the verifier, as done in the soundness attacks).

Definition 2.1. Let L be a language in $\mathcal{NP}$ and let R_L its associated relation. A

---

[a]Contrarily to how briefly discussed by Barak *et al.* [2], where the authors observe that an extractor would not need the verifier's secret key to return a witness for their particular constant-round protocol in the BPK model (this is only briefly discussed, and an attempt of defining proofs of knowledge in the BPK model was out of the scope of that paper).

complete pair $\langle P, V \rangle$ for L in the BPK model can enjoy $\texttt{wtype} \in \{$**one-time, sequential, concurrent, resettable**$\}$ **witness extraction with knowledge error** k if for all positive polynomials s, and any s-$\{$one-time, sequential, concurrent, resettable$\}$ malicious prover P^* performing an $\{$one-time, sequential, concurrent, resettable$\}$ witness extraction attack, there exists an algorithm $E = (E_1, E_2)$ and a polynomial-time function ρ with the following syntax and properties.

On input security parameter 1^n, E_1 generates a pair of public and secret keys (pk, sk), and pk is posted on the public file F. E_2 takes as input F and sk and interacts with P^*. The interaction between E_2 and P^* in session i implicitly defines a transcript tr_i of this interaction, for $i = 1, \ldots, s(n)$ (specifically, tr_i is the sequence of all messages referred to session i exchanged between E_2, using input x, pk, sk, and P^* on input x, pk; this includes messages involved in all rewindings of P^*, if any, and the random coins r_E used by E_1 and E_2). The function ρ takes as input (x, r_E, pk, tr_i), for some $i \in \{1, \ldots, s(n)\}$, and returns a string w_i.

For any sequence of n-bit strings $x_1, \ldots, x_{s(n)}$ returned by P^*, the sequence $(w_1, \ldots, w_{s(n)})$ returned by function ρ satisfies the following condition: denoting as $p_i(n)$ the probability that in the i-th session V accepts input x_i while interacting with P^*, if $p_i(n) > k(n)$ then (1) $R_L(x_i, w_i) = 1$, and (2) E_1 runs in time polynomial in n and E_2 runs in time at most $\max_{i=1}^{n} poly(n)/(p_i(n) - k(n))$.

We say that a complete pair $\langle P, V \rangle$ is a $\texttt{wtype}$ witness extractable argument of knowledge for relation R_L if it enjoys $\texttt{wtype}$ witness extraction.

We note that, as in the original work by Bellare and Goldreich [3], our definition is black-box as we require that there exists a single extractor E for any prover P^*, where E has oracle access to P^*. (Moreover, as also stressed in the more recent work by Bellare and Goldreich [4], by 'oracle access', we mean that the black-box extractor can provide all inputs, including messages and random bits on the random tape, to P^* and obtain all outputs.) In the rest of the paper we will only consider the black-box notion.

3. Separating the Notions of Witness Extraction

In this section we show that the four notions of witness extraction introduced in the previous section are not only meaningful but also *distinct*. Furthermore, we show that these notions are distinct *even when coupled with any soundness notion*. More formally, given the ordered sequence $Atk =$(*one-time, sequential, concurrent, resettable*), we show that, for any $s, e \in Atk$, if there exists an argument system in the BPK model with soundness type s and extraction type e, then there exists an argument system with soundness type s and extraction type e, that does not satisfy extraction type $e + 1$, where $e + 1$ is the next type in the sequence Atk, if type $e + 1$ is defined (that is, if e is not resettably witness-extractable). The separation is important since argument systems can be used for different purposes and thus in some cases only soundness is useful, while achieving witness extraction may be harder or make the construction more expensive. For applications requiring witness extraction, our separations show that just strengthening the soundness property may not be enough to achieve witness extraction, but more careful and separate design may be needed to achieve the latter.

The approach that we use is to transform a given argument system $\langle P, V \rangle$ into a new argument system $\langle P', V' \rangle$ by adding a few rounds in which the verifier sends to the prover some special information aux that depends on the verifier's key and on the input x. In doing this, we use techniques from a previous work [15] and add a crucial idea, informally described as follows. The information aux is only released at the end of a successful interaction (*i.e.*, an interaction in which the verifier accepts) and then showing aux on input x makes the verifier accepts. Since aux is released only at the end of a successful interaction, $\langle P', V' \rangle$ enjoys the same soundness type as $\langle P, V \rangle$. As we shall see in the proof of the separations, the auxiliary information aux is computed in such a way that the type of witness extraction is preserved but it is guaranteed that the next type is not enjoyed. Our separations are proved basing on the minimal assumption on the existence of one-way functions and the existence of a specific argument system for a non-trivial language L (that is, a language L not in BPP).

Theorem 3.1. *Let L be a non-trivial language. If there exist one-way functions and if L has an interactive argument $\langle P, V \rangle$ in the BPK model enjoying $\alpha \in \{one$-$time, sequential, concurrent, resettable\}$ soundness and $\beta \in \{one$-$time, sequential, concurrent\}$ witness extraction with negligible knowledge error, then there exists an interactive argument $\langle P', V' \rangle$ in the BPK model for L that enjoys the same soundness as $\langle P, V \rangle$, enjoys β witness extraction with negligible error but does not enjoy the next witness extraction with knowledge error k, for any constant $k < 1$.*

For lack of space, the proof can be found in the full version of the paper.

4. Concurrent Witness Extraction

In this section we propose one generalization of a 4-round concurrently sound and concurrently zero-knowledge argument system for any $\mathcal{NP}$-language in the BPK model [8], and show that it also satisfies concurrent witness extraction, according to Definition 2.1. The generalization allows to weaken the complexity assumption from the hardness of the Decisional Diffie Hellman problem to the existence of homomorphic one-way function families, without increasing the number of rounds.

Theorem 4.1. *Let* $k : \mathcal{N} \rightarrow [0, 1]$ *be a function having efficient output representation that is negligible in its input; also, let* L *be a language in* $\mathcal{NP}$ *and let* R_L *be its associated relation. Under the existence of homomorphic one-way function families, there exists (constructively) a 4-round concurrently sound, concurrently witness-extractable and concurrent zero-knowledge argument of knowledge with knowledge error* k *for* R_L.

We note that if L has a 3-round honest-verifier proof of knowledge, our construction is also efficient in the sense that it does not require any expensive $\mathcal{NP}$ reduction.

A formal description of the resulting protocol can be found along with the security proof in the full version of this paper.

Acknowledgments. The authors thank Giuseppe Persiano and Yunlei Zhao for many useful discussions about the definition of knowledge in the public-key model.

Bibliography

1. B. Barak. How to Go Beyond the Black-Box Simulation Barrier. In *42nd FOCS '01*, pages 106–115, 2001. IEEE Computer Society Press.
2. B. Barak, O. Goldreich, S. Goldwasser, and Y. Lindell. Resettably-Sound Zero-Znowledge and its Applications. In *42nd FOCS '01*, pages 116–125, 2001. IEEE Computer Society Press.
3. M. Bellare and O. Goldreich. On Defining Proofs of Knowledge. In *Crypto '92*, volume 740 of *LNCS*, pages 390–420. Springer Verlag, 1993.
4. M. Bellare and O. Goldreich. On Probabilistic versus Deterministic Provers in the Definition of Proofs of Knowledge. Technical Report ECCC Report TR06-136, ECCC, 2006.
5. R. Canetti, O. Goldreich, S. Goldwasser, and S. Micali. Resettable Zero-Knowledge. In *32nd STOC '00*, pages 235–244. ACM, 2000.
6. R. Canetti, J. Kilian, E. Petrank, and A. Rosen. Black-Box Concurrent Zero-Knowledge Requires $\omega(\log n)$ Rounds. In *33rd STOC '01*, pages 570–579. ACM, 2001.
7. G. Di Crescenzo, G. Persiano, and I. Visconti. Constant-Round Resettable Zero Knowledge with Concurrent Soundness in the Bare Public-Key Model. In *Crypto '04*, volume 3152 of *LNCS*, pages 237–253. Springer-Verlag, 2004.
8. G. Di Crescenzo and I. Visconti. Concurrent zero knowledge in the public-key model. In *32nd ICALP 05*, volume 3580 of *LNCS*, pages 816–827. Springer-Verlag, 2005.
9. C. Dwork, M. Naor, and A. Sahai. Concurrent Zero-Knowledge. In *30th STOC '98*, pages 409–418. ACM, 1998.

10. U. Feige, A. Fiat, and A. Shamir. Zero-Knowledge Proofs of Identity. *Journal of Cryptology*, 1:77–94, 1988.
11. U. Feige and A. Shamir. Zero-Knowledge Proofs of Knowledge in Two Rounds. In *Crypto '89*, volume 435 of *LNCS*, pages 526–544. Springer-Verlag, 1990.
12. O. Goldreich. *Foundations of Cryptography: Basic Tools*, volume 1. Cambridge University Press, Cambridge, UK, 2001.
13. O. Goldreich and Y. Oren. Definitions and Properties of Zero-Knowledge Proof Systems. *Journal of Cryptology*, 7:1–32, 1994.
14. S. Goldwasser, S. Micali, and C. Rackoff. The knowledge complexity of interactive proof-systems. In *21st STOC '85*, pages 291–304, 1985.
15. S. Micali and L. Reyzin. Soundness in the Public-Key Model. In *Crypto '01*, volume 2139 of *LNCS*, pages 542–565. Springer-Verlag, 2001.
16. L. Reyzin. *Zero-Knowledge with Public Keys, Ph.D. Thesis*. MIT, 2001.

AUTHOR INDEX

Thermal Physics

Entropy and Free Energies

Second Edition